THE BHAGAVADGĪTĀ

Kees W. Bolle

THE BHAGAVADGĪTĀ

A New Translation

UNIVERSITY OF CALIFORNIA PRESS
Berkeley Los Angeles London

University of California Press
Berkeley and Los Angeles, California

University of California Press, Ltd.
London, England

ISBN 0-520-03741-3
Library of Congress Catalog Card Number 78-59451

Printed in the United States of America

2 3 4 5 6 7 8 9 0

Contents

Part One: Text and Translation

Part Two: On Translating the Bhagavadgītā

Indices

PART ONE

TEXT AND TRANSLATION

I

dhṛtarāṣṭra uvāca

1. dharmakṣetre kurukṣetre
samavetā yuyutsavaḥ
māmakāḥ pāṇḍavāś caiva
kim akurvata saṃjaya

saṃjaya uvāca

2. dṛṣṭvā tu pāṇḍavānīkaṃ
vyūḍhaṃ duryodhanas tadā
ācāryam upasaṃgamya
rājā vacanam abravīt

3. paśyaitāṃ pāṇḍuputrāṇām
ācārya mahatīṃ camūm
vyūḍhāṃ drupadaputreṇa
tava śiṣyeṇa dhīmatā

4. atra śūrā maheṣvāsā
bhīmārjunasamā yudhi
yuyudhāno virāṭaś ca
drupadaś ca mahārathaḥ

5. dhṛṣṭaketuś cekitānaḥ
kāśirājaś ca vīryavān
purujit kuntibhojaś ca
śaibyaś ca narapuṃgavaḥ

6. yudhāmanyuś ca vikrānta
uttamaujāś ca vīryavān
saubhadro draupadeyāś ca
sarva eva mahārathāḥ

Dhṛtarāṣṭra:

1. In the land of the right tradition, the land of the Kurus,
   my men and the men of Pāṇḍu met,
   Ready to fight.
   What did they do, Saṃjaya?

Saṃjaya:

2. The king, Duryodhana, surveyed
   the Pāṇḍava army drawn up for battle.
   Then he went to his mentor
   and said:

3. "Master, see that mighty army
   of Pāṇḍu's men.
   Your skillful pupil, the son of Drupada,
   arrayed them.

4. They have heroes, mighty bowmen,
   matching Bhīma and Arjuna in battle:
   Yuyudhāna and Virāṭa,
   and Drupada, the great chariot fighter;

5. Dhṛṣṭaketu; Cekitāna;
   the valiant king of Kāśī;
   Purujit; Kuntibhoja;
   the Śibi king, foremost among men;

6. And the courageous Yudhāmanyu,
   and the heroic Uttamaujas,
   The son of Subhadrā, Draupadī's sons—
   all great chariot fighters.

7. asmākaṃ tu viśiṣṭā ye
   tān nibodha dvijottama
   nāyakā mama sainyasya
   saṃjñārthaṃ tān bravīmi te

8. bhavān bhīṣmaś ca karnaś ca
   kṛpaś ca samitiṃjayaḥ
   aśvatthāmā vikarṇaś ca
   saumadattis tathaiva ca

9. anye ca bahavaḥ śūrā
   madarthe tyaktajīvitāḥ
   nānāśastrapraharaṇāḥ
   sarve yuddhaviśāradāḥ

10. aparyāptaṃ tad asmākaṃ
    balaṃ bhīmābhirakṣitam
    paryāptaṃ tv idam eteṣāṃ
    balaṃ bhīṣmābhirakṣitam[1]

11. ayaneṣu ca sarveṣu
    yathābhāgam avasthitāḥ
    bhīṣmam evābhirakṣantu
    bhavantaḥ sarva eva hi

12. tasya saṃjanayan harṣaṃ
    kuruvṛddhaḥ pitāmahaḥ
    siṃhanādaṃ vinadyoccaiḥ
    śankhaṃ dadhmau pratāpavān

13. tataḥ śankhāś ca bheryaś ca
    paṇavānakagomukhāḥ
    sahasaivābhyahanyanta
    sa śabdas tumulo 'bhavat

[1]This is the only verse in this edition which differs from the text of the Critical Edition. See Note on the Text, p. 257.

7. But, most venerable nobleman,
   observe also those men of distinction
   Who are on our side, the captains of my army;
   let me identify them for you.

8. There are yourself, Bhīṣma, Karṇa,
   and the victorious Kṛpa;
   Aśvatthāman, Vikarṇa,
   and the son of Somadatta;

9. And many other heroes,
   willing to lay down their lives for me,
   Armed with various missiles and spears,
   all skilled in battle.

10. The other army is not equal to us
    in spite of its protection by Bhīma, the Terrible.
    This army of ours, commanded by Bhīṣma,
    the Awe-Inspiring, outnumbers them.

11. Let all of you, above all,
    guard Bhīṣma,
    In whatever division you are stationed,
    in all movements of the battle front."

12. Duryodhana listened with delight when Bhīṣma,
    the Kuru elder, the majestic grandsire,
    Blew his conch-shell,
    roaring loudly like a lion.

13. Then all at once, conch-shells,
    drums, cymbals, trumpets,
    Sounded forth,
    and the noise grew wild.

14. tataḥ śvetair hayair yukte
mahati syandane sthitau
mādhavaḥ pāṇḍavaś caiva
divyau śankhau pradadhmatuḥ

15. pāñcajanyaṃ hṛṣīkeśo
devadattaṃ dhanaṃjayaḥ
pauṇḍraṃ dadhmau mahāśankhaṃ
bhīmakarmā vṛkodaraḥ

16. anantavijayaṃ rājā
kuntīputro yudhiṣṭhiraḥ
nakulaḥ sahadevaś ca
sughoṣamaṇipuṣpakau

17. kāśyaś ca parameṣvāsaḥ
śikhaṇḍī ca mahārathaḥ
dhṛṣṭadyumno virāṭaś ca
sātyakiś cāparājitaḥ

18. drupado draupadeyāś ca
sarvaśaḥ pṛthivīpate
saubhadraś ca mahābāhuḥ
śankhān dadhmuḥ pṛthak pṛthak

19. sa ghoṣo dhārtarāṣṭrāṇāṃ
hṛdayāni vyadārayat
nabhaś ca pṛthivīṃ caiva
tumulo vyanunādayan

20. atha vyavasthitān dṛṣṭvā
dhārtarāṣṭrān kapidhvajaḥ
pravṛtte śastrasaṃpāte
dhanur udyamya pāṇḍavaḥ

21. hṛṣīkeśaṃ tadā vākyam
idam āha mahīpate
senayor ubhayor madhye
rathaṃ sthāpaya me 'cyuta

14. Kṛṣṇa and Arjuna,
    standing on their mighty chariot
Yoked with white steeds,
    blew their divine conch-shells.

15. Kṛṣṇa blew his "Horn of Pañcajana,"
    Arjuna blew his "Gift of God,"
And Wolf-Belly, the Worker of Terror
    blew his great shell "Wild One."

16. King Yudhiṣṭhira, Kuntī's son,
    blew "Everlasting Victory,"
And Nakula and Sahadeva blew
    "Sweet Tone" and "Gem-Flower."

17. The king of Kāśī—superb bowman—
    Sikhaṇḍin—the great chariot fighter—
Dhṛṣṭadyumna, Virāṭa,
    and the unvanquished Sātyaki,

18. Drupada, and Draupadī's sons,
    and the warrior son of Subhadrā
One by one sounded their conches
    in every direction at once.

19. The wild roar
    that made heaven and earth ring
Rent the hearts
    of Dhṛtarāṣṭra's men.

20–21. Arjuna, known by the monkey in his banner,
    looked upon Dhṛtarāṣṭra's men in battle order
—Arrows had already begun to fly—
    lifted his bow
And then spoke to Kṛṣṇa:
    "Unshakable One,
Halt my chariot
    between the two armies,

22. yāvad etān nirīkṣe 'haṃ
yoddhukāmān avasthitān
kair mayā saha yoddhavyam
asmin raṇasamudyame

23. yotsyamānān avekṣe 'haṃ
ya ete 'tra samāgatāḥ
dhārtarāṣṭrasya durbuddher
yuddhe priyacikīrṣavaḥ

24. evam ukto hṛṣīkeśo
guḍākeśena bhārata
senayor ubhayor madhye
sthāpayitvā rathottamam

25. bhīṣmadroṇapramukhataḥ
sarveṣām ca mahīkṣitām
uvāca pārtha paśyaitān
samavetān kurūn iti

26. tatrāpaśyat sthitān pārthaḥ
pitṝn atha pitāmahān
ācāryān mātulān bhrātṝn
putrān pautrān sakhīṃs tathā

27. śvaśurān suhṛdaś caiva
senayor ubhayor api
tān samīkṣya sa kaunteyaḥ
sarvān bandhūn avasthitān

28. kṛpayā parayāviṣṭo
viṣīdann idam abravīt
dṛṣṭvemān svajanān kṛṣṇa
yuyutsūn samavasthitān

29. sīdanti mama gātrāṇi
mukhaṃ ca pariśuṣyati
vepathuś ca śarīre me
romaharṣaś ca jāyate

22. While I survey
those pugnacious troops arrayed for battle
With whom I am to wage
this great war.

23. Let me look at those who are assembled here
and who will fight,
Who are eager to please in battle
Dhṛtarāṣṭra's perverse son."

24. Kṛṣṇa heeded
Arjuna's request.
He halted the superb chariot
between the two armies,

25. In front of Bhīṣma, Droṇa,
and all the princes of the earth,
And said: "See, Son of Pṛthā,
the assembled Kurus."

26. In that place Arjuna saw
fathers, grandfathers,
Mentors, uncles, brothers,
sons, grandsons, playmates,

27–28. Fathers-in-law, and close friends
in both armies.
Seeing all these kinsmen
in array, the son of Kuntī
Was overwhelmed by emotion
and in despair he said:
"O Kṛṣṇa, when I see my relatives here
who have come together and want to fight,

29. I feel paralyzed,
my mouth becomes dry,
I tremble within,
my hair stands on end;

30. gāṇḍīvaṃ sraṃsate hastāt
tvak caiva paridahyate
na ca śaknomy avasthātuṃ
bhramatīva ca me manaḥ

31. nimittāni ca paśyāmi
viparītāni keśava
na ca śreyo 'nupaśyāmi
hatvā svajanam āhave

32. na kāṅkṣe vijayaṃ kṛṣṇa
na ca rājyaṃ sukhāni ca
kiṃ no rājyena govinda
kiṃ bhogair jīvitena vā

33. yeṣām arthe kāṅkṣitaṃ no
rājyaṃ bhogāḥ sukhāni ca
ta ime 'vasthitā yuddhe
prāṇāṃs tyaktvā dhanāni ca

34. ācāryāḥ pitaraḥ putrās
tathaiva ca pitāmahāḥ
mātulāḥ śvaśurāḥ pautrāḥ
śyālāḥ saṃbandhinas tathā

35. etān na hantum icchāmi
ghnato 'pi madhusūdana
api trailokyarājyasya
hetoḥ kiṃ nu mahīkṛte

36. nihatya dhārtarāṣṭrān naḥ
kā prītiḥ syāj janārdana
pāpam evāśrayed asmān
hatvaitān ātatāyinaḥ

37. tasmān nārhā vayaṃ hantuṃ
dhārtarāṣṭrān svabāndhavān
svajanaṃ hi kathaṃ hatvā
sukhinaḥ syāma mādhava

30. The bow Gāṇḍīva slips from my hand,
 my skin feels hot,
I cannot keep steady,
 my mind whirls.

31. O Keśava, I see
 but evil signs.
I see nothing good resulting
 from slaying my own people in combat.

32. I have no desire for victory, Kṛṣṇa,
 nor for kingship and its joys.
What is kingship worth to us, Govinda,
 and pleasures, or life?

33. These men here drawn up in battle
 giving their lives and possessions
Are the ones for whose sake we desired
 kingship, pleasures, happiness.

34. Teachers, fathers, sons,
 grandfathers,
Uncles, fathers-in-law, grandsons,
 brothers-in-law, and other kinsmen—

35. If they killed me,
 I still would not wish to kill them,
Not for kingship over heaven, air and earth!
 How much less for the sake of the earth alone!

36. What joy could we have, Stirrer of Men,
 if we should slay Dhṛtarāṣṭra's party?
The atrocity would pursue us if we killed
 those men who are aiming their bows at us.

37. We do not have the right to slay
 Dhṛtarāṣṭra's men, our own kin.
For how could we be happy
 after slaying our relatives?

38. yady apy ete na paśyanti
lobhopahatacetasaḥ
kulakṣayakṛtaṃ doṣaṃ
mitradrohe ca pātakam

39. kathaṃ na jñeyam asmābhiḥ
pāpād asmān nivartitum
kulakṣayakṛtaṃ doṣaṃ
prapaśyadbhir janārdana

40. kulakṣaye praṇaśyanti
kuladharmāḥ sanātanāḥ
dharme naṣṭe kulaṃ kṛtsnam
adharmo 'bhibhavaty uta

41. adharmābhibhavāt kṛṣṇa
praduṣyanti kulastriyaḥ
strīṣu duṣṭāsu vārṣṇeya
jāyate varṇasaṃkaraḥ

42. saṃkaro narakāyaiva
kulaghnānāṃ kulasya ca
patanti pitaro hy eṣāṃ
luptapiṇḍodakakriyāḥ

43. doṣair etaiḥ kulaghnānāṃ
varṇasaṃkarakārakaiḥ
utsādyante jātidharmāḥ
kuladharmāś ca śāśvatāḥ

44. utsannakuladharmāṇāṃ
manuṣyāṇāṃ janārdana
narake niyataṃ vāso
bhavatīty anuśuśruma

45. aho bata mahat pāpam
kartuṃ vyavasitā vayam
yad rājyasukhalobhena
hantuṃ svajanam udyatāḥ

38. Even though they see no wickedness
    in annihilating their kin,
In betraying friends,
    since greed has clouded their wits,

39. Should we not be wise enough
    to turn back from this evil,
O Stirrer of Men, as we see before us
    the wickedness of annihilating the entire family?

40. With the disruption of the family,
    the eternal family tradition perishes.
With the collapse of the tradition
    chaos overtakes the whole race.

41. Such predominance of chaos leads to
    the corruption of women in the family.
When the women are corrupted
    the whole society erodes.

42. This erosion leads to hell
    for the family and those who destroyed it
Their ancestors end up in hell too,
    because the ancestral rites are discontinued.

43. The crimes of those who destroy their kinsfolk
    cause promiscuity;
They overturn the rules governing caste
    and the eternal family traditions.

44. Surely, Janārdana, men
    who overturn the family traditions
Will end up in hell.
    This is what we have been taught.

45. Alas! We are determined
    to commit a great crime,
Now that we have come out to kill our own people
    out of greed for kingship and pleasure.

46. yadi mām apratīkāram
aśastram śastrapāṇayaḥ
dhārtarāṣṭrā raṇe hanyus
tan me kṣemataraṃ bhavet

47. evam uktvārjunaḥ saṃkhye
rathopastha upāviśat
visṛjya saśaraṃ cāpaṃ
śokasaṃvignamānasaḥ

46. I would be happier
    if Dhṛtarāṣṭra's men killed me in the battle,
While I was unarmed
    and offered no resistance.

47. With these words Arjuna sank down on his seat
    in the midst of the battle.
He had let go of his bow and arrows.
    Sorrow had overwhelmed him.

II

saṃjaya uvāca

1. taṃ tathā kṛpayāviṣṭam
   aśrupūrṇākulekṣaṇam
   viṣīdantam idaṃ vākyam
   uvāca madhusūdanaḥ

śrībhagavān uvāca

2. kutas tvā kaśmalam idaṃ
   viṣame samupasthitam
   anāryajuṣṭam asvargyam
   akīrtikaram arjuna

3. klaibyaṃ mā sma gamaḥ pārtha
   naitat tvayy upapadyate
   kṣudraṃ hṛdayadaurbalyaṃ
   tyaktvottiṣṭha paraṃtapa

arjuna uvāca

4. kathaṃ bhīṣmam ahaṃ saṃkhye
   droṇaṃ ca madhusūdana
   iṣubhiḥ pratiyotsyāmi
   pūjārhāv arisūdana

5. gurūn ahatvā hi mahānubhāvān
   śreyo bhoktuṃ bhaikṣyam apīha loke
   hatvārthakāmāṃs tu gurūn ihaiva
   bhuñjīya bhogān rudhirapradigdhān

Samjaya:

1. When sentiment had thus overcome him,
   while he despaired—his sight blurred,
   His eyes filled with tears—
   Kṛṣṇa, the Slayer of Madhu, answered:

The Lord:

2. How is it possible that at a time of crisis
   you, Arjuna, should become so weak!
   Noblemen detest such weakness.
   It does not lead to heaven. It is degrading.

3. Be a man, Son of Pṛthā!
   This impotence does not suit you.
   Cast off this abject faintheartedness.
   Stand up, you Conqueror!

Arjuna:

4. O Slayer of Madhu, Slayer of Enemies,
   how can I fight Bhīṣma and Droṇa?
   How shall I send my arrows at those two,
   worthy of my worship?

5. It would be better
   To live on alms
   Without having slain
   Our spiritual guides,
   Men of authority—
   But after killing my elders,
   Even if they were greedy,
   My food here in this world
   Would taste of blood.

6. na caitad vidmaḥ kataran no garīyo
   yad vā jayema yadi vā no jayeyuḥ
   yān eva hatvā na jijīviṣāmas
   te 'vasthitāḥ pramukhe dhārtarāṣṭrāḥ

7. kārpaṇyadoṣopahatasvabhāvaḥ
   pṛcchāmi tvāṃ dharmasaṃmūḍhacetāḥ
   yac chreyaḥ syān niścitaṃ brūhi tan me
   śiṣyas te 'haṃ śādhi māṃ tvāṃ prapannam

8. na hi prapaśyāmi mamāpanudyād
   yac chokam ucchoṣaṇam indriyāṇām
   avāpya bhūmāv asapatnam ṛddhaṃ
   rājyaṃ surāṇām api cādhipatyam

samjaya uvāca

9. evam uktvā hṛṣīkeśaṃ
   guḍākeśaḥ paraṃtapaḥ
   na yotsya iti govindam
   uktvā tūṣṇīṃ babhūva ha

6. Still we do not know
Which is best,
Whether we should win
Or they.
There they are,
Dhṛtarāṣṭra's men,
Drawn up before us.
If we slay them,
We'll no longer wish to live.

7. I am not myself:
I am afflicted
With feelings of pity.
I am confused.
What should be done?
I ask you:
Which is best?
Tell me that
With certainty.
I am your pupil.
Teach me.
I have thrown myself at your feet.

8. For I cannot see
Anything at all
That could dispel this sorrow
Which lames me.
I cannot imagine
Anything to dispel it
Even if I attained
Prosperous kingship
Without a rival on earth,
Or even lordship
Of the gods.

Saṃjaya:

9. Thus the thick-haired warrior
spoke to Kṛṣṇa,
And he concluded: "I shall not fight!"
Then he was silent.

10. tam uvāca hṛṣīkeśaḥ
prahasann iva bhārata
senayor ubhayor madhye
viṣīdantam idaṃ vacaḥ

śrībhagavān uvāca

11. aśocyān anvaśocas tvaṃ
prajñāvādāṃś ca bhāṣase
gatāsūn agatāsūṃś ca
nānuśocanti paṇḍitāḥ

12. na tv evāham jātu nāsaṃ
na tvaṃ neme janādhipāḥ
na caiva na bhaviṣyāmaḥ
sarve vayam ataḥ param

13. dehino 'smin yathā dehe
kaumāraṃ yauvanaṃ jarā
tathā dehāntaraprāptir
dhīras tatra na muhyati

14. mātrāsparśās tu kaunteya
śītoṣṇasukhaduḥkhadāḥ
āgamāpāyino 'nityās
tāṃs titikṣasva bhārata

15. yaṃ hi na vyathayanty ete
puruṣaṃ puruṣarṣabha
samaduḥkhasukhaṃ dhīraṃ
so 'mṛtatvāya kalpate

16. nāsato vidyate bhāvo
nābhāvo vidyate sataḥ
ubhayor api dṛṣṭo 'ntas tv
anayos tattvadarśibhiḥ

17. avināśi tu tad viddhi
yena sarvam idaṃ tatam
vināśam avyayasyāsya
na kaścit kartum arhati

10. Hṛṣīkeśa seemed to smile
    when he answered
  The desperate man
    between the two armies:

The Lord:

11. You have spent your sorrow on beings who do not need it
    and pay lip-service to wisdom.
  Educated men do not sorrow
    for the dead nor the living.

12. There was no time at which I was not
    nor you nor these princes.
  Nor shall any of us
    ever cease to be.

13. Just as a person changes from
    childhood to youth to old age in the body,
  He changes bodies.
    This does not upset the composed man.

14. The world our senses touch, Son of Kuntī,
    is hot or cold, pleasant or unpleasant.
  Sensations come and go. They do not last.
    Learn to endure them, Son of Bharata!

15. They do not shake the composed man
    to whom unpleasantness
  And pleasure are alike.
    He is fit for immortality.

16. What is not cannot come into being,
    and what is has no end.
  Men who see things as they are
    perceive the limit of both.

17. But you must know that which is imperishable
    and which stretched forth the whole world.
  No one is able to destroy that
    which is everlasting.

18. antavanta ime dehā
nityasyoktāḥ śarīriṇaḥ
anāśino 'prameyasya
tasmād yudhyasva bhārata

19. ya enaṃ vetti hantāraṃ
yaś cainaṃ manyate hatam
ubhau tau na vijānīto
nāyaṃ hanti na hanyate

20. na jāyate mriyate vā kadācin
nāyaṃ bhūtvā bhavitā vā na bhūyaḥ
ajo nityaḥ śāśvato 'yaṃ purāṇo
na hanyate hanyamāne śarīre

21. vedāvināśinaṃ nityaṃ
ya enam ajam avyayam
kathaṃ sa puruṣaḥ pārtha
kaṃ ghātayati hanti kam

22. vāsāṃsi jīrṇāni yathā vihāya
navāni gṛhṇāti naro 'parāṇi
tathā śarīrāṇi vihāya jīrṇāny
anyāni saṃyāti navāni dehī

23. nainaṃ chindanti śastrāṇi
nainaṃ dahati pāvakaḥ
na cainaṃ kledayanty āpo
na śoṣayati mārutaḥ

18. Before you are the temporal bodies
    of the eternal, embodied one
Who does not perish and cannot be measured.
    Therefore you must fight.

19. Who thinks this one a slayer,
    or who thinks of him as slain,
Both lack understanding.
    He neither slays nor is slain.

20. He is never born.
He never dies.
You cannot say of him
He came to be
And will be no more.
Primeval, he is
Unborn,
Changeless,
Everlasting.
The body will be slain,
But he will not.

21. How can the man who knows him as imperishable,
    eternal, unborn, and changeless,
Kill anyone?
    Whom does he cause to be killed, Son of Pṛthā?

22. Just as a man discards
Worn-out clothes
And puts on others,
That are new,
The embodied leaves behind
Worn-out bodies
And enters others,
New ones.

23. Swords cannot wound him,
    the fire cannot burn him,
Water cannot dampen him
    nor the wind parch him.

24. acchedyo 'yam adāhyo 'yam
akledyo 'śoṣya eva ca
nityaḥ sarvagataḥ sthāṇur
acalo 'yaṃ sanātanaḥ

25. avyakto 'yam acintyo 'yam
avikāryo 'yam ucyate
tasmād evaṃ viditvainaṃ
nānuśocitum arhasi

26. atha cainaṃ nityajātaṃ
nityaṃ vā manyase mṛtam
tathāpi tvaṃ mahābāho
nainaṃ śocitum arhasi

27. jātasya hi dhruvo mṛtyur
dhruvaṃ janma mṛtasya ca
tasmād aparihārye 'rthe
na tvaṃ śocitum arhasi

28. avyaktādīni bhūtāni
vyaktamadhyāni bhārata
avyaktanidhanāny eva
tatra kā paridevanā

29. āścaryavat paśyati kaścid enam
āścaryavad vadati tathaiva cānyaḥ
āścaryavac cainam anyaḥ śṛṇoti
śrutvāpy enaṃ veda na caiva kaścit

24. He cannot be cut or burned,
    not moistened or dried.
Subsisting always, everywhere, immobile,
    fixed is the eternal one.

25. He is unmanifest, unthinkable,
    and not subject to change.
Therefore, once you have understood him in this way,
    you should not sorrow.

***

26. Or, even if you think he is born and dies
    continually,
Even then, O Warrior,
    you ought not to lament him.

27. Whoever is born will certainly die,
    and whoever dies will certainly be born.
Since this cannot be changed,
    your grief is inappropriate.

28. No one sees the beginning of things,
    but only the middle.
Their end also is unseen.
    There is no reason to lament.

29. As by a miracle
One may see him.
Likewise by miracle
One may
Name and discuss him,
And by miracle
One may hear
What is revealed of him.
But even having heard,
No one knows him.

30. dehī nityam avadhyo 'yaṃ
dehe sarvasya bhārata
tasmāt sarvāṇi bhūtāni
na tvaṃ śocitum arhasi

31. svadharmam api cāvekṣya
na vikampitum arhasi
dharmyād dhi yuddhāc chreyo 'nyat
kṣatriyasya na vidyate

32. yadṛcchayā copapannaṃ
svargadvāram apāvṛtam
sukhinaḥ kṣatriyāḥ pārtha
labhante yuddham īdṛśam

33. atha cet tvam imaṃ dharmyaṃ
saṃgrāmaṃ na kariṣyasi
tataḥ svadharmaṃ kīrtiṃ ca
hitvā pāpam avāpsyasi

34. akīrtiṃ cāpi bhūtāni
kathayiṣyanti te 'vyayām
saṃbhāvitasya cākīrtir
maraṇād atiricyate

35. bhayād raṇād uparataṃ
maṃsyante tvāṃ mahārathāḥ
yeṣāṃ ca tvaṃ bahumato
bhūtvā yāsyasi lāghavam

36. avācyavādāṃś ca bahūn
vadiṣyanti tavāhitāḥ
nindantas tava sāmarthyam
tato duḥkhataraṃ nu kim

37. hato vā prāpsyasi svargaṃ
jitvā vā bhokṣyase mahīm
tasmād uttiṣṭha kaunteya
yuddhāya kṛtaniścayaḥ

30. That person existing in everyone's body
    is for ever inviolable.
  Therefore you should not sorrow
    for any creatures.

***

31. Considering also the duty of your own class
    you should not waver.
  To a warrior nothing is better than
    a just battle.

32. Happy the warriors, Son of Pṛthā,
    who find such a battle
  Offered unsought—
    a gate to heaven wide open.

33. But if you will not engage
    in this just war,
  You give up your duty and your fame
    and will incur demerit.

34. Also, the world will talk
    of your everlasting dishonor,
  And dishonor is worse than death
    to a man of fame.

35. The great warriors will think
    you deserted out of fear.
  Those who held you in high esteem
    will snap their fingers at you.

36. Your detractors will say
    a number of unspeakable things,
  Reviling all you stand for.
    What could be worse than that?

37. Slain, you will gain heaven;
    victorious, you will enjoy the earth.
  Stand up, therefore, determined to fight,
    Son of Kuntī!

38. sukhaduḥkhe same kṛtvā
lābhālābhau jayājayau
tato yuddhāya yujyasva
naivaṃ pāpam avāpsyasi

39. eṣā te 'bhihitā sāṃkhye
buddhir yoge tv imāṃ śṛṇu
buddhyā yukto yayā pārtha
karmabandhaṃ prahāsyasi

40. nehābhikramanāśo 'sti
pratyavāyo na vidyate
svalpam apy asya dharmasya
trāyate mahato bhayāt

41. vyavasāyātmikā buddhir
ekeha kurunandana
bahuśākhā hy anantāś ca
buddhayo 'vyavasāyinām

42. yām imāṃ puṣpitāṃ vācaṃ
pravadanty avipaścitaḥ
vedavādaratāḥ pārtha
nānyad astīti vādinaḥ

43. kāmātmānaḥ svargaparā
janmakarmaphalapradām
kriyāviśeṣabahulāṃ
bhogaiśvaryagatiṃ prati

44. bhogaiśvaryaprasaktānāṃ
tayāpahṛtacetasām
vyavasāyātmikā buddhiḥ
samādhau na vidhīyate

38. Realizing that joy and grief, gain and loss,
    winning and losing are the same,
  Gird yourself for the battle.
    Thus you will not incur demerit.

***

39. I have given you this understanding through the teachings
    of Reason. Now hear it in the tradition of Discipline.
  Armed with its meditative knowledge you will be free
    from imprisonment by actions.

40. In Discipline no observance is lost,
    nor can any harm result from Discipline.
  Even the least practice on this path
    can protect you from grave danger.

41. The knowledge meditation attains on this path consists
    in commitment and is whole.
  Irresolute men have a fragmented
    and incomplete knowledge.

42–44. Undiscerning men, theologians
    preoccupied with Scriptural lore,
  Who claim there is nothing else,
    utter words with ephemeral results;

  Their words promise better births through cultic acts,
    dwell at length on various rites,
  And aim at pleasure and power.
    These men are full of desire, zealous for heaven.

  They cling to pleasures and power
    and are fooled by their own discourses.
  They have no knowledge consisting in commitment,
    fixed in concentration.

45. traiguṇyaviṣayā vedā
 nistraiguṇyo bhavārjuna
 nirdvandvo nityasattvastho
 niryogakṣema ātmavān

46. yāvān artha udapāne
 sarvataḥ saṃplutodake
 tāvān sarveṣu vedeṣu
 brāhmaṇasya vijānataḥ

47. karmaṇy evādhikāras te
 mā phaleṣu kadācana
 mā karmaphalahetur bhūr
 mā te sango 'stv akarmaṇi

48. yogasthaḥ kuru karmāṇi
 saṅgaṃ tyaktvā dhanaṃjaya
 siddhyasiddhyoḥ samo bhūtvā
 samatvaṃ yoga ucyate

49. dūreṇa hy avaraṃ karma
 buddhiyogād dhanaṃjaya
 buddhau śaraṇam anviccha
 kṛpaṇāḥ phalahetavaḥ

50. buddhiyukto jahātīha
 ubhe sukṛtaduṣkṛte
 tasmād yogāya yujyasva
 yogaḥ karmasu kauśalam

51. karmajaṃ buddhiyuktā hi
 phalaṃ tyaktvā manīṣiṇaḥ
 janmabandhavinirmuktāḥ
 padaṃ gacchanty anāmayam

52. yadā te mohakalilaṃ
 buddhir vyatitariṣyati
 tadā gantāsi nirvedaṃ
 śrotavyasya śrutasya ca

45. The Scriptures speak to the world's weave of integrity,
passion, and sloth. Transcend it, Arjuna,
Free from opposites, forever in integrity,
detached from things, in command of yourself.

46. All the Scriptures mean as much—no more, no less—
to the discerning spiritual man
As a water tank
in a universal flood.

47. You are entitled to perform rituals,
but not at all to their results.
The results of rituals should not be your motive.
Nor should you abstain from ritual.

48. Follow Discipline, and perform your rites
with detachment, Pursuer of Wealth,
Equal-minded to success or failure.
Discipline means equanimity,

49. For ritual [performed for its effect] is far inferior
to the Discipline of Meditation.
Seek refuge in meditative knowledge.
Wretched are men when results are their incentive.

50. A man with meditative knowledge
leaves behind him both good and evil deeds.
Therefore, practice Discipline.
Discipline is skill in works and rites.

51. Intelligent men with meditative knowledge
disregard the reward of cultic work,
And enter a blissful state,
freed from the imprisonment of births.

52. When your meditation gets across
the thicket of delusion,
You will no longer worry about
what the Scriptures have taught you or will teach you.

53. śrutivipratipannā te
    yadā sthāsyati niścalā
samādhāv acalā buddhis
    tadā yogam avāpsyasi

arjuna uvāca

54. sthitaprajñasya kā bhāṣā
    samādhisthasya keśava
sthitadhīḥ kiṃ prabhāṣeta
    kim āsīta vrajeta kim

śrībhagavān uvāca

55. prajahāti yadā kāmān
    sarvān pārtha manogatān
ātmany evātmanā tuṣṭaḥ
    sthitaprajñas tadocyate

56. duḥkheṣv anudvignamanāḥ
    sukheṣu vigataspṛhaḥ
vītarāgabhayakrodhaḥ
    sthitadhīr munir ucyate

57. yaḥ sarvatrānabhisnehas
    tat tat prāpya śubhāśubham
nābhinandati na dveṣṭi
    tasya prajñā pratiṣṭhitā

58. yadā saṃharate cāyaṃ
    kūrmo 'ṅgānīva sarvaśaḥ
indriyāṇīndriyārthebhyas
    tasya prajñā pratiṣṭhitā

59. viṣayā vinivartante
    nirāhārasya dehinaḥ
rasavarjaṃ raso 'py asya
    paraṃ dṛṣṭvā nivartate

53. When your meditating mind, now bewildered
 by conflicting views of Revelation,
Shall stand firm, unmoved in concentration,
 then will you attain Discipline.

Arjuna:

54. Please describe the man of firm judgment
 who is established in concentration.
How would a man of firm mind speak,
 or sit, or move about?

The Lord:

55. A man is of firm judgment
 when he has abandoned all inner desires
And the self is content,
 at peace with itself.

56. When unpleasant things do not perturb him
 nor pleasures beguile him,
When longing, fear, and anger have left,
 he is a sage of firm mind.

57. That man has a firm judgment
 who feels no desire toward anything.
Whatever good or bad he incurs,
 he never delights in it nor hates it.

58. When on all sides he withdraws his senses
 from the sensual world,
As a tortoise draws in its legs,
 his judgment has become stable.

59. The realm of the senses recedes
 for the person who fasts.
Only an inclination, a flavor, lingers.
 That leaves him only when he has seen the highest.

60. yatato hy api kaunteya
puruṣasya vipaścitaḥ
indriyāṇi pramāthīni
haranti prasabhaṃ manaḥ

61. tāni sarvāṇi saṃyamya
yukta āsīta matparaḥ
vaśe hi yasyendriyāṇi
tasya prajñā pratiṣṭhitā

62. dhyāyato viṣayān puṃsaḥ
saṅgas teṣūpajāyate
saṅgāt saṃjāyate kāmaḥ
kāmāt krodho 'bhijāyate

63. krodhād bhavati saṃmohaḥ
saṃmohāt smṛtivibhramaḥ
smṛtibhraṃśād buddhināśo
buddhināśāt praṇaśyati

64. rāgadveṣaviyuktais tu
viṣayān indriyaiś caran
ātmavaśyair vidheyātmā
prasādam adhigacchati

65. prasāde sarvaduḥkhānāṃ
hānir asyopajāyate
prasannacetaso hy āśu
buddhiḥ paryavatiṣṭhate

66. nāsti buddhir ayuktasya
na cāyuktasya bhāvanā
na cābhāvayataḥ śāntir
aśāntasya kutaḥ sukham

67. indriyāṇāṃ hi caratāṃ
yan mano 'nuvidhīyate
tad asya harati prajñāṃ
vāyur nāvam ivāmbhasi

60. Even the wise man who exerts himself
  to attain perfection
Has senses that harass him
  and carry away his mind.

61. One should sit down, restraining all senses,
  intent on me.
Whoever controls his senses
  has a firm judgment.

62. A man gets attached to what the senses tell him
  if he does not turn his mind away.
Attachment gives rise to desire,
  desire to anger.

63. Anger leads to a state of delusion;
  delusion distorts one's memory.
Distortion of memory distorts consciousness,
  and then a man perishes.

64. But when a man wholly governing himself
  is roaming the sensual world
With his senses under control, freed
  from likes and dislikes, he attains clarity.

65. In clarity, he is liberated
  from all unpleasantness,
For the judgment of clear-minded men
  is unerringly steadfast.

66. The undisciplined does not meditate;
  he has no means of mental realization.
And there is no peace for one without such means.
  Without peace, how can there be happiness for him?

67. For when a man allows his mind to obey
  the whims of the senses,
It destroys his judgment
  like a storm destroys a ship.

68. tasmād yasya mahābāho
 nigṛhītāni sarvaśaḥ
indriyāṇīndriyārthebhyas
 tasya prajñā pratiṣṭhitā

69. yā niśā sarvabhūtānāṃ
 tasyāṃ jāgarti saṃyamī
yasyāṃ jāgrati bhūtāni
 sā niśā paśyato muneḥ

70. āpūryamāṇam acalapratiṣṭhaṃ
 samudram āpaḥ praviśanti yadvat
tadvat kāmā yaṃ praviśanti sarve
 sa śāntim āpnoti na kāmakāmī

71. vihāya kāmān yaḥ sarvān
 pumāṃś carati niḥspṛhaḥ
nirmamo nirahaṃkāraḥ
 sa śāntim adhigacchati

72. eṣā brāhmī sthitiḥ pārtha
 naināṃ prāpya vimuhyati
sthitvāsyām antakāle 'pi
 brahmanirvāṇam ṛcchati

68. Therefore, O Warrior,
having your senses entirely withdrawn
From the world of the senses
means attaining a steadfast judgment.

69. The man of self-control is awake
in what is night for all creatures;
And when they are awake,
it is night for the seer.

70. The sea gathers the waters;
It fills and fills itself . . .
Its equilibrium
Is undisturbed.
So also
The man into whom
All desires enter—
Not he who goes after desires—
Finds peace.

71. The man who has given up all desire
and moves about without wanting anything,
Who says neither *mine* nor *I*,
wins peace.

72. This, Son of Pṛthā, is divine stability.
Whoso reaches it is not again confused.
Whoso abides in it even at death
gains the freedom that is God's.

III

arjuna uvāca

1. jyāyasī cet karmaṇas te
   matā buddhir janārdana
   tat kiṃ karmaṇi ghore māṃ
   niyojayasi keśava

2. vyāmiśreṇaiva vākyena
   buddhiṃ mohayasīva me
   tad ekaṃ vada niścitya
   yena śreyo 'ham āpnuyām

śrībhagavān uvāca

3. loke 'smin dvividhā niṣṭhā
   purā proktā mayānagha
   jñānayogena sāṃkhyānāṃ
   karmayogena yoginām

4. na karmaṇām anārambhān
   naiṣkarmyaṃ puruṣo 'śnute
   na ca saṃnyasanād eva
   siddhiṃ samadhigacchati

5. na hi kaścit kṣanam api
   jātu tiṣṭhaty akarmakṛt
   kāryate hy avaśaḥ karma
   sarvaḥ prakṛtijair guṇaiḥ

6. karmendriyāṇi saṃyamya
   ya āste manasā smaran
   indriyārthān vimūḍhātmā
   mithyācāraḥ sa ucyate

Arjuna:

1. If meditative knowledge
   or right judgment is superior to action,
   Why do you urge me
   to do this work of violence, Keśava?

2. You confuse me
   with a tangle of words.
   Teach me the one thing
   by which I can attain what is highest.

The Lord:

3. O Blameless One, long ago have I revealed
   the twofold rule basic to this world:
   For men of reason, the way of Knowledge;
   for men of discipline, the way of Cultic Work.

4. Man does not overcome activity
   by refraining from ritual.
   He does not become successful
   by renunciation alone.

5. For no one remains inactive
   even for a moment.
   The states of all existence make everyone act
   in spite of himself.

6. A man who restrains his body's powers and functions,
   but who sits, turning over in his mind
   The objects of sense, deludes himself.
   His conduct is pointless.

7. yas tv indriyāṇi manasā
niyamyārabhate 'rjuna
karmendriyaiḥ karmayogam
asaktaḥ sa viśiṣyate

8. niyataṃ kuru karma tvam
karma jyāyo hy akarmaṇaḥ
śarīrayātrāpi ca te
na prasidhyed akarmaṇaḥ

9. yajñārthāt karmano 'nyatra
loko 'yam karmabandhanaḥ
tadarthaṃ karma kaunteya
muktasaṅgaḥ samācara

10. sahayajñāḥ prajāḥ sṛṣṭvā
purovāca prajāpatiḥ
anena prasaviṣyadhvam
eṣa vo 'stv iṣṭakāmadhuk

11. devān bhāvayatānena
te devā bhāvayantu vaḥ
parasparaṃ bhāvayantaḥ
śreyaḥ param avāpsyatha

12. iṣṭān bhogān hi vo devā
dāsyante yajñabhāvitāḥ
tair dattān apradāyaibhyo
yo bhuṅkte stena eva saḥ

13. yajñaśiṣṭāśinaḥ santo
mucyante sarvakilbiṣaiḥ
bhuñjate te tv aghaṃ pāpā
ye pacanty ātmakāraṇāt

14. annād bhavanti bhūtāni
parjanyād annasaṃbhavaḥ
yajñād bhavati parjanyo
yajñaḥ karmasamudbhavaḥ

7. He is superior who with his mind
   restrains the senses, Arjuna, and engages
In the discipline of work
   with all his powers, not anxious for results.

8. Perform the required ritual work.
   Action is better than inaction.
Without action, the body
   would stop functioning.

9. It is true, this world is enslaved by activity,
   but the exception is work for the sake of sacrifice.
Therefore, Son of Kuntī, free from attachment,
   act for that purpose.

10. Long ago, the Lord of men brought forth
   men together with sacrifice and said:
"By this you shall multiply;
   let this be the source of your abundance.

11. Please the gods by sacrifice
   and they must make you prosper.
While you and the gods sustain each other,
   you will reach the highest good.

12. Sustained by sacrifice
   the gods will fulfill your desires.
Only a thief consumes their gifts
   without giving to them."

13. Good men eat the remnants of sacrifice
   and are cleansed of all impurities.
The wicked, who cook merely for themselves,
   partake of evil.

14. From food, creatures arise.
   Rain produces food.
Sacrifice brings rain.
   Cultic work is the root of sacrifice.

15. karma brahmodbhavaṃ viddhi
brahmākṣarasamudbhavam
tasmāt sarvagataṃ brahma
nityaṃ yajñe pratiṣṭhitam

16. evaṃ pravartitaṃ cakraṃ
nānuvartayatīha yaḥ
aghāyur indriyārāmo
moghaṃ pārtha sa jīvati

17. yas tv ātmaratir eva syād
ātmatṛptaś ca mānavaḥ
ātmany eva ca saṃtuṣṭas
tasya kāryaṃ na vidyate

18. naiva tasya kṛtenārtho
nākṛteneha kaścana
na cāsya sarvabhūteṣu
kaścid arthavyapāśrayaḥ

19. tasmād asaktaḥ satataṃ
kāryaṃ karma samācara
asakto hy ācaran karma
param āpnoti pūruṣaḥ

20. karmaṇaiva hi samsiddhim
āsthitā janakādayaḥ
lokasaṃgraham evāpi
saṃpaśyan kartum arhasi

21. yad yad ācarati śreṣṭhas
tat tad evetaro janaḥ
sa yat pramāṇaṃ kurute
lokas tad anuvartate

22. na me pārthāsti kartavyaṃ
triṣu lokeṣu kiṃcana
nānavāptam avāptavyaṃ
varta eva ca karmaṇi

15. Cultic work comes from the Divine,
    the Divine from the one supreme, subtle sound.
Hence the Divine, although omnipresent,
    is ever established in the sacrifice.

16. Whoever does not turn with the wheel
    thus set in motion—
That man lives in vain, Son of Pṛthā.
    He is of evil intent, engrossed in the senses.

17. But the man who takes pleasure in the self
    and is satisfied in its reality
And is wholly content in it,
    has no real need for action.

18. For him there is no sense whatever in action
    nor in inaction.
He does not rely on anything in this world
    for any end.

19. Therefore, do the work that is required, always
    free from attachments.
Acting in that freedom
    man reaches the highest.

20. By cultic work Janaka and others
    attained complete success.
Concerned alone with the upholding of the world,
    you should act.

21. Whatever the best man does,
    others do that also.
The world follows
    the standard he sets for himself.

22. There is nothing at all I need to do
    in the worlds, heaven, air, and earth.
There is nothing I need that I do not have.
    And yet I am engaged in work.

23. yadi hy ahaṃ na varteyaṃ
 jātu karmaṇy atandritaḥ
mama vartmānuvartante
 manuṣyāḥ pārtha sarvaśaḥ

24. utsīdeyur ime lokā
 na kuryāṃ karma ced aham
saṃkarasya ca kartā syām
 upahanyām imāḥ prajāḥ

25. saktāḥ karmaṇy avidvāṃso
 yathā kurvanti bhārata
kuryād vidvāṃs tathāsaktaś
 cikīrṣur lokasaṃgraham

26. na buddhibhedaṃ janayed
 ajñānāṃ karmasaṅginām
joṣayet sarvakarmāṇi
 vidvān yuktaḥ samācaran

27. prakṛteḥ kriyamāṇāni
 guṇaiḥ karmāṇi sarvaśaḥ
ahaṃkāravimūḍhātmā
 kartāham iti manyate

28. tattvavit tu mahābāho
 guṇakarmavibhāgayoḥ
guṇā guṇeṣu vartanta
 iti matvā na sajjate

29. prakṛter guṇasaṃmūḍhāḥ
 sajjante guṇakarmasu
tān akṛtsnavido mandān
 kṛtsnavin na vicālayet

30. mayi sarvāṇi karmāṇi
 saṃnyasyādhyātmacetasā
nirāśīr nirmamo bhūtvā
 yudhyasva vigatajvaraḥ

23. For if I did not engage in action,
    tirelessly,
  People everywhere
    would follow my example.

24. If I did no work,
    these worlds would go down,
  And I would surely wreak havoc;
    I would destroy these people.

25. Fools are wedded to cultic work.
    A wise man should act as they do,
  But unattached,
    envisaging the totality of the world.

26. Unwise men are attached to ritual,
    and he should not unsettle their minds.
  Being himself disciplined in his acts,
    the wise should encourage them in all their rites.

27. Always and everywhere, acts are done
    by the states arising in primal matter.
  A man totally confused in his self-consciousness
    imagines: *I act*.

28. But he who knows how the forces of nature
    and cultic work are really divided, O Warrior,
  Is free from them, for he is aware
    that nature's forces always move one another.

29. A man of full knowledge should not interfere
    with dullards, who know only part.
  They are obsessed by the forces of nature
    and entranced by their motions.

30. Cast all works on me, directing
    your thought to the reality of your self.
  Become free from desires, from selfishness,
    and fight without anxiety.

31. ye me matam idaṃ nityam
anutiṣṭhanti mānavāḥ
śraddhāvanto 'nasūyanto
mucyante te 'pi karmabhiḥ

32. ye tv etad abhyasūyanto
nānutiṣṭhanti me matam
sarvajñānavimūḍhāṃs tān
viddhi naṣṭān acetasaḥ

33. sadṛśaṃ ceṣṭate svasyāḥ
prakṛter jñānavān api
prakṛtiṃ yānti bhūtāni
nigrahaḥ kiṃ kariṣyati

34. indriyasyendriyasyārthe
rāgadveṣau vyavasthitau
tayor na vaśam āgacchet
tau hy asya paripanthinau

35. śreyān svadharmo viguṇaḥ
paradharmāt svanuṣṭhitāt
svadharme nidhanaṃ śreyaḥ
paradharmo bhayāvahaḥ

arjuna uvāca

36. atha kena prayukto 'yaṃ
pāpaṃ carati pūruṣaḥ
anicchann api vārṣṇeya
balād iva niyojitaḥ

śrībhagavān uvāca

37. kāma eṣa krodha eṣa
rajoguṇasamudbhavaḥ
mahāśano mahāpāpmā
viddhy enam iha vairiṇam

31. Men who hold to this my teaching
    with full confidence,
Without caviling,
    are no longer imprisoned by their acts.

32. But those who are irritated by my teaching
    and do not follow it
Are fools; they are lost;
    they are estranged from insight.

33. Even a wise man moves
    according to his nature.
All creatures follow their nature.
    Coercion will accomplish nothing.

34. Likes and dislikes are arrayed
    in whatever our senses grasp.
A man should not come under the sway
    of likes and dislikes. They are his opponents.

35. One's own duty in its imperfection
    is better than someone else's duty well-performed.
It is better to die in one's own duty. . . .
    Another's duty is perilous.

Arjuna:

36. Then what or who makes man do wrong
    even without wanting to,
As if he were driven by force,
    Son of Vṛṣṇi?

The Lord:

37. It is desire, and it is anger, and arises
    from the state of being known as passion.
It devours much and is a great evil.
    That is the enemy.

38. dhūmenāvriyate vahnir
    yathādarśo malena ca
yathōlbenāvṛto garbhas
    tathā tenedam āvṛtam

39. āvṛtaṃ jñānam etena
    jñānino nityavairiṇā
kāmarūpeṇa kaunteya
    duṣpūreṇānalena ca

40. indriyāṇi mano buddhir
    asyādhiṣṭhānam ucyate
etair vimohayaty eṣa
    jñānam āvṛtya dehinam

41. tasmāt tvam indriyāṇy ādau
    niyamya bharatarṣabha
pāpmānaṃ prajahi hy enaṃ
    jñānavijñānanāśanam

42. indriyāṇi parāṇy āhur
    indriyebhyaḥ paraṃ manaḥ
manasas tu parā buddhir
    yo buddheḥ paratas tu saḥ

43. evaṃ buddheḥ paraṃ buddhvā
    saṃstabhyātmānam ātmanā
jahi śatruṃ mahābāho
    kāmarūpaṃ durāsadam

38. This enemy covers the world
as smoke conceals the fire,
As dirt clouds a mirror,
or a membrane envelops an embryo.

39. This constant enemy of the wise
keeps wisdom hidden.
It appears as desire.
It is an insatiable fire.

40. The senses, the mind, our concentration,
uphold this enemy.
By means of them the enemy conceals
wisdom and deludes a man.

41. Hence you must slay that destroyer
of wisdom and discrimination.
You must slay it after first
conquering your senses, Strongest of Bharatas.

42. They say the senses are high,
yet the mind higher than the senses.
The power of concentration transcends the mind.
Still, there is he who is beyond that power.

43. Thus understanding him who is beyond concentration,
you yourself, gaining strength by yourself,
You, Warrior, must slay
the formidable enemy in the form of desire.

IV

śrībhagavān uvāca

1. imaṃ vivasvate yogaṃ
   proktavān aham avyayam
   vivasvān manave prāha
   manur ikṣvākave 'bravīt

2. evaṃ paramparāprāptam
   imaṃ rājarṣayo viduḥ
   sa kāleneha mahatā
   yogo naṣṭaḥ paraṃtapa

3. sa evāyaṃ mayā te 'dya
   yogaḥ proktaḥ purātanaḥ
   bhakto 'si me sakhā ceti
   rahasyaṃ hy etad uttamam

arjuna uvāca

4. aparaṃ bhavato janma
   paraṃ janma vivasvataḥ
   katham etad vijānīyāṃ
   tvam ādau proktavān iti

śrībhagavān uvāca

5. bahūni me vyatītāni
   janmāni tava cārjuna
   tāny ahaṃ veda sarvāṇi
   na tvaṃ vettha paraṃtapa

6. ajo 'pi sann avyayātmā
   bhūtānām īśvaro 'pi san
   prakṛtiṃ svām adhiṣṭhāya
   saṃbhavāmy ātmamāyayā

The Lord:

1. Long long ago I taught Vivasvant [the man of
   mythic times] this ceaseless discipline.
   Vivasvant gave it to Manu [the first perfectly righteous man]
   and Manu gave it to Ikṣvāku [who founded one of the
   two royal dynasties].

2. The discipline thus sacredly handed down
   was understood by the royal seers.
   Then, after a long presence in this world,
   it was lost.

3. This same discipline of ancient days
   today I give to you,
   Because you are my devotee and friend.
   And indeed, this highest of all matters is secret.

Arjuna:

4. Your birth is something recent;
   Vivasvant's happened long ago.
   How can I make sense of what you say,
   that you taught this long, long ago, in the beginning?

The Lord:

5. You and I have had
   many births, Arjuna.
   I know them all.
   You do not.

6. Unborn, imperishable in my own being,
   and Lord over finite lives,
   Still I take as my basis material existence
   and appear through my own power.

7. yadā yadā hi dharmasya
glānir bhavati bhārata
abhyutthānam adharmasya
tadātmānaṃ sṛjāmy aham

8. paritrāṇāya sādhūnāṃ
vināśāya ca duṣkṛtām
dharmasaṃsthāpanārthāya
saṃbhavāmi yuge yuge

9. janma karma ca me divyam
evaṃ yo vetti tattvataḥ
tyaktvā dehaṃ punarjanma
naiti mām eti so 'rjuna

10. vītarāgabhayakrodhā
manmayā mām upāśritāḥ
bahavo jñānatapasā
pūtā madbhāvam āgatāḥ

11. ye yathā māṃ prapadyante
tāṃs tathaiva bhajāmy aham
mama vartmānuvartante
manuṣyāḥ pārtha sarvaśaḥ

12. kāṅkṣantaḥ karmaṇāṃ siddhiṃ
yajanta iha devatāḥ
kṣipraṃ hi mānuṣe loke
siddhir bhavati karmajā

13. cāturvarṇyaṃ mayā sṛṣṭaṃ
guṇakarmavibhāgaśaḥ
tasya kartāram api māṃ
viddhy akartāram avyayam

14. na māṃ karmāṇi limpanti
na me karmaphale spṛhā
iti māṃ yo 'bhijānāti
karmabhir na sa badhyate

7. For whenever
   right languishes
   And unright ascends,
   I manifest myself.

8. Age after age I appear
   to establish the right and true,
   So that the good are saved
   and the evildoers perish.

9. When a man knows my divine birth and work
   thus, as they really are,
   After this life he is not reborn,
   but comes to me.

10. Many people, freed of passion, fear, and anger,
    full of me and relying on me,
    Have been purified by the fire of wisdom
    and have come to my mansion.

11. Men seek refuge with me in various ways.
    I grant them grace.
    All around you,
    men are following my path.

12. Wanting their cultic acts to succeed,
    they offer sacrifices to the gods,
    For here in the world of men successful results
    come quickly and easily through ritual.

13. I brought forth the four great divisions of men
    according to their qualities and rituals.
    Although I made all this,
    know that I never act at all.

14. Actions do not pollute me;
    desire for results is unknown to me.
    He who understands me thus
    is not ensnared by his ritual acts.

15. evaṃ jñātvā kṛtaṃ karma
    pūrvair api mumukṣubhiḥ
    kuru karmaiva tasmāt tvaṃ
    pūrvaiḥ pūrvataraṃ kṛtam

16. kiṃ karma kim akarmeti
    kavayo 'py atra mohitāḥ
    tat te karma pravakṣyāmi
    yaj jñātvā mokṣyase 'śubhāt

17. karmaṇo hy api boddhavyaṃ
    boddhavyaṃ ca vikarmaṇaḥ
    akarmaṇaś ca boddhavyaṃ
    gahanā karmaṇo gatiḥ

18. karmaṇy akarma yaḥ paśyed
    akarmaṇi ca karma yaḥ
    sa buddhimān manuṣyeṣu
    sa yuktaḥ kṛtsnakarmakṛt

19. yasya sarve samārambhāḥ
    kāmasaṃkalpavarjitāḥ
    jñānāgnidagdhakarmāṇaṃ
    tam āhuḥ paṇḍitaṃ budhāḥ

20. tyaktvā karmaphalāsaṅgaṃ
    nityatṛpto nirāśrayaḥ
    karmaṇy abhipravṛtto 'pi
    naiva kiṃcit karoti saḥ

21. nirāśīr yatacittātmā
    tyaktasarvaparigrahaḥ
    śārīraṃ kevalaṃ karma
    kurvan nāpnoti kilbiṣam

22. yadṛcchālābhasaṃtuṣṭo
    dvandvātīto vimatsaraḥ
    samaḥ siddhāv asiddhau ca
    kṛtvāpi na nibadhyate

15. With this in mind, men in ancient days did cultic acts
    while aspiring for release.
    And therefore you must imitate
    the men of ancient times.

16. Even sages have been confused
    by the meaning of "active" and "inactive."
    Therefore I shall explain what action is.
    Knowing this will free you from evil.

17. One must understand what right action is
    and what wrong action is.
    One must know also about nonaction. It is difficult
    to understand the nature of action.

18. Whoever sees quiescence in the prescribed cultic acts
    and effective acts in inaction,
    He is understanding among men.
    Doing all right acts, he is disciplined.

19. The man whose undertakings have lost
    desire and calculation
    Is called educated by those with understanding.
    His actions are consumed in the fire of wisdom.

20. Not caring for the results of his work,
    always content, not in need of support,
    Even when he becomes engaged in action,
    he does not really do anything.

21. Without wishes, with mind and body under control,
    with no claim upon anything,
    Involved in no activity other than that
    of the body alone, he cannot incur demerit.

22. Pleased by whatever comes his way, outside the realm
    of opposites, free from selfishness,
    Even-minded in success and failure,
    even when he has acted, his act does not imprison him.

23. gatasaṅgasya muktasya
 jñānāvasthitacetasaḥ
yajñāyācarataḥ karma
 samagraṃ pravilīyate

24. brahmārpaṇaṃ brahma havir
 brahmāgnau brahmaṇā hutam
brahmaiva tena gantavyaṃ
 brahmakarmasamādhinā

25. daivam evāpare yajñaṃ
 yoginaḥ paryupāsate
brahmāgnāv apare yajñaṃ
 yajñenaivopajuhvati

26. śrotrādīnīndriyāṇy anye
 saṃyamāgniṣu juhvati
śabdādīn viṣayān anya
 indriyāgniṣu juhvati

27. sarvāṇīndriyakarmāṇi
 prāṇakarmāṇi cāpare
ātmasaṃyamayogāgnau
 juhvati jñānadīpite

28. dravyayajñās tapoyajñā
 yogayajñās tathāpare
svādhyāyajñānayajñāś ca
 yatayaḥ saṃśitavratāḥ

23. The actions of this man all vanish.
    He has no attachment anymore. He is free.
His mind is held steady in wisdom. He does
    what should be done for the sacrifices.

24. The dedication of the sacrifice is God.
    The oblation itself is God. God pours it into God's fire.
God is bound to be attained by one
    who concentrates on God's cultic work.

25. The discipline of some is to revere
    the sacrifice itself.
Some follow the rules of sacrifice
    but offer it upon God's spiritual fire.

26. Some offer up their sense of hearing
    and the other senses upon the fires of self-restraint.
And some offer up sound and the other objects
    of their senses to the fire of the senses.

27. Some offer up all sensual acts
    and all activities of life
Upon the fire that is lit by wisdom,
    the fire of the discipline of self-control.

28. Next to those who sacrifice things,
    those who sacrifice with asceticism,
And those who sacrifice
    through discipline,
There are still others,
    devotees faithful to their vows
Whose sacrifice goes on
    through study or the pursuit of wisdom.

29. apāne juhvati prāṇaṃ
prāṇe 'pānaṃ tathāpare
prāṇāpānagatī ruddhvā
prāṇāyāmaparāyaṇāh

30. apare niyatāhārāḥ
prāṇān prāṇeṣu juhvati
sarve 'py ete yajñavido
yajñakṣapitakalmaṣāh

31. yajñaśiṣṭāmṛtabhujo
yānti brahma sanātanam
nāyaṃ loko 'sty ayajñasya
kuto 'nyaḥ kurusattama

32. evaṃ bahuvidhā yajñā
vitatā brahmaṇo mukhe
karmajān viddhi tān sarvān
evaṃ jñātvā vimokṣyase

33. śreyān dravyamayād yajñāj
jñānayajñaḥ paraṃtapa
sarvaṃ karmākhilaṃ pārtha
jñāne parisamāpyate

34. tad viddhi praṇipātena
paripraśnena sevayā
upadekṣyanti te jñānaṃ
jñāninas tattvadarśinaḥ

35. yaj jñātvā na punar moham
evaṃ yāsyasi pāṇḍava
yena bhūtāny aśeṣeṇa
drakṣyasy ātmany atho mayi

29. There there are those who give themselves
 to breath control,
 Checking the course of their breath
 up and down.
 They offer the life-breath they inhale
 in the exhalation,
 And, likewise, their exhalation
 in their breathing-in.

30. Others abstain from eating, and thus
 offer nothing but their breathing.
 All these truly know sacrifice.
 Their impurities are taken away by sacrifice.

31. Enjoying the food of immortality left over
 from sacrifice, they go to the eternal godhead.
 A man who does not sacrifice
 has no part in this world. How could he enter the other?

32. Thus many kinds of sacrifice are made
 and give direct access to God.
 Know them as born from action,
 and knowing this you will be freed.

33. Better than sacrifice of matter alone
 is sacrifice carried out through understanding.
 All action, Conqueror, without exception,
 is contained and completed in understanding.

34. You must learn this by humbly submitting yourself,
 by asking questions and rendering service.
 Then those who have understanding,
 who see things as they are, will teach you.

35. When you have learned it,
 you will not be confused like this again.
 This understanding will show you that all exists,
 in yourself and also in me.

36. api ced asi pāpebhyah
    sarvebhyaḥ pāpakṛttamaḥ
sarvam jñānaplavenaiva
    vṛjinaṃ saṃtariṣyasi

37. yathaidhāṃsi samiddho 'gnir
    bhasmasāt kurute 'rjuna
jñānāgniḥ sarvakarmāṇi
    bhasmasāt kurute tathā

38. na hi jñānena sadṛśaṃ
    pavitram iha vidyate
tat svayaṃ yogasaṃsiddhaḥ
    kālenātmani vindati

39. śraddhāvāṃl labhate jñānaṃ
    tatparaḥ saṃyatendriyaḥ
jñānaṃ labdhvā parāṃ śāntim
    acireṇādhigacchati

40. ajñaś cāśraddadhānaś ca
    saṃśayātmā vinaśyati
nāyaṃ loko 'sti na paro
    na sukhaṃ saṃśayātmanaḥ

41. yogasaṃnyastakarmāṇaṃ
    jñānasaṃchinnasaṃśayam
ātmavantaṃ na karmāṇi
    nibadhnanti dhanaṃjaya

42. tasmād ajñānasaṃbhūtaṃ
    hṛtsthaṃ jñānāsinātmanaḥ
chittvainaṃ saṃśayaṃ yogam
    ātiṣṭhottiṣṭha bhārata

36. Even if you are the worst
    of all evildoers,
You will cross over evil and deceit
    with the boat of understanding.

37. Once the fire is kindled,
    it reduces the firewood to ashes.
Just so, understanding
    consumes all action.

38. There is no purifier like understanding.
    Accomplished in discipline,
A man has all he needs to find it
    in himself in the course of time.

39. He who trusts in his spiritual guide
    gains understanding. He holds it highest, constantly,
Controlling his senses. Having gained understanding,
    he soon reaches supreme peace.

40. But a man full of doubts, lacking
    understanding and trust, perishes.
The man full of doubts has neither this world
    nor the next, nor happiness.

41. Actions do not imprison him who
    through discipline has renounced action.
Understanding has dissolved his doubts.
    He has control of himself.

42. Therefore, with the sword of understanding
    put an end to the product of your ignorance—
That wavering in your heart. And then,
    begin your discipline. Arise!

V

arjuna uvāca

1. saṃnyāsaṃ karmaṇāṃ kṛṣṇa
   punar yogaṃ ca śaṃsasi
   yac chreya etayor ekaṃ
   tan me brūhi suniścitam

śrībhagavān uvāca

2. saṃnyāsaḥ karmayogaś ca
   niḥśreyasakarāv ubhau
   tayos tu karmasaṃnyāsāt
   karmayogo viśiṣyate

3. jñeyaḥ sa nityasaṃnyāsī
   yo na dveṣṭi na kāṅkṣati
   nirdvandvo hi mahābāho
   sukhaṃ bandhāt pramucyate

4. sāṃkhyayogau pṛthag bālāḥ
   pravadanti na paṇḍitāḥ
   ekam apy āsthitaḥ samyag
   ubhayor vindate phalam

5. yat sāṃkhyaiḥ prāpyate sthānaṃ
   tad yogair api gamyate
   ekaṃ sāṃkhyaṃ ca yogaṃ ca
   yaḥ paśyati sa paśyati

6. saṃnyāsas tu mahābāho
   duḥkham āptum ayogataḥ
   yogayukto munir brahma
   nacireṇādhigacchati

Arjuna:

1. You praise the renunciation of acts, and then,
   you speak in praise of discipline!
   Tell me plainly, without ambiguity,
   which of the two is better?

The Lord:

2. Both, renunciation and discipline of action,
   lead to supreme bliss.
   Yet discipline of action
   surpasses the renunciation of it.

3. Clearly, constant renunciation is part of a man
   when he knows neither disgust nor desire.
   Free from the sway of opposites,
   he is easily freed from his prison.

4. Not the educated, but foolish men speak of
   reason and discipline as separate.
   Whoever has made a serious beginning with only one,
   gains the fruit of both.

5. The place men of reason arrive at
   is reached also by men of discipline.
   Reason and discipline are one.
   Who sees this is wide awake.

6. However, renunciation is difficult
   to achieve without discipline.
   Trained in some discipline,
   a wise man soon reaches God.

7. yogayukto viśuddhātmā
   vijitātmā jitendriyaḥ
   sarvabhūtātmabhūtātmā
   kurvann api na lipyate

8. naiva kiṃcit karomīti
   yukto manyeta tattvavit
   paśyañ śṛṇvan spṛśañ jighrann
   aśnan gacchan svapañ śvasan

9. pralapan visṛjan gṛhṇann
   unmiṣan nimiṣann api
   indriyāṇīndriyārtheṣu
   vartanta iti dhārayan

10. brahmaṇy ādhāya karmāṇi
    saṅgaṃ tyaktvā karoti yaḥ
    lipyate na sa pāpena
    padmapattram ivāmbhasā

11. kāyena manasā buddhyā
    kevalair indriyair api
    yoginaḥ karma kurvanti
    saṅgaṃ tyaktvātmaśuddhaye

12. yuktaḥ karmaphalaṃ tyaktvā
    śāntim āpnoti naiṣṭhikīm
    ayuktaḥ kāmakāreṇa
    phale sakto nibadhyate

13. sarvakarmāṇi manasā
    saṃnyasyāste sukhaṃ vaśī
    navadvāre pure dehī
    naiva kurvan na kārayan

7. If a man is trained in a discipline,
   becomes wholly purified,
   Learns to control himself
   and his senses,
   His own individual existence
   now being the existence of all—
   Even when he acts,
   he is not stained.

8. Disciplined, knowing the nature of things,
   he will think: "I don't do anything!"
   When all the while he sees, hears, touches, smells,
   eats, goes about, sleeps, breathes,

9. Talks, voids, grasps something,
   opens and shuts his eyes;
   He knows full well
   that the senses merely play on the objects of sense.

10. Resting his acts in God,
    he has lost his attachment. He acts,
    But evil clings to him no more
    than water to a lotus leaf.

11. Disciplined men do act with their body, thought,
    meditation, or even their senses alone,
    But they do so to purify themselves,
    and without attachment.

12. The disciplined man gives up the results of his acts
    and attains perfect peace.
    The undisciplined man acts out of desire; he is
    attached to the results; his acts imprison him.

13. Mentally freed from all acts,
    the person dwells happily in the body—
    Lord in the city of nine gates—
    not acting at all, nor causing action.

14. na kartrtvaṃ na karmāṇi
   lokasya sṛjati prabhuḥ
na karmaphalasaṃyogaṃ
   svabhāvas tu pravartate

15. nādatte kasyacit pāpaṃ
   na caiva sukṛtaṃ vibhuḥ
ajñānenāvṛtaṃ jñānaṃ
   tena muhyanti jantavaḥ

16. jñānena tu tad ajñānaṃ
   yeṣāṃ nāśitam ātmanaḥ
teṣām ādityavaj jñānaṃ
   prakāśayati tat param

17. tadbuddhayas tadātmānas
   tanniṣṭhās tatparāyaṇāḥ
gacchanty apunarāṛvrttiṃ
   jñānanirdhūtakalmaṣāḥ

18. vidyāvinayasaṃpanne
   brāhmaṇe gavi hastini
śuni caiva śvapāke ca
   paṇḍitāḥ samadarśinaḥ

19. ihai 'va tair jitaḥ sargo
   yeṣāṃ sāmye sthitaṃ manaḥ
nirdoṣaṃ hi samaṃ brahma
   tasmād brahmaṇi te sthitāḥ

20. na prahṛṣyet priyaṃ prāpya
   no 'dvijet prāpya cāpriyam
sthirabuddhir asaṃmūḍho
   brahmavid brahmaṇi sthitaḥ

21. bāhyasparśeṣv asaktātmā
   vindaty ātmani yat sukham
sa brahmayogayuktātmā
   sukham akṣayam aśnute

14. Neither acting nor acts nor
 the link of people with the result of their acts
 Comes from the lord.
 They are the dominion of material nature.

15. The lord does not take on
 the fault or merit of anyone.
 Ignorance veils wisdom,
 and misleads people,

16. But when knowledge of the self destroys
 that ignorance in men,
 Their knowledge like the sun
 lights up that which is highest.

17. They direct their meditation, their whole being, toward it.
 They make it their whole aim.
 They are wholly intent on it. Cleansed by wisdom,
 they enter the estate of no return.

18. The educated see no difference between
 men of purest birth, of knowledge and good conduct,
 And cows, elephants,
 foul dogs, and foul eaters of dogs.

19. Men who can hold their thought in such balance
 have overcome the world of birth right here.
 God is flawless and in balance,
 so they live in God.

20. Such a man will not exult when he is lucky
 nor be afflicted when unlucky.
 Steady of mind, wide awake,
 the knower of God abides in God.

21. When wholly free from outer contacts
 a man finds happiness in himself,
 He is fully trained in God's discipline
 and reaches unending bliss.

22. ye hi saṃsparśajā bhogā
duḥkhayonaya eva te
ādyantavantaḥ kaunteya
na teṣu ramate budhaḥ

23. śaknotīhaiva yaḥ soḍhuṃ
prāk śarīravimokṣaṇāt
kāmakrodhodbhavaṃ vegaṃ
sa yuktaḥ sa sukhī naraḥ

24. yo 'ntaḥsukho 'ntarārāmas
tathāntarjyotir eva yaḥ
so yogī brahmanirvāṇaṃ
brahmabhūto 'dhigacchati

25. labhante brahmanirvāṇam
ṛṣayaḥ kṣīṇakalmaṣāḥ
chinnadvaidhā yatātmānaḥ
sarvabhūtahite ratāḥ

26. kāmakrodhaviyuktānāṃ
yatīnāṃ yatacetasām
abhito brahmanirvāṇaṃ
vartate viditātmanām

27. sparśān kṛtvā bahir bāhyāṃś
cakṣuś caivāntare bhruvoḥ
prāṇāpānau samau kṛtvā
nāsābhyantaracāriṇau

28. yatendriyamanobuddhir
munir mokṣaparāyaṇaḥ
vigatecchābhayakrodho
yaḥ sadā mukta eva saḥ

29. bhoktāraṃ yajñatapasāṃ
sarvalokamaheśvaram
suhṛdaṃ sarvabhūtānāṃ
jñātvā māṃ śāntim ṛcchati

22. The experiences we owe to our sense of touch
are only sources of unpleasantness.
They have a beginning and an end.
A wise man takes no pleasure in them.

23. That man is disciplined and happy
who can prevail over the turmoil
That springs from desire and anger,
here on earth, before he leaves his body.

24. That disciplined man
with joy and light within,
Becomes one with God
and reaches the freedom that is God's.

25. Seers whose stains are washed away
win the freedom that is God's.
Their doubts are ended. They have dominion
over themselves. They delight in the well-being
of all beings.

26. God's freedom surrounds men of sustained efforts,
who release themselves from desire and anger,
Who control their thought
and know themselves.

27, 28. The wise man who dispells outer contacts,
who concentrates his sight between his brows,
Who evens out his breathing
in and out,
Who masters his senses, thought, and meditation,
and is intent on freedom,
And is already freed from desire, fear and anger,
who is like this always; he is set free.

29. Knowing me, the enjoyer of sacrifice
and spiritual exertion, the great lord
Of the universe and friend of all beings,
he enters peace.

VI

śrībhagavān uvāca

1. anāśritaḥ karmaphalaṃ
   kāryaṃ karma karoti yaḥ
   sa saṃnyāsī ca yogī ca
   na niragnir na cākriyaḥ

2. yaṃ saṃnyāsam iti prāhur
   yogaṃ taṃ viddhi pāṇḍava
   na hy asaṃnyastasaṃkalpo
   yogī bhavati kaścana

3. ārurukṣor muner yogaṃ
   karma kāraṇam ucyate
   yogārūḍhasya tasyaiva
   śamaḥ kāraṇam ucyate

4. yadā hi nendriyārtheṣu
   na karmasv anuṣajjate
   sarvasaṃkalpasaṃnyāsī
   yogārūḍhas tadocyate

5. uddhared ātmanātmānaṃ
   nātmānam avasādayet
   ātmaiva hy ātmano bandhur
   ātmaiva ripur ātmanaḥ

6. bandhur ātmātmanas tasya
   yenātmaivātmanā jitaḥ
   anātmanas tu śatrutve
   vartetātmaiva śatruvat

The Lord:

1. That man knows renunciation and is disciplined
   who does the required cultic acts not counting on their results,
   Not he whose sacrificial fire is extinct
   and who avoids all liturgy.

2. What people call renunciation
   is really liturgical discipline,
   For a man acquires no discipline whatever
   without detaching himself from the purpose of the ritual.

3. Cult is the way for the sage
   who aspires to discipline.
   When he has advanced to discipline,
   his way is stillness.

4. He has advanced to discipline
   and has renounced all purpose,
   When he is no longer obsessed
   with sense objects and ritual works.

5. Man should discover his own reality
   and not thwart himself.
   For he has the self as his only friend,
   or as his only enemy.

6. A person has the self as friend
   when he has conquered himself,
   But if he rejects his own reality,
   the self will war against him.

7. jitātmanaḥ praśāntasya
   paramātmā samāhitaḥ
   śītoṣṇasukhaduḥkheṣu
   tathā mānāvamānayoḥ

8. jñānavijñānatṛptātmā
   kūṭastho vijitendriyaḥ
   yukta ity ucyate yogī
   samaloṣṭāśmakāñcanaḥ

9. suhṛnmitrāryudāsīna-
   madhyasthadveṣyabandhuṣu
   sādhuṣv api ca pāpeṣu
   samabuddhir viśiṣyate

10. yogī yuñjīta satatam
   ātmānaṃ rahasi sthitaḥ
   ekākī yatacittātmā
   nirāśīr aparigrahaḥ

11. śucau deśe pratiṣṭhāpya
   sthiram āsanam ātmanaḥ
   nātyucchritam nātinīcaṃ
   cailājinakuśottaram

12. tatraikāgraṃ manaḥ kṛtvā
   yatacittendriyakriyaḥ
   upaviśyāsane yuñjyād
   yogam ātmaviśuddhaye

13. samaṃ kāyaśirogrīvaṃ
   dhārayann acalaṃ sthiraḥ
   saṃprekṣya nāsikāgraṃ svaṃ
   diśaś cānavalokayan

14. praśāntātmā vigatabhīr
   brahmacārivrate sthitaḥ
   manaḥ saṃyamya maccitto
   yukta āsīta matparaḥ

7. A man who has conquered himself
   has a self that is fully present,
In heat and cold, comfort and discomfort,
   in honor, and disgrace also.

8. The man of discipline, abundantly endowed
   with wisdom and sense, solitary
And unshakable, controlled, has true harmony.
   Lumps of earth, rocks, gold, are alike to him.

9. Honor to him who is disposed equally
   toward personal friends, allies, and opponents,
Those standing aside or caught between,
   foes, kinsmen, the good, and the wicked even.

10. The man of discipline will train himself,
   continually, in a secret place,
Alone, restraining himself and his thoughts completely,
   without having or wishing for anything.

11. In a clean place he prepares a firm seat for himself,
   neither too high nor too low,
Covered with cloth, a skin, and sacred grass
   [such as one sits on at sacrifices].

12. On this seat, restraining the function
   of his thought and senses,
he fixes his mind on one point. He will practice
   discipline to purify himself.

13–14. He is immobile, holding body, head, and neck straight,
   motionless.
He rests his gaze between his eyebrows
   without attention to the world around him;
In total peace, without any fear,
   faithful to the vow of his sacred study,
He will sit disciplined, intent on me,
   controlling his mind, his thought set on me.

15. yuñjann evaṃ sadātmānaṃ
    yogī niyatamānasaḥ
    śāntiṃ nirvāṇaparamāṃ
    matsaṃsthām adhigacchati

16. nātyaśnatas tu yogo 'sti
    na caikāntam anaśnataḥ
    na cātisvapnaśīlasya
    jāgrato naiva cārjuna

17. yuktāhāravihārasya
    yuktaceṣṭasya karmasu
    yuktasvapnāvabodhasya
    yogo bhavati duḥkhahā

18. yadā viniyataṃ cittam
    ātmany evāvatiṣṭhate
    niḥspṛhaḥ sarvakāmebhyo
    yukta ity ucyate tadā

19. yathā dīpo nivātastho
    neṅgate sopamā smṛtā
    yogino yatacittasya
    yuñjato yogam ātmanaḥ

20. yatroparamate cittaṃ
    niruddhaṃ yogasevayā
    yatra caivātmanātmānaṃ
    paśyann átmani tuṣyati

21. sukham ātyantikaṃ yat tad
    buddhigrāhyam atīndriyam
    vetti yatra na caivāyaṃ
    sthitaś calati tattvataḥ

22. yaṃ labdhvā cāparaṃ lābhaṃ
    manyate nādhikaṃ tataḥ
    yasmin sthito na duḥkhena
    guruṇāpi vicālyate

15. The man of discipline who in this manner
    incessantly disciplines himself,
  Controlling his mind, attains the summit of freedom,
    the peace that is in me.

16. A man who overeats has no discipline,
    nor does a man who does not eat at all.
  Likewise a man addicted to sleep,
    and one who wants to be forever awake.

17. Only he acquires the discipline that ends sorrow
    who is disciplined in eating, relaxation,
  Disciplined in acts, disciplined
    in sleep and wakefulness.

18. When thought is checked and focuses
    on one's own reality alone,
  Then a person is called disciplined.
    He is freed from all desires.

19. A lamp in a windless place has a still flame.
    This is the traditional image
  For the disciplined man of controlled mind
    who practices the discipline of the self.

20. His thought comes to rest
    checked by the practice of discipline,
  And he is happy in himself
    perceiving his self's reality;

21. He knows that boundless bliss
    beyond the senses which meditation can grasp;
  He holds on and does not swerve
    from its truth;

22. And having seized upon it,
    he prizes nothing more.
  Abiding in it, he is not moved
    by sorrow, however heavy;

23. taṃ vidyād duḥkhasaṃyogaviyogaṃ yogasaṃjñitam
sa niścayena yoktavyo
yogo 'nirviṇṇacetasā

24. saṃkalpaprabhavān kāmāṃs
tyaktvā sarvān aśeṣataḥ
manasaivendriyagrāmaṃ
viniyamya samantataḥ

25. śanaiḥ śanair uparamed
buddhyā dhṛtigṛhītayā
ātmasaṃsthaṃ manaḥ kṛtvā
na kiṃcid api cintayet

26. yato yato niścarati
manaś cañcalam asthiram
tatas tato niyamyaitad
ātmany eva vaśaṃ nayet

27. praśāntamanasaṃ hy enaṃ
yoginaṃ sukham uttamam
upaiti śāntarajasaṃ
brahmabhūtam akalmaṣam

28. yuñjann evaṃ sadātmānaṃ
yogī vigatakalmaṣaḥ
sukhena brahmasaṃsparśam
atyantaṃ sukham aśnute

29. sarvabhūtastham ātmānaṃ
sarvabhūtāni cātmani
īkṣate yogayuktātmā
sarvatra samadarśanaḥ

30. yo māṃ paśyati sarvatra
sarvaṃ ca mayi paśyati
tasyāhaṃ na praṇaśyāmi
sa ca me na praṇaśyati

23. He will know that this loosening
of sorrowful ties is discipline.
He must practice it resolutely,
without losing heart.

24. He gives up all desires, regardless,
that are the outgrowth of conscious, stated purposes.
His will restrains the horde
of the senses completely.

25. Gradually he will come to rest through
his firm meditative power.
He fixes his mind on the self,
and he will think of nothing.

26. Whenever the fickle, unstable mind
goes astray,
He subdues it and brings it
under control in himself.

27. For utmost joy comes to that disciplined man
whose thought is at peace.
Passion has quieted. He has
become one with God, pure.

28. Thus the man of discipline, cleansed,
constantly trains himself.
He easily reaches God
and tastes limitless joy.

29. Wholly immersed in discipline
seeing the same in all things,
He sees himself in all beings,
and all beings in himself.

30. I do not let him go;
I never desert him
Who sees me in all there is
and sees all in me.

31. sarvabhūtasthitaṃ yo māṃ
bhajaty ekatvam āsthitaḥ
sarvathā vartamāno 'pi
sa yogī mayi vartate

32. ātmaupamyena sarvatra
samaṃ paśyati yo 'rjuna
sukhaṃ vā yadi vā duḥkhaṃ
sa yogī paramo mataḥ

arjuna uvāca

33. yo 'yaṃ yogas tvayā proktaḥ
sāmyena madhusūdana
etasyāhaṃ na paśyāmi
cañcalatvāt sthitiṃ sthirām

34. cañcalaṃ hi manaḥ kṛṣṇa
pramāthi balavad dṛḍham
tasyāhaṃ nigrahaṃ manye
vāyor iva suduṣkaram

śrībhagavān uvāca

35. asaṃśayaṃ mahābāho
mano durnigrahaṃ calam
abhyāsena tu kaunteya
vairāgyeṇa ca gṛhyate

36. asaṃyatātmanā yogo
duṣprāpa iti me matiḥ
vaśyātmanā tu yatatā
śakyo 'vāptum upāyataḥ

arjuna uvāca

37. ayatiḥ śraddhayopeto
yogāc calitamānasaḥ
aprāpya yogasaṃsiddhiṃ
kāṃ gatiṃ kṛṣṇa gacchati

31. Who has attained oneness and loves me
    who am in all beings—
Whatever his circumstances,
    that man of discipline lives in me.

32. Who sees the same in all there is,
    whether pleasant or unpleasant,
And in the image of his own reality,
    that man of discipline is supreme, I say.

Arjuna:

33. Man is fickle. Hence I fail to see
    how this discipline
That you describe as sameness
    could be firmly established.

34. Man's will is fickle,
    stirring about, impetuous, set in its ways.
It is quite difficult to restrain it, I think.
    It is like curbing the wind.

The Lord:

35. Surely, the mind or will
    is hard to control and fickle.
But by training and ascetic practice
    it is possible to control it.

36. In my opinion discipline
    is difficult for a man without self-control;
But a man with self-control who makes an effort
    can attain it by some means.

Arjuna:

37. If a man is full of trust, yet makes no effort,
    and his mind strays from discipline,
And he achieves no enduring success—
    where does he end up, Kṛṣṇa?

38. kaccin nobhayavibhraṣṭaś
    chinnābhram iva naśyati
    apratiṣṭho mahābāho
    vimūḍho brahmaṇaḥ pathi

39. etan me saṃśayaṃ kṛṣṇa
    chettum arhasy aśeṣataḥ
    tvadanyaḥ saṃśayasyāsya
    chettā na hy upapadyate

śrībhagavān uvāca

40. pārtha naiveha nāmutra
    vināśas tasya vidyate
    na hi kalyāṇakṛt kaścid
    durgatiṃ tāta gacchati

41. prāpya puṇyakṛtāṃl lokān
    uṣitvā śāśvatīḥ samāḥ
    śucīnāṃ śrīmatāṃ gehe
    yogabhraṣṭo 'bhijāyate

42. athavā yoginām eva
    kule bhavati dhīmatām
    etad dhi durlabhataraṃ
    loke janma yad īdṛśam

43. tatra taṃ buddhisaṃyogaṃ
    labhate paurvadehikam
    yatate ca tato bhūyaḥ
    saṃsiddhau kurunandana

44. pūrvābhyāsena tenaiva
    hriyate hy avaśo 'pi saḥ
    jijñāsur api yogasya
    śabdabrahmātivartate

45. prayatnād yatamānas tu
    yogī saṃśuddhakilbiṣaḥ
    anekajanmasaṃsiddhas
    tato yāti parāṃ gatim

38. Could it not be that he is lost both ways
    and fades like a torn cloud [emptied of its rain]?
  He has no sure foothold
    and he is lost on God's path.

39. Please, Kṛṣṇa, resolve my uncertainty
    once and for all,
  For there is no one but you
    to sweep away this uncertainty.

The Lord:

40. That man will not be ruined, Pārtha,
    whether in this world or beyond it,
  For no one who has done anything salutary
    ends up badly, dear friend.

41. He reaches the regions of the meritorious
    and he lives there for endless years.
  Then he who strayed from discipline is reborn
    in the home of pure, auspicious folk.

42. Or else, he grows up in the house
    of wise people, men of discipline.
  For such a birth is still more difficult
    to attain on earth.

43. There he takes up that inclination
    that was within him before.
  He strives still more toward complete success,
    Joy of the Kurus,

44. For his former training carries him on
    even without his will.
  The mere desire to know discipline
    takes him beyond the externals of religion.

45. However, the man of discipline makes
    a serious effort. He becomes pure.
  After a number of births, perfected,
    he reaches the highest goal.

46. tapasvibhyo 'dhiko yogī
jñānibhyo 'pi mato 'dhikaḥ
karmibhyaś cādhiko yogī
tasmād yogī bhavārjuna

47. yoginām api sarveṣāṃ
madgatenāntarātmanā
śraddhāvān bhajate yo māṃ
sa me yuktatamo mataḥ

46. The man of discipline is more than the ascetics,
    more also than men of wisdom.
    He excels the men of ritual work.
    Therefore, become a man of discipline!

47. Of all men of discipline,
    the one who trusts me and loves me
    With his inmost self,
    him I hold most disciplined.

VII

śrībhagavān uvāca

1. mayy āsaktamanāḥ pārtha
   yogaṃ yuñjan madāśrayaḥ
   asaṃśayaṃ samagraṃ māṃ
   yathā jñāsyasi tac chṛṇu

2. jñānaṃ te 'haṃ savijñānam
   idaṃ vakṣyāmy aśeṣataḥ
   yaj jñātvā neha bhūyo 'nyaj
   jñātavyam avaśiṣyate

3. manuṣyāṇāṃ sahasreṣu
   kaścid yatati siddhaye
   yatatām api siddhānāṃ
   kaścin māṃ vetti tattvataḥ

4. bhūmir āpo 'nalo vāyuḥ
   khaṃ mano buddhir eva ca
   ahaṃkāra itīyaṃ me
   bhinnā prakṛtir aṣṭadhā

5. apareyam itas tv anyāṃ
   prakṛtiṃ viddhi me parām
   jīvabhūtāṃ mahābāho
   yayedaṃ dhāryate jagat

6. etadyonīni bhūtāni
   sarvāṇīty upadhāraya
   ahaṃ kṛtsnasya jagataḥ
   prabhavaḥ pralayas tathā

The Lord:

1. There is no doubt that you will know me
   in my total being when you persist
   In discipline, and rely on me,
   and when your thought clings to me. Listen.

2. Without holding back anything, I shall teach you
   wisdom, and explain how it can be attained,
   Knowing which,
   there is nothing left to be known.

3. One out of thousands
   may strive for success.
   And even of these only a few
   may know me as I really am.

4. My earthly world is eightfold,
   divided into earth, water,
   Fire, air, ether, mind, the faculty
   of meditation, and self-awareness.

5. This is lower nature. My higher
   nature is different.
   It is the very life
   that sustains the world.

6. Do not forget that this is the source
   of all existence.
   I am the genesis and the end
   of the entire world.

7. mattaḥ parataraṃ nānyat
   kiṃcid asti dhanaṃjaya
   mayi sarvam idaṃ protaṃ
   sūtre maṇigaṇā iva

8. raso 'ham apsu kaunteya
   prabhāsmi śaśisūryayoḥ
   praṇavaḥ sarvavedeṣu
   śabdaḥ khe pauruṣaṃ nṛṣu

9. puṇyo gandhaḥ pṛthivyāṃ ca
   tejaś cāsmi vibhāvasau
   jīvanaṃ sarvabhūteṣu
   tapaś cāsmi tapasviṣu

10. bījaṃ māṃ sarvabhūtānāṃ
    viddhi pārtha sanātanam
    buddhir buddhimatām asmi
    tejas tejasvinām aham

11. balaṃ balavatāṃ cāhaṃ
    kāmarāgavivarjitam
    dharmāviruddho bhūteṣu
    kāmo 'smi bharatarṣabha

12. ye caiva sāttvikā bhāvā
    rājasās tāmasāś ca ye
    matta eveti tān viddhi
    na tv ahaṃ teṣu te mayi

13. tribhir guṇamayair bhāvair
    ebhiḥ sarvam idaṃ jagat
    mohitaṃ nābhijānāti
    mām ebhyaḥ param avyayam

14. daivī hy eṣā guṇamayī
    mama māyā duratyayā
    mām eva ye prapadyante
    māyām etāṃ taranti te

7. There is nothing higher than I am,
   O Conqueror of Wealth!
The world is strung on me
   like pearls on a string.

8. I am the flavor in water,
   the radiance in the sun and moon,
The basic, sacred word in sacred texts,
   the sound in the highest element,
And, Arjuna, I am
   what makes men *men*.

9. I am the scent of promise in the earth
   and the burning strength in the fire,
The life in all creatures
   and the ascetic fire in holy men.

10. Son of Pṛthā, know me as the
   perennial seed in all that lives.
I am the understanding of those who understand,
   the majesty of the majestic.

11. I am the strength of the strong,
   free from lust and passion,
And I am, Strongest of Bharatas,
   the right desire in living beings.

12. States of mind arise from
   integrity, passion, and sloth.
They come from me, for certain, yet
   I am not in them; they are in me.

13. These three states, made up of integrity,
   passion, and sloth, mislead the world.
It does not recognize me, because
   I am different and unchanging.

14. My veil, woven of these three strands,
   is divine and difficult to pierce.
Yet those who seek my grace do get
   beyond its wizardry.

15. na māṃ duṣkṛtino mūḍhāḥ
prapadyante narādhamāḥ
māyayāpahṛtajñānā
āsuraṃ bhāvam āśritāḥ

16. caturvidhā bhajante māṃ
janāḥ sukṛtino 'rjuna
ārto jijñāsur arthārthī
jñānī ca bharatarṣabha

17. teṣāṃ jñānī nityayukta
ekabhaktir viśiṣyate
priyo hi jñānino 'tyartham
ahaṃ sa ca mama priyaḥ

18. udārāḥ sarva evaite
jñānī tv ātmaiva me matam
āsthitaḥ sa hi yuktātmā
mām evānuttamāṃ gatim

19. bahūnāṃ janmanām ante
jñānavān māṃ prapadyate
vāsudevaḥ sarvam iti
sa mahātmā sudurlabhaḥ

20. kāmais tais tair hṛtajñānāḥ
prapadyante 'nyadevatāḥ
taṃ taṃ niyamam āsthāya
prakṛtyā niyatāḥ svayā

21. yo yo yāṃ yāṃ tanuṃ bhaktaḥ
śraddhayārcitum icchati
tasya tasyācalāṃ śraddhāṃ
tām eva vidadhāmy aham

22. sa tayā śraddhayā yuktas
tasyārādhanam īhate
labhate ca tataḥ kāmān
mayaiva vihitān hi tān

15. Workers of evil, people with obsessions,
    and vile men do not seek my grace.
Because of this wizardry they have no wisdom.
    They are in an infernal state.

16, 17. People act properly and worship me
    when they have fallen into misfortune,
Or when they are eager for wisdom,
    or eager for wealth, or when they are wise.

Always disciplined, among these four types, the wise man
    stands supreme, devoted to me alone.
The wise man loves me ardently,
    and I love him.

18. All four are worthy. Still I think
    of the wise man as my self,
For he has trained himself,
    has come to me and entered upon the highest way.

19. The wise man submits to my grace
    at the end of many births.
He realizes: God is all.
    This exalted person is exceptional.

20. When varied desires damage their wisdom,
    people seek grace in other gods than me.
They resort to various regimens
    to satisfy their nature's need.

21. Any devotee may draw near
    any divine form in full trust.
In each case, I endow him with
    unfailing confidence.

22. Filled with this trust he attends to
    the worship of his god,
And he obtains his desires from him,
    for in fact I grant these desires.

23. antavat tu phalaṃ teṣāṃ
 tad bhavaty alpamedhasām
devān devayajo yānti
 madbhaktā yānti mām api

24. avyaktaṃ vyaktim āpannaṃ
 manyante mām abuddhayaḥ
paraṃ bhāvam ajānanto
 mamāvyayam anuttamam

25. nāhaṃ prakāśaḥ sarvasya
 yogamāyāsamāvṛtaḥ
mūḍho 'yaṃ nābhijānāti
 loko mām ajam avyayam

26. vedāhaṃ samatītāni
 vartamānāni cārjuna
bhaviṣyāṇi ca bhūtāni
 māṃ tu veda na kaścana

27. icchādveṣasamutthena
 dvandvamohena bhārata
sarvabhūtāni saṃmohaṃ
 sarge yānti paraṃtapa

28. yeṣāṃ tv antagataṃ pāpaṃ
 janānāṃ puṇyakarmaṇām
te dvandvamohanirmuktā
 bhajante māṃ dṛḍhavratāḥ

29. jarāmaraṇamokṣāya
 mām āśritya yatanti ye
te brahma tad viduḥ kṛtsnam
 adhyātmaṃ karma cākhilam

30. sādhibhūtādhidaivaṃ māṃ
 sādhiyajñaṃ ca ye viduḥ
prayāṇakāle 'pi ca māṃ
 te vidur yuktacetasaḥ

23. Lacking in wisdom, men do attain
    their goals, but their goals have a limit.
Making offerings to other gods, they go to other gods.
    My devotees ultimately come to me.

24. Men without understanding think I was
    unmanifest first and then came to exist.
They do not know my supreme,
    changeless, most perfect being.

25. I am not given for everyone to see.
    I am concealed by the wizardry I apply.
This perplexed world does not recognize
    me, the unborn and unchanging.

26. I know previous existences
    and present and future ones,
But not a single person
    knows me.

27. All creatures enter delusion at birth—
    Conqueror of Enemies!—
For they are obsessed by the opposites,
    haunted by likes and dislikes.

28. But when men cultivate merit
    and the impure is exhausted,
They are set free from the delusion of opposites.
    They commune with me, steady in their vow.

29. Those who rely on me and strive for
    liberation from old age and death
Know the divine secret fully, and the entire
    ordained work, bearing on the self.

30. Who concentrate their minds and know me
    in my relationship to the principles of existence,
To the gods and sacrifice,
    truly know me, even at the time of their death.

VIII

arjuna uvāca

1. kiṃ tad brahma kim adhyātmaṃ
   kiṃ karma puruṣottama
   adhibhūtaṃ ca kiṃ proktam
   adhidaivaṃ kim ucyate

2. adhiyajñaḥ kathaṃ ko 'tra
   dehe 'smin madhusūdana
   prayāṇakāle ca kathaṃ
   jñeyo 'si niyatātmabhiḥ

śrībhagavān uvāca

3. akṣaraṃ brahma paramaṃ
   svabhāvo 'dhyātmam ucyate
   bhūtabhāvodbhavakaro
   visargaḥ karmasaṃjñitaḥ

4. adhibhūtaṃ kṣaro bhāvaḥ
   puruṣaś cādhidaivatam
   adhiyajño 'ham evātra
   dehe dehabhṛtāṃ vara

5. antakāle ca mām eva
   smaran muktvā kalevaram
   yaḥ prayāti sa madbhāvaṃ
   yāti nāsty atra saṃśayaḥ

6. yaṃ yaṃ vāpi smaran bhāvaṃ
   tyajaty ante kalevaram
   taṃ tam evaiti kaunteya
   sadā tadbhāvabhāvitaḥ

Arjuna:

1. What is that "divine secret?" What affects
   the self? What work is ordained?
   What can be said of the principles of existence?
   What relates to the gods?

2. How is one related to
   the sacrifice, here, in this body?
   And how shall men of self-control
   know you at their death?

The Lord:

3. The divine secret is the imperishable [—the supreme,
   subtle sound behind the sacred texts].
   Highest nature affects the self.
   The world in its birth and existence
   Brings forth creatures and orders of being
   and is the ordained cultic work.

4. Historical circumstances make for
   the principles of existence.
   Man's spirit relates to the gods.
   Indeed, I myself,
   Here in body, relate to sacrifice,
   O you, supreme mortal!

5. And when a man leaves the body,
   thinking of me at the time of his death,
   There is no doubt that he
   will come to my estate.

6. Whatever estate he has in mind
   when in the end he leaves the body,
   That is the estate he enters, for that
   is the estate he has always dwelt on in his mind.

7. tasmāt sarveṣu kāleṣu
   mām anusmara yudhya ca
mayy arpitamanobuddhir
   mām evaiṣyasy asaṃśayaḥ

8. abhyāsayogayuktena
   cetasā nānyagāminā
paramaṃ puruṣaṃ divyaṃ
   yāti pārthānucintayan

9. kaviṃ purāṇam anuśāsitāram
   aṇor aṇīyāṃsam anusmared yaḥ
sarvasya dhātāram acintyarūpam
   ādityavarṇaṃ tamasaḥ parastāt

10. prayāṇakāle manasācalena
   bhaktyā yukto yogabalena caiva
bhruvor madhye prāṇam āveśya samyak
   sa taṃ paraṃ puruṣam upaiti divyam

11. yad akṣaraṃ vedavido vadanti
   viśanti yad yatayo vītarāgāḥ
yad icchanto brahmacaryaṃ caranti
   tat te padaṃ saṃgraheṇa pravakṣye

7. Therefore you must meditate on me
 always, and you must fight.
 No doubt you will come to me when your mind
 and meditation are fixed on me.

8. Meditating, with a practiced mind,
 if seduced
 By nothing else, man reaches
 the Divine Being.

9. Who only meditates on the primordial Lord,
 The Ruler,
 Smaller than the smallest,
 Who ordained everything,
 Whom thought cannot fathom,
 Whose luster is like the sun's,
 In whom there is no darkness—

10. He who meditates on the Lord
 at the time of death,
 With unwavering mind,
 Trained in devotion
 And in the strength of discipline,
 Concentrating well
 His breath,
 His life,
 Between
 His brows—
 That man reaches
 The supreme, Divine Being.

11. Men who know Scripture
 Call it
 The imperishable, the subtle sound.
 Ascetics who have
 Vanquished passion
 Enter it.
 Those who seek it lead
 A life of chastity.
 I shall tell you concisely
 About that state.

12. sarvadvārāṇi saṃyamya
mano hṛdi nirudhya ca
mūrdhny ādhāyātmanaḥ prāṇam
āsthito yogadhāraṇām

13. om ity ekākṣaraṃ brahma
vyāharan mām anusmaran
yaḥ prayāti tyajan dehaṃ
sa yāti paramāṃ gatim

14. ananyacetāḥ satataṃ
yo māṃ smarati nityaśaḥ
tasyāhaṃ sulabhaḥ pārtha
nityayuktasya yoginaḥ

15. mām upetya punarjanma
duhkḥālayam aśāśvatam
nāpnuvanti mahātmanaḥ
saṃsiddhiṃ paramāṃ gatāḥ

16. ā brahmabhuvanāl lokāḥ
punarāvartino 'rjuna
mām upetya tu kaunteya
punarjanma na vidyate

17. sahasrayugaparyantam
ahar yad brahmaṇo viduḥ
rātriṃ yugasahasrāntāṃ
te 'horātravido janāḥ

18. avyaktād vyaktayaḥ sarvāḥ
prabhavanty aharāgame
rātryāgame pralīyante
tatraivāvyaktasaṃjñake

19. bhūtagrāmaḥ sa evāyaṃ
bhūtvā bhūtvā pralīyate
rātryāgame 'vaśaḥ pārtha
prabhavaty aharāgame

12. One should control all the openings of the body,
    check the thoughts of his heart,
  Concentrate his life's breath in his head,
    in short, concentrate on discipline.

13. He goes to the highest goal
    who leaves the body,
  Meditating on me, saying the divine secret,
    one syllable, OM.

14. I am easy to reach for him
    who is ever disciplined,
  Who thinks of nothing, ever, but of me,
    who meditates on me constantly.

15. Great men reach me and do not take a new birth
    fleeting and miserable.
  They have attained their
    perfect fulfillment.

16. On this side of God's abode
    worlds are cycles,
  Arjuna, but for those who reach me
    there is no repetition.

17. Who knows the Eternal's day
    and the Eternal's night,
  Each lasting a thousand ages, truly
    knows day and night.

18. At daybreak all things are disclosed.
    They arise from the unmanifest.
  At dusk they dissolve into
    the very same unmanifest.

19. Again and again, the whole multitude
    of creatures is born, and when night falls,
  Is dissolved, without their will,
    and at daybreak, is born again.

20. paras tasmāt tu bhāvo 'nyo
    'vyakto 'vyaktāt sanātanaḥ
yaḥ sa sarveṣu bhūteṣu
    naśyatsu na vinaśyati

21. avyakto 'kṣara ity uktas
    tam āhuḥ paramāṃ gatim
yaṃ prāpya na nivartante
    tad dhāma paramaṃ mama

22. puruṣaḥ sa paraḥ pārtha
    bhaktyā labhyas tv ananyayā
yasyāntaḥsthāni bhūtāni
    yena sarvam idaṃ tatam

23. yatra kāle tv anāvṛttim
    āvṛttiṃ caiva yoginaḥ
prayātā yānti taṃ kālaṃ
    vakṣyāmi bharatarṣabha

24. agnir jyotir ahaḥ śuklaḥ
    ṣaṇmāsā uttarāyaṇam
tatra prayātā gacchanti
    brahma brahmavido janāḥ

25. dhūmo rātris tathā kṛṣṇaḥ
    ṣaṇmāsā dakṣiṇāyanam
tatra cāndramasaṃ jyotir
    yogī prāpya nivartate

26. śuklakṛṣṇe gatī hy ete
    jagataḥ śāśvate mate
ekayā yāty anāvṛttim
    anyayāvartate punaḥ

27. naite sṛtī pārtha jānan
    yogī muhyati kaścana
tasmāt sarveṣu kāleṣu
    yogayukto bhavārjuna

20. Beyond that unmanifest is
    another, everlasting unmanifest
Which has no end, although
    every creature perish.

21. This is called the imperishable
    unmanifest and the highest goal.
Who reaches it does not return.
    It is my supreme abode.

22. It is he,
    accessible through unswerving devotion.
All creatures have their being in him.
    Through him the world was made.

23. I shall tell you at what time,
    upon dying,
Disciplined men will not return,
    and when they will return.

24. People who know God reach God when they die
    at the time of fire, light, day,
The bright half of the month, and the six months
    when the sun rises from the North.

25. When a man of discipline passes on
    to the light of the moon at the time of smoke and night,
The dark half of the month, the half year
    of the sun's southern course, he returns.

26. For the world takes these two eternal
    courses, the light and the dark.
By one a man leaves, not to return.
    By the other does he return.

27. Knowing about these two courses,
    no disciplined man becomes lost.
Therefore, see to it that you are
    disciplined at all times.

28. vedeṣu yajñeṣu tapaḥsu caiva
dāneṣu yat puṇyaphalaṃ pradiṣṭam
atyeti tat sarvam idaṃ viditvā
yogī paraṃ sthānam upaiti cādyam

28. Whatever merit is laid down
For study of Scripture,
For sacrifices, ascetic life,
And alms giving—
The disciplined man who understands
The lesson goes beyond all of it
And reaches the highest, the very first place.

IX

śrībhagavān uvāca

1. idaṃ tu te guhyatamaṃ
   pravakṣyāmy anasūyave
   jñānaṃ vijñānasahitaṃ
   yaj jñātvā mokṣyase 'śubhāt

2. rājavidyā rājaguhyaṃ
   pavitram idam uttamam
   pratyakṣāvagamaṃ dharmyaṃ
   susukhaṃ kartum avyayam

3. aśraddadhānāḥ puruṣā
   dharmasyāsya paraṃtapa
   aprāpya māṃ nivartante
   mṛtyusaṃsāravartmani

4. mayā tatam idaṃ sarvaṃ
   jagad avyaktamūrtinā
   matsthāni sarvabhūtāni
   na cāhaṃ teṣv avasthitaḥ

5. na ca matsthāni bhūtāni
   paśya me yogam aiśvaram
   bhūtabhṛn na ca bhūtastho
   mamātmā bhūtabhāvanaḥ

6. yathākāśasthito nityaṃ
   vāyuḥ sarvatrago mahān
   tathā sarvāṇi bhūtāni
   matsthānīty upadhāraya

The Lord:

1. You are a man of good will, and I shall tell you
    the most secret wisdom,
   And explain how it can be attained.
    Then nothing will stand in your way.

2. It is the supreme purifier,
    the master science, the sovereign mystery.
   It is right and perfectly obvious,
    easy to do, and everlasting.

3. Men who do not trust
    in this which is right, O Conqueror,
   Do not reach me, and return
    to the endless round of deaths.

4. My shape is unmanifest, but I
    pervade the world.
   All beings have their being in me,
    but I do not rest in them.

5. See my sovereign technique:
    creatures both in me and not in me.
   Supporting beings, my person brings
    beings to life, without living in them.

6. I am omnipresent as the stormwind
    which resides in space.
   All beings exist in me.
    Remember that.

7. sarvabhūtāni kaunteya
   prakṛtiṃ yānti māmikām
   kalpakṣaye punas tāni
   kalpādau visṛjāmy aham

8. prakṛtiṃ svām avaṣṭabhya
   visṛjāmi punaḥ punaḥ
   bhūtagrāmam imaṃ kṛtsnam
   avaśaṃ prakṛter vaśāt

9. na ca māṃ tāni karmāṇi
   nibadhnanti dhanaṃjaya
   udāsīnavad āsīnam
   asaktaṃ teṣu karmasu

10. mayādhyakṣeṇa prakṛtiḥ
    sūyate sacarācaram
    hetunānena kaunteya
    jagad viparivartate

11. avajānanti māṃ mūḍhā
    mānuṣīṃ tanum āśritam
    paraṃ bhāvam ajānanto
    mama bhūtamaheśvaram

12. moghāśā moghakarmāṇo
    moghajñānā vicetasaḥ
    rākṣasīṃ āsurīṃ caiva
    prakṛtiṃ mohinīṃ śritāḥ

13. mahātmānas tu māṃ pārtha
    daivīṃ prakṛtim āśritāḥ
    bhajanty ananyamanaso
    jñātvā bhūtādim avyayam

14. satataṃ kīrtayanto māṃ
    yatantaś ca dṛḍhavratāḥ
    namasyantaś ca māṃ bhaktyā
    nityayuktā upāsate

7. All creatures enter into my nature
   at the end of an aeon.
In another beginning
   I send them forth again.

8. Establishing my own nature,
   time after time I send them forth,
This host of beings, without
   their will, by dint of that nature.

9. This activity does not
   imprison me, O Fighter for Wealth!
I appear as an onlooker, detached
   in the midst of this work.

10. Nature gives birth to all moving
   and unmoving things. I supervise.
That is how the world keeps turning,
   Son of Kuntī!

11. Fools misjudge me when I take
   a human form,
Because they do not know my supreme
   state as Lord of Beings.

12. Unconscious, they fall prey to beguiling nature
   such as belongs to ogres and demons,
For their hopes are vain, and so
   are their rituals and their search for wisdom.

13. But great men resort to me,
   to divine nature.
Thinking of no one else, they worship me,
   for they know me as the changeless source of existence.

14. Making my name great always,
   firm, not straying from their vow,
Revering me in their devotion, constant
   in discipline, in reverence they know me.

15. jñānayajñena cāpy anye
    yajanto mām upāsate
ekatvena pṛthaktvena
    bahudhā viśvatomukham

16. ahaṃ kratur ahaṃ yajñaḥ
    svadhāham aham auṣadham
mantro 'ham aham evājyam
    aham agnir ahaṃ hutam

17. pitāham asya jagato
    mātā dhātā pitāmahaḥ
vedyaṃ pavitram oṃkāra
    ṛk sāma yajur eva ca

18. gatir bhartā prabhuḥ sākṣī
    nivāsaḥ śaraṇaṃ suhṛt
prabhavaḥ pralayaḥ sthānaṃ
    nidhānaṃ bījam avyayam

19. tapāmy aham ahaṃ varṣaṃ
    nigṛhṇāmy utsṛjāmi ca
amṛtaṃ caiva mṛtyuś ca
    sad asac cāham arjuna

20. traividyā māṃ somapāḥ pūtapāpā
    yajñair iṣṭvā svargatiṃ prārthayante
te puṇyam āsādya surendralokam
    aśnanti divyān divi devabhogān

15. Others know me in reverence,
    when thirsting for wisdom they bring their sacrifices,
Knowing my unique form, my many and successive
    forms, my face turned toward everyone.

16. I am the rite, I am the sacrifice,
    the libation for the ancestors and the juice for the gods,
The priest's verse and the sacrificial butter.
    I take the offering, I am the offering.

17. I am father and mother of the world.
    In ancient days I established it.
I am what need be known, what purifies,
    the sacred syllable OM,
The verse of the sacred books,

18. Your way and goal, upholder, ruler,
    witness, dwelling, refuge, friend,
The world's origin, continuance
    and dissolution, abiding
Essence, changeless seed.

19. I scorch. I stop and send the rain.
    I am deathlessness and death.
O Arjuna, I am
    the entire world.

20. Cleansed of evil,
Knowers of the holy Scriptures,
Drinkers of sacred libations,
Make sacrifice to me
And seek to attain heaven.
They reach the blessed world
Of the Lord of the gods
And in the divine world
Taste the gods' divine enjoyments.

21. te taṃ bhuktvā svargalokaṃ viśālaṃ
  kṣīṇe puṇye martyalokaṃ viśanti
evaṃ trayīdharmam anuprapannā
  gatāgataṃ kāmakāmā labhante

22. ananyāś cintayanto māṃ
  ye janāh paryupāsate
teṣāṃ nityābhiyuktānāṃ
  yogakṣemaṃ vahāmy aham

23. ye 'py anyadevatā bhaktā
  yajante śraddhayānvitāḥ
te 'pi mām eva kaunteya
  yajanty avidhipūrvakam

24. ahaṃ hi sarvayajñānāṃ
  bhoktā ca prabhur eva ca
na tu mām abhijānanti
  tattvenātaś cyavanti te

25. yānti devavratā devān
  pitṝn yānti pitṛvratāḥ
bhūtāni yānti bhūtejyā
  yānti madyājino 'pi mām

26. pattraṃ puṣpaṃ phalaṃ toyaṃ
  yo me bhaktyā prayacchati
tad ahaṃ bhaktyupahṛtam
  aśnāmi prayatātmanaḥ

27. yat karoṣi yad aśnāsi
  yaj juhoṣi dadāsi yat
yat tapasyasi kaunteya
  tat kuruṣva madarpaṇam

21. But after they have enjoyed
The wide expanse of heaven,
Their merit exhausted,
They return to mortal life.
Thus they follow the practice
Of the Scriptures,
They lust and desire
And get what comes and goes.

22. Those who think on me with reverence,
and think of nothing else,
When their zeal is constant—I grant them
a sure prize.

23. And when devotees have other gods
and full of trust bring sacrifices
Outside the established liturgy,
they sacrifice to none but me.

24. For I receive and I command
all sacrifices.
But not all sacrificers recognize me
as I am. Hence they fail.

25. The gods' devotees go to the gods.
Who vow to ancestral spirits go to those.
Sacrificers to demons go to the demons.
Who sacrifice to me come to me.

26. When you offer with love a leaf,
a flower, or water to me,
I accept that offer of love
from the giver who gives himself.

27. Whatever you do, or eat,
or sacrifice, or offer,
Whatever you do in self-restraint,
do as an offering to me.

28. śubhāśubhaphalair evaṃ
  mokṣyase karmabandhanaiḥ
saṃnyāsayogayuktātmā
  vimukto mām upaiṣyasi

29. samo 'haṃ sarvabhūteṣu
  na me dveṣyo 'sti na priyaḥ
ye bhajanti tu māṃ bhaktyā
  mayi te teṣu cāpy aham

30. api cet sudurācāro
  bhajate mām ananyabhāk
sādhur eva sa mantavyaḥ
  samyag vyavasito hi saḥ

31. kṣipraṃ bhavati dharmātmā
  śaśvacchāntiṃ nigacchati
kaunteya pratijānīhi
  na me bhaktaḥ praṇaśyati

32. māṃ hi pārtha vyapāśritya
  ye 'pi syuḥ pāpayonayaḥ
striyo vaiśyās tathā śūdrās
  te 'pi yānti parāṃ gatim

33. kiṃ punar brāhmaṇāḥ puṇyā
  bhaktā rājarṣayas tathā
anityam asukhaṃ lokam
  imaṃ prāpya bhajasva mām

34. manmanā bhava madbhakto
  madyājī māṃ namaskuru
mām evaiṣyasi yuktvaivam
  ātmānaṃ matparāyaṇaḥ

28. Thus you will be freed from the prison
 of deeds and their results, good and evil.
 Wholly trained in renunciation,
 released, you will come to me.

29. I am equal-minded toward all beings.
 They neither enrapture me nor enrage me.
 But if they worship me lovingly,
 they are in me and I in them.

30. Even if a very wicked man worships,
 loving none but me—
 That man should be considered wise
 and good. He knows what he is about.

31. He soon becomes completely righteous.
 He is bound for everlasting peace.
 I am speaking to *you*. *Understand*:
 No devotee of mine gets lost.

32. For all who rely on me,
 no matter how vile their birth—
 Women, artisans, laborers—
 go to the highest goal.

33. How much more my devotees
 who have merit by birth or are rulers with vision!
 You have entered this fleeting, joyless world.
 Worship and love me!

34. Think of me, be devoted to me.
 Revere me while sacrificing to me.
 Thus disciplining yourself, wholly
 intent on me, you will come to me.

X

śrībhagavān uvāca

1. bhūya eva mahābāho
   śṛṇu me paramaṃ vacaḥ
   yat te 'haṃ prīyamāṇāya
   vakṣyāmi hitakāmyayā

2. na me viduḥ suragaṇāḥ
   prabhavaṃ na maharṣayaḥ
   aham ādir hi devānāṃ
   maharṣīṇāṃ ca sarvaśaḥ

3. yo māṃ ajam anādiṃ ca
   vetti lokamaheśvaram
   asaṃmūḍhaḥ sa martyeṣu
   sarvapāpaiḥ pramucyate

4. buddhir jñānam asaṃmohaḥ
   kṣamā satyaṃ damaḥ śamaḥ
   sukhaṃ duhkhaṃ bhavo 'bhāvo
   bhayaṃ cābhayam eva ca

5. ahiṃsā samatā tuṣṭis
   tapo dānaṃ yaśo 'yaśaḥ
   bhavanti bhāvā bhūtānāṃ
   matta eva pṛthagvidhāḥ

6. maharṣayaḥ sapta pūrve
   catvāro manavas tathā
   madbhāvā mānasā jātā
   yeṣāṃ loka imāḥ prajāḥ

The Lord:

1. Listen again, warrior, to my supreme word,
   because you delight in it,
   And I shall present it to you,
   for I desire what is best for you.

2. The multitudes of gods do not know where I come from,
   neither do the great seers,
   For I am the universal beginning
   of the gods and the great seers.

3. When a man knows me as the unborn
   beginningless Lord of worlds and peoples,
   He is free among mortals from all obsessions,
   released at once from all evil.

4. Understanding, wisdom, clarity,
   forbearance and truthfulness, inner control and peace,
   Joy, grief, the arising and passing away of things,
   anxiety and courage,

5. Gentleness, equanimity, happiness,
   austerity, generosity, glory and shame—
   Whatever exists is disposed to such states of mind,
   and all these varieties come from me.

6. The seven timeless sages
   and the four ancestors of mankind
   Are born of my will and have their disposition in me
   and all creatures on earth are theirs.

7. etāṃ vibhūtiṃ yogaṃ ca
mama yo vetti tattvataḥ
so 'vikampena yogena
yujyate nātra saṃśayaḥ

8. ahaṃ sarvasya prabhavo
mattaḥ sarvaṃ pravartate
iti matvā bhajante māṃ
budhā bhāvasamanvitāḥ

9. maccittā madgataprāṇā
bodhayantaḥ parasparam
kathayantaś ca māṃ nityaṃ
tuṣyanti ca ramanti ca

10. teṣāṃ satatayuktānāṃ
bhajatāṃ prītipūrvakam
dadāmi buddhiyogaṃ taṃ
yena mām upayānti te

11. teṣām evānukampārtham
aham ajñānajaṃ tamaḥ
nāśayāmy ātmabhāvastho
jñānadīpena bhāsvatā

arjuna uvāca

12. paraṃ brahma paraṃ dhāma
pavitraṃ paramaṃ bhavān
puruṣaṃ śāśvataṃ divyam
ādidevam ajaṃ vibhum

13. āhus tvām ṛṣayaḥ sarve
devarṣir nāradas tathā
asito devalo vyāsaḥ
svayaṃ caiva bravīṣi me

14. sarvam etad ṛtaṃ manye
yam māṃ vadasi keśava
na hi te bhagavan vyaktiṃ
vidur devā na dānavāḥ

7. Who knows this dominion of mine
   and its use as they really are,
Is sure to be truly disciplined
   by applying himself without wavering.

8. I am the origin of all.
   Because of me everything lives.
Intelligent men in the right state of mind
   know this and sing my praise.

9. They are happy and joyful, thinking of me,
   their whole life going out toward me,
Instructing one another,
   constantly narrating my acts.

10. They never cease to be disciplined,
   delight in worshiping,
And I bestow on them the right mind
   which leads them to me.

11. Tenderly—remaining in my true state—
   I put an end to their sloth,
Which comes from ignorance.
   I do so with the bright light of wisdom.

Arijuna:

12–13. You are God, the highest abode,
   the supreme sanctifier.
All seers, and also the divine seer Nārada,
   and Asita Devala, and Vyāsa
Call you the everlasting Divine Being
   who existed before the gods,
The Lord without birth—
   and you yourself tell me so.

14. I believe
   all this you teach me is true.
Neither gods nor demons, O Lord,
   are able to envision your form.

15. svayam evātmanātmānaṃ
vettha tvaṃ puruṣottama
bhūtabhāvana bhūteśa
devadeva jagatpate

16. vaktum arhasy aśeṣeṇa
divyā hy ātmavibhūtayaḥ
yābhir vibhūtibhir lokān
imāṃs tvaṃ vyāpya tiṣṭhasi

17. kathaṃ vidyām ahaṃ yogiṃs
tvāṃ sadā paricintayan
keṣu keṣu ca bhāveṣu
cintyo 'si bhagavan mayā

18. vistareṇātmano yogaṃ
vibhūtiṃ ca janārdana
bhūyaḥ kathaya tṛptir hi
śṛṇvato nāsti me 'mṛtam

śrībhagavān uvāca

19. hanta te kathayiṣyāmi
divyā hy ātmavibhūtayaḥ
prādhānyataḥ kuruśreṣṭha
nāsty anto vistarasya me

20. aham ātmā guḍākeśa
sarvabhūtāśayasthitaḥ
aham ādiś ca madhyaṃ ca
bhūtānām anta eva ca

21. ādityānām ahaṃ viṣṇur
jyotiṣāṃ ravir aṃśumān
marīcir marutām asmi
nakṣatrāṇām ahaṃ śaśī

22. vedānāṃ sāmavedo 'smi
devānām asmi vāsavaḥ
indriyāṇāṃ manaś cāsmi
bhūtānām asmi cetanā

15. You, Highest Being, who
   to yourself alone are known,
O source of living beings, Lord of life,
   God of gods, Lord of the world!

16. The abundant forms of yourself are divine.
   Please tell me then, and hold back nothing,
By what forms you continue
   to pervade this multiple world.

17. Meditating on you always,
   how may I know you—you in your mystic power?
And in what states of being
   should I envisage you?

18. Tell me more, and in detail,
   of your mystic power and mighty forms,
For I cannot listen enough, O Stirrer of Men,
   to your immortal word.

The Lord:

19. My mighty forms are indeed divine, and
   of course I shall tell you
What they are in essence.
   My total extent has no end.

20. I am the reality that abides
   in the soul of all creatures,
And of all creatures I am
   the beginning, middle, and end.

21. Of the Gods of Heaven, I am Viṣṇu,
   of lights the brilliant sun.
I am the leading storm god.
   I am the moon among the stars.

22. Of Sacred Scriptures, I am the Book of Songs.
   I am king of the celestial race.
I am the mind presiding over the senses.
   Of all that evolved, I am awareness.

23. rudrāṇāṃ śaṃkaraś cāsmi
    vitteśo yakṣarakṣasām
    vasūnāṃ pāvakaś cāsmi
    meruḥ śikhariṇām aham

24. purodhasāṃ ca mukhyaṃ māṃ
    viddhi pārtha bṛhaspatim
    senānīnām ahaṃ skandaḥ
    sarasām asmi sāgaraḥ

25. maharṣīṇāṃ bhṛgur ahaṃ
    girām asmy ekam akṣaram
    yajñānāṃ japayajño 'smi
    sthāvarāṇāṃ himālayaḥ

26. aśvatthaḥ sarvavṛkṣāṇāṃ
    devarṣīṇāṃ ca nāradaḥ
    gandharvāṇāṃ citrarathaḥ
    siddhānāṃ kapilo muniḥ

27. uccaiḥśravasam aśvānāṃ
    viddhi mām amṛtodbhavam
    airāvataṃ gajendrāṇāṃ
    narāṇāṃ ca narādhipam

28. āyudhānām ahaṃ vajraṃ
    dhenūnām asmi kāmadhuk
    prajanaś cāsmi kandarpaḥ
    sarpāṇām asmi vāsukiḥ

29. anantaś cāsmi nāgānāṃ
    varuṇo yādasām aham
    pitṝṇām aryamā cāsmi
    yamaḥ saṃyamatām aham

30. prahlādaś cāsmi daityānāṃ
    kālaḥ kalayatām aham
    mṛgāṇāṃ ca mṛgendro 'haṃ
    vainateyaś ca pakṣiṇām

23. I am Śiva among the Terrifying Gods,
  Lord of Wealth among elves and goblins.
 Of the Radiant Gods I am Fire,
  of mountain peaks, Meru.

24. Know me as the chief of house-priests—
  the chaplain of the gods.
 Among generals I am the God of War,
  among great waters the ocean.

25. Of the great seers I am the greatest, Bhṛgu,
  of speech the one supreme, subtle sound,
 Of sacrifices the offering of whispered chants,
  of mountain-ranges Himālaya,

26. Of all trees the sacred fig-tree,
  of divine seers Nārada,
 Of the heavenly musicians Citraratha,
  of perfect wise men the sage Kapila.

27. Know me among horses as charger of Indra
  sprung from Immortality,
 Among elephants as the elephant of Indra,
  and among men as king.

28. Of weapons I am Indra's thunderbolt,
  of cattle Kāmaduh [the Cow of Plenty].
 Regarding procreation, I am the God of Love.
  Of serpents I am Vāsuki [their prince].

29. I am the primeval watersnake.
  Of the mighty beings of the waters I am Varuṇa.
 I am Aryaman heading the ancestral spirits.
  In restraint I am Yama [lord of death].

30. I am the devout prince of the gods' foes.
  Among men marking the seasons I am Time.
 Among wild beasts I am the lion.
  Of all that has wings I am [Viṣṇu's bird] Garuḍa.

31. pavanaḥ pavatām asmi
rāmaḥ śastrabhṛtām aham
jhaṣāṇāṃ makaraś cāsmi
srotasām asmi jāhnavī

32. sargāṇām ādir antaś ca
madhyaṃ caivāham arjuna
adhyātmavidyā vidyānāṃ
vādaḥ pravadatām aham

33. aksarāṇām akāro 'smi
dvandvaḥ sāmāsikasya ca
aham evākṣayaḥ kālo
dhātāhaṃ viśvatomukhaḥ

34. mṛtyuḥ sarvaharaś cāham
udbhavaś ca bhaviṣyatām
kīrtiḥ śrīr vāk ca nārīṇāṃ
smṛtir medhā dhṛtiḥ kṣamā

35. bṛhatsāma tathā sāmnāṃ
gāyatrī chandasām aham
māsānāṃ mārgaśīrṣo 'ham
ṛtūnāṃ kusumākaraḥ

36. dyūtaṃ chalayatām asmi
tejas tejasvinām aham
jayo 'smi vyavasāyo 'smi
sattvaṃ sattvavatām aham

37. vrṣṇīnāṃ vāsudevo smi
pāṇḍavānāṃ dhanaṃjayaḥ
munīnām apy ahaṃ vyāsaḥ
kavīnām uśanā kaviḥ

38. daṇḍo damayatām asmi
nītir asmi jigīṣatām
maunaṃ caivāsmi guhyānāṃ
jñānaṃ jñānavatām aham

31. I am the purifier in ritual purification,
   Rāma among warriors,
Of the sea's prodigies the Makara,
   among rivers the Ganges.

32. Of every world brought forth I am
   beginning, middle, and end.
I am that knowledge that affects the self,
   the true subject of learned debaters.

33. I am the A of the alphabet,
   in grammar the compound of perfect balance.
I alone am imperishable time
   and I turn everywhere sustaining the world.

34. I am death that snatches all
   and the birth of all yet to be born.
Of feminine names Glory, Fortune, Divine Speech,
   Memory, Prudence, Constancy, Patience.

35. In ritual I am the perfect chant
   and the perfectly scanned verse
I am the first of months,
   among seasons the spring.

36. I am the dice-roll of the cunning,
   the majesty of the majestic,
The victory and the determined struggle,
   the integrity of courageous men.

37. I am Kṛṣṇa of the Vṛṣṇis,
   Arjuna of the Pāṇḍavas!
Of saintly hermits I am Vyāsa,
   of seers Uśanas

38. I am the justice stern masters mete,
   the statecraft of leaders who desire victory;
I am the silence of mysteries,
   the wisdom of the wise.

39. yac cāpi sarvabhūtānāṃ
bījaṃ tad aham arjuna
na tad asti vinā yat syān
mayā bhūtaṃ carācaram

40. nānto 'sti mama divyānāṃ
vibhūtīnāṃ paraṃtapa
eṣa tūddeśataḥ prokto
vibhūter vistaro mayā

41. yad yad vibhūtimat sattvaṃ
śrīmad ūrjitam eva vā
tat tad evāvagaccha tvaṃ
mama tejoṃśasaṃbhavam

42. athavā bahunaitena
kiṃ jñātena tavārjuna
viṣṭabhyāham idaṃ kṛtsnam
ekāṃśena sthito jagat

39. I am all that is
    the nucleus of any being.
Nothing moving or unmoving
    could exist without me.

40. There is no end to my divine,
    abundant, mighty forms,
But I have given you a view
    of my dominion.

41. Learn this: Whatever radiates power
    or shows fortune or valor
Surely reflects a small portion
    of my glory.

42. But there is no need to know everything!
    I have spread out this entire world
And continue to support it
    with one fraction of myself.

XI

arjuna uvāca

1. madanugrahāya paramaṃ
guhyam adhyātmasaṃjñitam
yat tvayoktaṃ vacas tena
moho 'yaṃ vigato mama

2. bhavāpyayau hi bhūtānāṃ
śrutau vistaraśo mayā
tvattaḥ kamalapattrākṣa
māhātmyam api cāvyayam

3. evam etad yathāttha tvam
ātmānaṃ parameśvara
draṣṭum icchāmi te rūpam
aiśvaraṃ puruṣottama

4. manyase yadi tac chakyaṃ
mayā draṣṭum iti prabho
yogeśvara tato me tvaṃ
darśayātmānam avyayam

śrībhagavān uvāca

5. paśya me pārtha rūpāṇi
śataśo 'tha sahasraśaḥ
nānāvidhāni divyāni
nānāvarṇākṛtīni ca

6. paśyādityān vasūn rudrān
aśvinau marutas tathā
bahūny adṛṣṭapūrvāṇi
paśyāścaryāṇi bhārata

Arjuna:

1. You have favored me by disclosing
   the highest secret, concerning the self.
   Your words have cleared away
   the darkness of my mind,

2. For you have taught me at length
   the origin and end of creatures,
   And also about your glory,
   which is endless.

3. O highest Lord, I wish I could see you,
   your form as Lord,
   Just as you yourself say you are,
   Supreme Divine Being.

4. O Lord, if you think it is possible
   that I might see you—
   Then, Lord of mystic power,
   show to me your changeless self.

The Lord:

5. Open your eyes and see
   my hundreds, my thousands of forms,
   In all their variety, heavenly splendor,
   in all their colors and semblances.

6. Look upon the Gods of Heaven, the Radiant Gods,
   the Terrifying Gods, the Kind Celestial Twins.
   See, Arjuna, countless marvels
   never seen before.

7. ihaikasthaṃ jagat kṛtsnaṃ
paśyādya sacarācaram
mama dehe guḍākeśa
yac cānyad draṣṭum icchasi

8. na tu māṃ śakyase draṣṭum
anenaiva svacakṣuṣā
divyaṃ dadāmi te cakṣuḥ
paśya me yogam aiśvaram

saṃjaya uvāca

9. evam uktvā tato rājan
mahāyogeśvaro hariḥ
darśayām āsa pārthāya
paramaṃ rūpam aiśvaram

10. anekavaktranayanam
anekādbhutadarśanam
anekadivyābharaṇaṃ
divyānekodyatāyudham

11. divyamālyāmbaradharaṃ
divyagandhānulepanam
sarvāścaryamayaṃ devam
anantaṃ viśvatomukham

12. divi sūryasahasrasya
bhaved yugapad utthitā
yadi bhāḥ sadṛśī sā syād
bhāsas tasya mahātmanaḥ

13. tatraikasthaṃ jagat kṛtsnaṃ
pravibhaktam anekadhā
apaśyad devadevasya
śarīre pāṇḍavas tadā

14. tataḥ sa vismayāviṣṭo
hṛṣṭaromā dhanaṃjayaḥ
praṇamya śirasā devaṃ
kṛtāñjalir abhāṣata

7. Here in my body, in one place, now
   the whole world—
All that moves and does not move—
   and whatever else you want to see.

8. Of course, with the ordinary eye
   you cannot see me.
I give you divine vision.
   Behold my absolute power!

Saṃjaya:

9. With these words, Viṣṇu,
   the great Lord of mystic power,
Gave Arjuna the vision
   of his highest, absolute form—

10. His form with many mouths and eyes,
   appearing in many miraculous ways,
With many divine ornaments
   and divine, unsheathed weapons.

11. He wore garlands and robes
   and ointments of divine fragrance.
He was a wholly wonderful god,
   infinite, facing in every direction.

12. If the light of a thousand suns
   should effulge all at once,
It would resemble the radiance
   of that god of overpowering reality.

13. Then and there, Arjuna saw
   the entire world unified,
Yet divided manifold,
   embodied in the God of gods.

14. Bewildered and enraptured,
   Arjuna, the Pursuer of Wealth,
Bowed his head to the god,
   joined his palms, and said:

arjuna uvāca

15. paśyāmi devāṃs tava deva dehe
sarvāṃs tathā bhūtaviśesasaṃghān
brahmāṇam īśaṃ kamalāsanastham
ṛṣīṃś ca sarvān uragāṃś ca divyān

16. anekabāhūdaraṿaktranetraṃ
paśyāmi tvāṃ sarvato 'nantarūpam
nāntaṃ na madhyaṃ na punas tavādiṃ
paśyāmi viśveśvara viśvarūpa

17. kirīṭinaṃ gadinaṃ cakriṇaṃ ca
tejorāśiṃ sarvato dīptimantam
paśyāmi tvāṃ durnirīkṣyaṃ samantād
dīptānalārkadyutim aprameyam

18. tvam akṣaraṃ paramaṃ veditavyaṃ
tvam asya viśvasya paraṃ nidhānam
tvam avyayaḥ śāśvatadharmagoptā
sanātanas tvaṃ puruṣo mato me

19. anādimadhyāntam anantavīryam
anantabāhuṃ śaśisūryanetram
paśyāmi tvāṃ dīptahutāśavaktraṃ
svatejasā viśvam idaṃ tapantam

Arjuna:

15. Master! Within you
I see the gods, and
All classes of beings, the Creator
On his lotus seat,
And all seers and divine serpents.

16. Far and near, I see you
without limit,
Reaching, containing everything, and
With innumerable mouths and eyes.
I see no end to you, no middle,
And no beginning—
O universal Lord and form of all!

17. You, Wearer
Of Crown, Mace, and Discus,
You are a deluge of brilliant light
All around.
I see you,
Who can hardly be seen,
With the splendor of radiant fires and suns,
Immeasurable.

18. You are the one imperishable
Paramount necessary core of knowledge,
The world's ultimate foundation;
You never cease to guard the eternal tradition.
You are the everlasting
Divine Being.

19. There is no telling what is
Beginning, middle, or end in you.
Your power is infinite.
Your arms reach infinitely far.
Sun and moon are your eyes.
This is how I see you.
Your mouth is a flaming sacrificial fire.
You burn up the world with your radiance.

20. dyāvāpṛthivyor idam antaraṃ hi
vyāptaṃ tvayaikena diśaś ca sarvāḥ
dṛṣṭvādbhutaṃ rūpam idaṃ tavograṃ
lokatrayaṃ pravyathitaṃ mahātman

21. amī hi tvāṃ surasaṃghā viśanti
kecid bhītāḥ prāñjalayo gṛṇanti
svastīty uktvā maharṣisiddhasaṃghāḥ
stuvanti tvāṃ stutibhiḥ puṣkalābhiḥ

22. rudrādityā vasavo ye ca sādhyā
viśve 'śvinau marutaś coṣmapāś ca
gandharvayakṣāsurasiddhasaṃghā
vīkṣante tvā vismitāś caiva sarve

23. rūpaṃ mahat te bahuvaktranetraṃ
mahābāho bahubāhūrupādam
bahūdaraṃ bahudaṃṣṭrākarālaṃ
dṛṣṭvā lokāḥ pravyathitās tathāham

24. nabhaḥspṛśaṃ dīptam anekavarṇaṃ
vyāttānanaṃ dīptaviśālanetram
dṛṣṭvā hi tvā pravyathitāntarātmā
dhṛtiṃ na vindāmi śamaṃ ca viṣṇo

20. For you alone fill the quarters of heaven
And the space between heaven and earth.
The world above,
Man's world,
And the world in between
Are frightened at the awesome sight of you,
O mighty being!

21. There I see throngs of gods entering you.
Some are afraid,
They join their palms
And call upon your name.
Throngs of great seers and perfect sages hail you
With magnificent hymns.

22. The Terrifying Gods,
The Gods of Heaven, the Radiant Gods,
Also the Celestial Spirits,
The All-Gods, the Celestial Twins,
The Storm Gods and the Ancestors;
Multitudes of heavenly musicians,
Good sprites, demons and perfect sages
All look upon you in wonder.

23. When the worlds see your form
Of many mouths and eyes,
Of many arms, legs, feet,
Many torsos, many terrible tusks,
They tremble,
As do I.

24. For seeing you
Ablaze with all the colors of the rainbow,
Touching the sky,
With gaping mouths and wide, flaming eyes,
My heart in me is shaken.
O God,
I have lost all certainty, all peace.

25. daṃṣṭrākarālāni ca te mukhāni
dṛṣṭvaiva kālānalasaṃnibhāni
diśo na jāne na labhe ca śarma
prasīda deveśa jagannivāsa

26. amī ca tvāṃ dhṛtarāṣṭrasya putrāḥ
sarve sahaivāvanipālasaṃghaiḥ
bhīṣmo droṇaḥ sūtaputras tathāsau
sahāsmadīyair api yodhamukhyaiḥ

27. vaktrāṇi te tvaramāṇā viśanti
daṃṣṭrākarālāni bhayānakāni
kecid vilagnā daśanāntareṣu
saṃdṛśyante cūrṇitair uttamāṅgaiḥ

28. yathā nadīnāṃ bahavo 'mbuvegāḥ
samudram evābhimukhā dravanti
tathā tavāmī naralokavīrā
viśanti vaktrāṇy abhivijvalanti

29. yathā pradīptaṃ jvalanaṃ pataṅgā
viśanti nāśāya samṛddhavegāḥ
tathaiva nāśāya viśanti lokās
tavāpi vaktrāṇi samṛddhavegāḥ

25. Your mouths and their terrible tusks
Evoke
The world in conflagration.
Looking at them
I can no longer
Orient myself.
There is no refuge.
O Lord of gods,
Dwelling place of the world,
Give me your grace.

26. And there the sons of Dhṛtarāṣṭra
Enter you,
All of them,
Together with a host of kings,
Bhīṣma,
Droṇa,
And also the charioteer's son, Karṇa—
And our own commanders,
Even they are with them!

27. They rush into your awful mouths
With those terrible tusks.
Some can be seen
Stuck
Between your teeth,
Their heads crushed.

28. As the many river torrents
Rush toward one sea,
Those worldly heroes
Enter
Your flaming mouths.

29. As moths hasten frantically
Into the fire
To meet their end,
So men enter
Your jaws.

30. lelihyase grasamānaḥ samantāl
lokān samagrān vadanair jvaladbhiḥ
tejobhir āpūrya jagat samagraṃ
bhāsas tavogrāḥ pratapanti viṣṇo

31. ākhyāhi me ko bhavān ugrarūpo
namo 'stu te devavara prasīda
vijñātum icchāmi bhavantam ādyaṃ
na hi prajānāmi tava pravṛttim

śrībhagavān uvāca

32. kālo 'smi lokakṣayakṛt pravṛddho
lokān samāhartum iha pravṛttaḥ
ṛte 'pi tvāṃ na bhaviṣyanti sarve
ye 'vasthitāḥ pratyanīkeṣu yodhāḥ

33. tasmāt tvam uttiṣṭha yaśo labhasva
jitvā śatrūn bhunkṣva rājyaṃ samṛddham
mayaivaite nihatāḥ pūrvam eva
nimittamātraṃ bhava savyasācin

30. Devouring all
With the flames of your mouths
Lapping and licking all around,
You fill the world
With effulgence,
And your awesome splendor is scorching,
O God!

31. I bow before you, supreme God.
Be gracious.
You, who are so awesome to see,
Tell me, who are you?
I want to know you, the very first Lord,
For I do not understand what it is you are doing.

The Lord:

32. I am Time who destroys man's world.
I am the time that is now ripe
To gather in the people here;
That is what I am doing.
Even without you,
All these warriors
Drawn up for battle
In opposing ranks
Will cease to exist.

33. Therefore
Rise up!
Win glory!
When you conquer your enemies,
Your kingship will be fulfilled.
Enjoy it.
Be just an instrument,
You, who can draw the bow
With the left as well as the right hand!
I myself have slain
Your enemies
Long ago.

34. droṇaṃ ca bhīṣmaṃ ca jayadrathaṃ ca
karṇaṃ tathānyān api yodhavīrān
mayā hatāṃs tvaṃ jahi mā vyathiṣṭhā
yudhyasva jetāsi raṇe sapatnān

saṃjaya uvāca

35. etac chrutvā vacanaṃ keśavasya
kṛtāñjalir vepamānaḥ kirīṭī
namaskṛtvā bhūya evāha kṛṣṇaṃ
sagadgadaṃ bhītabhītaḥ praṇamya

arjuna uvāca

36. sthāne hṛṣīkeśa tava prakīrtyā
jagat prahṛṣyaty anurajyate ca
rakṣāṃsi bhītāni diśo dravanti
sarve namasyanti ca siddhasaṃghāḥ

37. kasmāc ca te na nameran mahātman
garīyase brahmaṇo 'py ādikartre
ananta deveśa jagannivāsa
tvam akṣaraṃ sad asat tatparaṃ yat

34. Do not waver.
Conquer the enemies
Whom I have already slain—
Droṇa and Bhīṣma and Jayadratha,
And Karṇa also, and the other heroes at arms.
Fight!
You are about to defeat
Your rivals in war.

Saṃjaya:

35. After these words of Kṛṣṇa,
The wearer of the crown was overwhelmed.
Joining his palms he honored Kṛṣṇa.
He bowed down, then spoke again,
Stammering, overcome by fear:

Arjuna:

36. It is right, Kṛṣṇa, that the world
Revels in your glory,
That demons are frightened
And flee in all directions,
And all the host of perfect sages
Honor you.

37. Why should they not bow to you,
O mighty one!
For you are most worthy of honor;
You impelled even the creator.
O infinite Lord of the gods
And abode of the world,
You are the imperishable beginning,
You are what exists and what does not exist,
And you are beyond both.

38. tvam ādidevaḥ puruṣaḥ purāṇas
tvam asya viśvasya paraṃ nidhānam
vettāsi vedyaṃ ca paraṃ ca dhāma
tvayā tataṃ viśvam anantarūpa

39. vāyur yamo 'gnir varuṇaḥ śaśāṅkaḥ
prajāpatis tvaṃ prapitāmahaś ca
namo namas te 'stu sahasrakṛtvaḥ
punaś ca bhūyo 'pi namo namas te

40. namaḥ purastād atha pṛṣṭhatas te
namo 'stu te sarvata eva sarva
anantavīryāmitavikramas tvaṃ
sarvaṃ samāpnoṣi tato 'si sarvaḥ

41. sakheti matvā prasabhaṃ yad uktaṃ
he kṛṣṇa he yādava he sakheti
ajānatā mahimānaṃ tavedaṃ
mayā pramādāt praṇayena vāpi

42. yac cāvahāsārtham asatkṛto 'si
vihāraśayyāsanabhojaneṣu
eko 'thavāpy acyuta tatsamakṣaṃ
tat kṣāmaye tvām aham aprameyam

38. You are the very first god,
The primal Divine Being,
The absolute foundation of all things,
Knower and known,
And the highest estate.
You of infinite form
Stretched out the world.

39. You who are Wind, Death, Fire,
The God of Streams, the Moon,
The Lord of living beings,
Of creation,
You should receive honor
A thousandfold—Time and again,
Honor, honor to you!

40. Let honor be given to you
Before you and behind
And on all sides.
You who are all,
Your might is boundless,
Your strength unmeasured.
You are all,
For you fulfill all.

41. Whatever I blurted out,
Carelessly or out of affection—
Kṛṣṇa! Son of Yadhu! My friend!—
Thinking of you as my companion,
And unaware of this,
Of your greatness,

42. And whatever I did improperly to you,
Jokingly,
In playing, resting, sitting, or eating,
Either by myself or in public—
O imperishable Lord,
I ask your pardon for it.
You are immeasurable.

43. pitāsi lokasya carācarasya
tvam asya pūjyaś ca gurur garīyān
na tvatsamo 'sty abhyadhikaḥ kuto 'nyo
lokatraye 'py apratimaprabhāva

44. tasmāt praṇamya praṇidhāya kāyaṃ
prasādaye tvām aham īśam īḍyam
piteva putrasya sakheva sakhyuḥ
priyaḥ priyāyārhasi deva soḍhum

45. adṛṣṭapūrvaṃ hṛṣito 'smi dṛṣṭvā
bhayena ca pravyathitaṃ mano me
tad eva me darśaya deva rūpaṃ
prasīda deveśa jagannivāsa

46. kirīṭinaṃ gadinaṃ cakrahastam
icchāmi tvāṃ draṣṭum ahaṃ tathaiva
tenaiva rūpeṇa caturbhujena
sahasrabāho bhava viśvamūrte

43. You are the father of the world
With all its moving and unmoving things.
You are its spiritual guide,
Most venerable and worthy of worship.
There is none like you.
How could there be anyone higher
In the world above, in man's world,
And in the realm between the two,
O paramount Lord!

44. Therefore, I bow,
I prostrate myself,
I beg your grace,
For you are the Lord to be worshiped.
Please, God, be patient with me
As a father with his son, a friend with his friend
A lover with his beloved.

45. I have seen
What no one saw before,
And I rejoice.
But my heart is stricken with fear.
Show me
That one usual form of yours,
O God,
Be gracious, Lord of gods,
Refuge of the world.

46. I would like to see you
Just like that
With your crown and club
And the discus in your hand.
O you with thousand arms
And of all forms,
Appear again
In that four-armed shape of yours.

śrībhagavān uvāca

47. mayā prasannena tavārjunedaṃ
rūpaṃ paraṃ darśitam ātmayogāt
tejomayaṃ viśvam anantam ādyaṃ
yan me tvadanyena na dṛṣṭapūrvam

48. na vedayajñādhyayanair na dānair
na ca kriyābhir na tapobhir ugraiḥ
evaṃrūpaḥ śakya ahaṃ nṛloke
draṣṭuṃ tvadanyena kurupravīra

49. mā te vyathā mā ca vimūḍhabhāvo
dṛṣṭvā rūpaṃ ghoram īdṛṅ mamedam
vyapetabhīḥ prītamanāḥ punas tvaṃ
tad eva me rūpam idaṃ prapaśya

saṃjaya uvāca

50. ity arjunaṃ vāsudevas tathoktvā
svakaṃ rūpaṃ darśayām āsa bhūyaḥ
āśvāsayām āsa ca bhītam enaṃ
bhūtvā punaḥ saumyavapur mahātmā

arjuna uvāca

51. dṛṣṭvedaṃ mānuṣaṃ rūpaṃ
tava saumyaṃ janārdana
idānīm asmi saṃvṛttaḥ
sacetāḥ prakṛtiṃ gataḥ

The Lord:

47. I am pleased with you, Arjuna,
And by my own will
I have shown you my supreme form.
This is the form of my majesty.
It is my universal form,
Primordial and endless.
No one but you has ever seen it.

48. No one but you, foremost of the Kurus,
In the world of men
Can see me in this form,
Whether by knowledge of Sacred Texts,
Or by sacrifices,
Study, or acts of generosity,
Or rituals, or grim austerities.

49. Have no fear, no anxieties,
When you see this shape of mine,
However terrifying it is.
See, here is my usual form again.
Your fear is dispelled,
Your heart at ease.

Saṃjaya:

50. Thus Kṛṣṇa spoke to Arjuna
And showed his own form again.
The mighty being
Took on his agreeable form,
And he comforted that frightened man.

Arjuna:

51. Now that I see this pleasant,
human shape of yours, Kṛṣṇa,
I regain my senses
and become normal again.

śrībhagavān uvāca

52\. sudurdarśam idaṃ rūpaṃ
   dṛṣṭavān asi yan mama
devā apy asya rūpasya
   nityaṃ darśanakānkṣiṇaḥ

53\. nāhaṃ vedair na tapasā
   na dānena na cejyayā
śakya evaṃvidho draṣṭuṃ
   dṛṣṭavān asi māṃ yathā

54\. bhaktyā tv ananyayā śakya
   aham evaṃvidho 'rjuna
jñātuṃ draṣṭuṃ ca tattvena
   praveṣṭuṃ ca paraṃtapa

55\. matkarmakṛn matparamo
   madbhaktaḥ saṅgavarjitaḥ
nirvairaḥ sarvabhūteṣu
   yaḥ sa mām eti pāṇḍava

The Lord:

52. Even the gods long
   to see this form of mine
That is very difficult to see
   and that you have seen.

53. The way you have seen me
   I cannot be seen
By knowing sacred texts, by austerity,
   generosity, or sacrifice,

54. But I can be known and seen in this way,
   as I really am;
I am accessible through devotion
   directed to me alone.

55. Who does his rites for me and is intent on me,
   who loves me without other desires,
And has no ill will toward any creatures at all,
   he comes to me.

XII

arjuna uvāca

1. evaṃ satatayuktā ye
   bhaktās tvāṃ paryupāsate
   ye cāpy akṣaram avyaktaṃ
   teṣāṃ ke yogavittamāḥ

śrībhagavān uvāca

2. mayy āveśya mano ye māṃ
   nityayuktā upāsate
   śraddhayā parayopetās
   te me yuktatamā matāḥ

3. ye tv akṣaram anirdeśyam
   avyaktaṃ paryupāsate
   sarvatragam acintyaṃ ca
   kūṭastham acalaṃ dhruvam

4. saṃniyamyendriyagrāmaṃ
   sarvatra samabuddhayaḥ
   te prāpnuvanti mām eva
   sarvabhūtahite ratāḥ

5. kleśo 'dhikataras teṣām
   avyaktāsaktacetasām
   avyaktā hi gatir duḥkhaṃ
   dehavadbhir avāpyate

6. ye tu sarvāṇi karmāṇi
   mayi saṃnyasya matparāḥ
   ananyenaiva yogena
   māṃ dhyāyanta upāsate

Arjuna:

1. I understand how some devotees of steady
   discipline see and revere you,
   And others the very nucleus, the invisible nucleus
   of all things. But who knows discipline best?

The Lord:

2. Those are most disciplined
   who are endowed with greatest trust.
   They concentrate on me,
   and see and revere me, in constant discipline.

3, 4. Still, those who see and revere the unmanifest,
   which is imperishable, incomparable,
   Onmipresent, passing beyond understanding,
   the highest, changeless, lasting,
   They also reach me. They take pleasure
   in the well-being of all creatures.
   They have attained equanimity toward all
   and restrained their senses.

5. These men, who focus their attention
   on the unmanifest, go through greater affliction,
   For souls in their human form have difficulty
   reaching an invisible goal.

6. But those who are intent on me
   and dedicate all their rituals and doings to me,
   Who meditate on me, who revere and see me,
   disciplined toward none but me—

7. teṣām aham samuddhartā
   mṛtyusaṃsārasāgarāt
bhavāmi nacirāt pārtha
   mayy āveśitacetasām

8. mayy eva mana ādhatsva
   mayi buddhiṃ niveśaya
nivasiṣyasi mayy eva
   ata ūrdhvaṃ na saṃśayaḥ

9. atha cittaṃ samādhātuṃ
   na śaknoṣi mayi sthiram
abhyāsayogena tato
   mām icchāptuṃ dhanaṃjaya

10. abhyāse 'py asamartho 'si
   matkarmaparamo bhava
madartham api karmāṇi
   kurvan siddhim avāpsyasi

11. athaitad apy aśakto 'si
   kartuṃ madyogam āśritaḥ
sarvakarmaphalatyāgaṃ
   tataḥ kuru yatātmavān

12. śreyo hi jñānam abhyāsāj
   jñānād dhyānaṃ viśiṣyate
dhyānāt karmaphalatyāgas
   tyāgāc chāntir anantaram

13. adveṣṭā sarvabhūtānāṃ
   maitraḥ karuṇa eva ca
nirmamo nirahaṃkāraḥ
   samaduḥkhasukhaḥ kṣamī

14. saṃtuṣṭaḥ satataṃ yogī
   yatātmā dṛḍhaniścayaḥ
mayy arpitamanobuddhir
   yo madbhaktaḥ sa me priyaḥ

7. Them I lift up from the ocean
   of the round of deaths
As soon as they direct
   their thought to me.

8. Keep your mind centered on me. Make
   your meditation enter me.
From now on you will dwell in me
   for certain.

9. Or, if you are not able to concentrate
   on me fixedly,
You, Winner of Wealth, must try
   to win me by training.

10. And if you are not disciplined enough for training,
   give yourself wholly to rites for me.
You will be successful
   just doing cultic acts for my sake.

11. If you are not able to do even that,
   rely on the mystery of my devotion.
Keep yourself in check, and cease anticipating
   the effects of all your rituals.

12. Although wisdom is better than training,
   and meditation excels the search for knowledge,
Abandoning the outcome of rituals is worth more
   than meditating. It brings peace at once.

13, 14. I love my devotee—
   the man of discipline always happy,
Controlling himself, firm of will,
   accepting all creatures
With solidarity and compassion,
   not selfish, not self-centered,
With equanimity toward pleasant and unpleasant things,
   thought and meditation directed toward me.

15. yasmān nodvijate loko
lokān nodvijate ca yaḥ
harṣāmarṣabhayodvegair
mukto yaḥ sa ca me priyaḥ

16. anapekṣaḥ śucir dakṣa
udāsīno gatavyathaḥ
sarvārambhaparityāgī
yo madbhaktaḥ sa me priyaḥ

17. yo na hṛṣyati na dveṣṭi
na śocati na kāṅkṣati
śubhāśubhaparityāgī
bhaktimān yaḥ sa me priyaḥ

18. samaḥ śatrau ca mitre ca
tathā mānāvamānayoḥ
śītoṣṇasukhaduḥkheṣu
samaḥ saṅgavivarjitaḥ

19. tulyanindāstutir maunī
saṃtuṣṭo yena kenacit
aniketaḥ sthiramatir
bhaktimān me priyo naraḥ

20. ye tu dharmyāmṛtam idaṃ
yathoktaṃ paryupāsate
śraddadhānā matparamā
bhaktās te 'tīva me priyāḥ

15. And I love the man who is free from the turmoil
of joy, impatience, and fear,
Who does not frighten the world
and is not afraid of the world.

16. I love my devotee—the unperturbed
onlooker, carefree, pure, intelligent,
Able to give up
all he undertakes.

17. I love that man of devotion who shows
neither exhilaration nor disgust,
Neither regret nor desire, and who can
give up good as well as evil things.

18, 19. I love the man of devotion. He is
equal-minded to friend and foe,
To honor and shame, heat and cold,
to pleasant and unpleasant things.
He is a silent sage, equally unaffected
by praise and blame. He is content
With whatever comes his way.
He has no home. His mind is steadfast.

20. I love those devotees who see and revere
what I have set forth
As true immortality.
They trust me beyond all the world.

XIII

śrībhagavān uvāca

1. idaṃ śarīraṃ kaunteya
   kṣetram ity abhidhīyate
   etad yo vetti taṃ prāhuḥ
   kṣetrajña iti tadvidaḥ

2. kṣetrajñaṃ cāpi māṃ viddhi
   sarvakṣetreṣu bhārata
   kṣetrakṣetrajñayor jñānaṃ
   yat taj jñānaṃ mataṃ mama

3. tat kṣetraṃ yac ca yādṛk ca
   yadvikāri yataś ca yat
   sa ca yo yatprabhāvaś ca
   tat samāsena me śṛṇu

4. ṛṣibhir bahudhā gītaṃ
   chandobhir vividhaiḥ pṛthak
   brahmasūtrapadaiś caiva
   hetumadbhir viniścitaiḥ

5. mahābhūtāny ahaṃkāro
   buddhir avyaktam eva ca
   indriyāṇi daśaikaṃ ca
   pañca cendriyagocarāḥ

6. icchā dveṣaḥ sukhaṃ duḥkhaṃ
   saṃghātaś cetanā dhṛtiḥ
   etat kṣetraṃ samāsena
   savikāram udāhṛtam

The Lord:

1. The human body is a field,
   and someone knows this field.
   Those who know him
   call him the knower of the field.

2. I am knower of the field in all fields.
   Knowledge of the field
   And of him who knows the field—
   that I call wisdom.

3. Learn from me in brief about this field,
   what it is, its nature, how it changes,
   How it came about, and learn
   of the knower and his powers.

4. Often and in many ways seers
   have sung of the field in sacred verses,
   And in didactic verses about God,
   well founded and certain.

5, 6. This sums up the field with its changes:
   the gross elements; self-awareness;
   The Great Principle and the unmanifest;
   the ten senses of action and perception;

   With these, thought; the five ranges of the senses;
   desire, hate, pleasantness, unpleasantness;
   The aggregates of sense and matter;
   consciousness; mental steadiness.

7. amānitvam adambhitvam
   ahiṃsā kṣāntir ārjavam
   ācāryopāsanaṃ śaucaṃ
   sthairyam ātmavinigrahaḥ

8. indriyārtheṣu vairāgyam
   anahaṃkāra eva ca
   janmamṛtyujarāvyādhi-
   duḥkhadoṣānudarśanam

9. asaktir anabhiṣvangaḥ
   putradāragṛhādiṣu
   nityaṃ ca samacittatvam
   iṣṭāniṣṭopapattiṣu

10. mayi cānanyayogena
    bhaktir avyabhicāriṇī
    viviktadeśasevitvam
    aratir janasaṃsadi

11. adhyātmajñānanityatvaṃ
    tattvajñānārthadarśanam
    etaj jñānam iti proktam
    ajñānaṃ yad ato 'nyathā

12. jñeyaṃ yat tat pravakṣyāmi
    yaj jñātvāmṛtam aśnute
    anādimat paraṃ brahma
    na sat tan nāsad ucyate

13. sarvataḥpāṇipādaṃ tat
    sarvatokṣiśiromukham
    sarvataḥśrutimal loke
    sarvam āvṛtya tiṣṭhati

7–11. To be wise, you should be modest,
sincere, gentle, forbearing, just.
You should venerate your spiritual guide
and be pure, steadfast, self-controlled;

Turn away from what the senses tell you;
stop seeing yourself in the center;
Watch the evils of birth, death, old age,
disease, and all unpleasantness;

Do not be attached, do not be fond
of your son, wife, house, and the like,
Practice equanimity always,
whether luck grants your wishes or not.

And, to be wise, practice unswerving love
as a discipline toward me alone.
Visit solitary places and stay a while.
Do not delight in crowds.

Cultivate knowledge pertaining to the self
and a view of the meaning of reality.
All this together constitutes wisdom.
What deviates from this is ignorance.

***

12. I shall teach you the goal of wisdom.
When you know it you reach the immortal.
It is called "neither existent nor inexistent,"
It is the beginningless, the supreme, God.

13. It reaches and moves in all directions.
It sees, rules, faces everywhere.
It hears universally.
It never ceases to envelop all.

14. sarvendriyaguṇābhāsaṃ
sarvendriyavivarjitam
asaktaṃ sarvabhṛc caiva
nirguṇaṃ guṇabhoktṛ ca

15. bahir antaś ca bhūtānām
acaraṃ caram eva ca
sūkṣmatvāt tad avijñeyaṃ
dūrasthaṃ cāntike ca tat

16. avibhaktaṃ ca bhūteṣu
vibhaktam iva ca sthitam
bhūtabhartṛ ca taj jñeyaṃ
grasiṣṇu prabhaviṣṇu ca

17. jyotiṣām api taj jyotis
tamasaḥ param ucyate
jñānaṃ jñeyaṃ jñānagamyaṃ
hṛdi sarvasya dhiṣṭhitam

18. iti kṣetraṃ tathā jñānaṃ
jñeyaṃ coktaṃ samāsataḥ
madbhakta etad vijñāya
madbhāvāyopapadyate

19. prakṛtiṃ puruṣaṃ caiva
viddhy anādī ubhāv api
vikārāṃś ca guṇāṃś caiva
viddhi prakṛtisaṃbhavān

20. kāryakāraṇakartṛtve
hetuḥ prakṛtir ucyate
puruṣaḥ sukhaduḥkhānāṃ
bhoktṛtve hetur ucyate

21. puruṣaḥ prakṛtistho hi
bhuṅkte prakṛtijān guṇān
kāraṇaṃ guṇasaṅgo 'sya
sadasadyonijanmasu

14. Without senses, it appears
    sentient in all its modes.
Transcendent and immanent at the same time,
    unattached, it supports all.

15. External, yet inside creatures,
    immobile and yet moving,
It is too subtle to be explained.
    It is distant and yet near.

16. Creatures have it undivided,
    and yet it seems divided among them.
The goal of wisdom, it is their support.
    It consumes them. It creates them.

17. It is the very light of lights.
    It is beyond darkness.
Knowledge, the goal of knowledge, of wisdom
    is seated in everyone's heart.

18. I have presented to you in short
    the field, wisdom, and its goal.
My devotee understands
    and is fit for my estate.

***

19. Primal matter and spirit
    are both without beginning.
The underlying states and changes in all things
    have a material origin.

20. A person acts and effects things
    on the basis of primal matter.
He has his experiences because of the spirit
    in all unpleasantness and pleasure.

21. For when the spirit exists in primal matter
    it enjoys the states matter brings about.
Its attachment to those states
    effects good and evil births.

22. upadraṣṭānumantā ca
bhartā bhoktā maheśvaraḥ
paramātmeti cāpy ukto
dehe 'smin puruṣaḥ paraḥ

23. ya evaṃ vetti puruṣaṃ
prakṛtiṃ ca guṇaiḥ saha
sarvathā vartamāno 'pi
na sa bhūyo 'bhijāyate

24. dhyānenātmani paśyanti
kecid ātmānam ātmanā
anye sāṃkhyena yogena
karmayogena cāpare

25. anye tv evam ajānantaḥ
śrutvānyebhya upāsate
te 'pi cātitaranty eva
mṛtyuṃ śrutiparāyaṇāḥ

26. yāvat saṃjāyate kiṃcit
sattvaṃ sthāvarajaṅgamam
kṣetrakṣetrajñasaṃyogāt
tad viddhi bharatarṣabha

27. samaṃ sarveṣu bhūteṣu
tiṣṭhantaṃ parameśvaram
vinaśyatsv avinaśyantaṃ
yaḥ paśyati sa paśyati

28. samaṃ paśyan hi sarvatra
samavasthitam īśvaram
na hinasty ātmanātmānaṃ
tato yāti parāṃ gatim

29. prakṛtyaiva ca karmāṇi
kriyamāṇāni sarvaśaḥ
yaḥ paśyati tathātmānam
akartāraṃ sa paśyati

22. With respect to the human body
    the supreme spirit is
The great Lord who observes, approves,
    supports and enjoys.

23. Who thus knows the spirit
    and primal matter with its states
Is not born again,
    no matter what he does in life.

24. Some perceive the reality of the self
    by themselves and in themselves
Through meditation, some through reason,
    some through ritual.

25. But others have a different understanding.
    They hear the word from others and accept it with reverence.
Their ultimate guide is revelation.
    These men also cross the ocean of death.

***

26. Know that any and every being
    moving or motionless that is born
Is born from the joining of the field
    and the master who knows the field.

27. He has the right vision who sees
    in all creatures alike the supreme Lord
Who remains and does not die
    when they die.

28. For when he sees the Lord dwelling
    in all and everything alike,
He cannot be at war with himself.
    Thus he is on his way to the highest goal.

29. Primal matter alone is at work
    in all that is done.
Who sees this and sees that he himself
    is not engaged in acts has true insight.

30. yadā bhūtapṛthagbhāvam
ekastham anupaśyati
tata eva ca vistāraṃ
brahma saṃpadyate tadā

31. anāditvān nirguṇatvāt
paramātmāyam avyayaḥ
śarīrastho 'pi kaunteya
na karoti na lipyate

32. yathā sarvagataṃ saukṣmyād
ākāśaṃ nopalipyate
sarvatrāvasthito dehe
tathātmā nopalipyate

33. yathā prakāśayaty ekaḥ
kṛtsnaṃ lokam imaṃ raviḥ
kṣetraṃ kṣetrī tathā kṛtsnaṃ
prakāśayati bhārata

34. kṣetrakṣetrajñayor evam
antaraṃ jñānacakṣuṣā
bhūtaprakṛtimokṣaṃ ca
ye vidur yānti te param

30. When he sees that creatures different in state
    and habitat are really in one place
And that they spread forth from there,
    he reaches the Eternal.

31. The changeless, supreme self, though dwelling in the body,
    does not act and is not affected by action,
For it has no beginning and is not subject
    to the states of matter.

32. Just as the ether, present everywhere,
    is too subtle to be polluted by anything,
The self, though pervading the whole body,
    is not polluted.

33. One sun illumines
    the entire world.
Likewise, the Lord of the field
    illumines the entire field.

34. Those who have the insight to know about this distinction
    between field and master of the field,
And about freedom from existence and matter,
    are on their way to the highest goal.

XIV

śrībhagavān uvāca

1. paraṃ bhūyaḥ pravakṣyāmi
   jñānānāṃ jñānam uttamam
   yaj jñātvā munayaḥ sarve
   parāṃ siddhim ito gatāḥ

2. idaṃ jñānam upāśritya
   mama sādharmyam āgatāḥ
   sarge 'pi nopajāyante
   pralaye na vyathanti ca

3. mama yonir mahad brahma
   tasmin garbhaṃ dadhāmy aham
   saṃbhavaḥ sarvabhūtānāṃ
   tato bhavati bhārata

4. sarvayoniṣu kaunteya
   mūrtayaḥ saṃbhavanti yāḥ
   tāsāṃ brahma mahad yonir
   aham bījapradaḥ pitā

5. sattvaṃ rajas tama iti
   guṇāḥ prakṛtisaṃbhavāḥ
   nibadhnanti mahābāho
   dehe dehinam avyayam

6. tatra sattvaṃ nirmalatvāt
   prakāśakam anāmayam
   sukhasaṅgena badhnāti
   jñānasaṅgena cānagha

The Lord:

1. Again, I shall set forth supreme knowledge,
   the very highest wisdom.
   All sages who reached it, on departing from this world
   have reached supreme perfection.

2. They are not born when the world is born;
   they are not shaken when the world is destroyed;
   They resort to this wisdom
   and have become just like myself.

3. The Great Principle, the Divine, is my womb;
   I cast the seed into it;
   There is the origin
   of all creatures.

4. Whatever forms originate
   in any wombs,
   The real womb is the Divine, the Great Principle.
   I am the father that gives the seed.

5. Integrity, passion, sloth; these are
   the states arising in primal matter.
   They tie the changeless soul
   down to the body, O warrior.

6. Integrity gives light and health
   because it is pure.
   It binds through the love for happiness
   and for knowledge, Blameless One.

7. rajo rāgātmakaṃ viddhi
tṛṣṇāsaṅgasamudbhavam
tan nibadhnāti kaunteya
karmasaṅgena dehinam

8. tamas tv ajñānajaṃ viddhi
mohanaṃ sarvadehinām
pramādālasyanidrābhis
tan nibadhnāti bhārata

9. sattvaṃ sukhe sañjayati
rajaḥ karmaṇi bhārata
jñānam āvṛtya tu tamaḥ
pramāde sañjayaty uta

10. rajas tamaś cābhibhūya
sattvaṃ bhavati bhārata
rajaḥ sattvaṃ tamaś caiva
tamaḥ sattvaṃ rajas tathā

11. sarvadvāreṣu dehe 'smin
prakāśa upajāyate
jñānaṃ yadā tadā vidyād
vivṛddhaṃ sattvam ity uta

12. lobhaḥ pravṛttir ārambhaḥ
karmaṇām aśamaḥ spṛhā
rajasy etāni jāyante
vivṛddhe bharatarṣabha

13. aprakāśo 'pravṛttiś ca
pramādo moha eva ca
tamasy etāni jāyante
vivṛddhe kurunandana

14. yadā sattve pravṛddhe tu
pralayaṃ yāti dehabhṛt
tadottamavidāṃ lokān
amalān pratipadyate

7. Passion consists in desire
   arising from cravings and attachments.
   It binds the soul, son of Kuntī,
   by the love for action.

8. Sloth is born from ignorance.
   It deludes all souls.
   It binds, man of Bharata,
   by carelessness, idleness, sleep.

9. Integrity fastens the world to happiness,
   and passion to action, Bhārata,
   But sloth clouds wisdom
   and ties the world to carelessness.

10. Integrity arises
    growing beyond passion and sloth.
    Passion and sloth in turn arise
    by growing beyond the other two.

11. When the flood of light appears
    at all the gates of the body,
    Then you can tell
    the growth of integrity.

12. Greed, activities,
    initiative in actions, uneasiness, desire—
    These come about
    when passion is on the increase.

13. When sloth takes over,
    these things come about:
    Darkness and inertia,
    negligence and mere delusion.

14. Now if a person dies
    when integrity holds sway,
    He attains to the pure worlds
    of those who know the highest.

15. rajasi pralayaṃ gatvā
    karmasaṅgiṣu jāyate
tathā pralīnas tamasi
    mūḍhayoniṣu jāyate

16. karmaṇaḥ sukṛtasyāhuḥ
    sāttvikaṃ nirmalaṃ phalam
rajasas tu phalaṃ duḥkham
    ajñānaṃ tamasaḥ phalam

17. sattvāt saṃjāyate jñānaṃ
    rajaso lobha eva ca
pramādamohau tamaso
    bhavato 'jñānam eva ca

18. ūrdhvaṃ gacchanti sattvasthā
    madhye tiṣṭhanti rājasāḥ
jaghanyaguṇavṛttisthā
    adho gacchanti tāmasāḥ

19. nānyaṃ guṇebhyaḥ kartāraṃ
    yadā draṣṭānupaśyati
guṇebhyaś ca paraṃ vetti
    madbhāvaṃ so 'dhigacchati

20. guṇān etān atītya trīn
    dehī dehasamudbhavān
janmamṛtyujarāduḥkhair
    vimukto 'mṛtam aśnute

arjuna uvāca

21. kair liṅgais trīn guṇān etān
    atīto bhavati prabho
kimācāraḥ kathaṃ caitāṃs
    trīn guṇān ativartate

15. Dying under the sway of passion,
    he is born among people loving action,
  And dying under the rule of sloth,
    he is bound for an inert, misguided existence.

16. They say that rightly done works or cultic acts
    have a result of purity and integrity.
  The consequence of passion is pain.
    Sloth leads to ignorance.

17. Wisdom is born from integrity,
    and greed from passion.
  Carelessness and delusions, obsessions,
    and ignorance itself come from sloth.

18. Men of integrity ascend;
    men of passion remain in the middle;
  Men of sloth, who move in the lowest state,
    end up below.

19. When a man opens his eyes and observes
    that the states alone are the root of all activity,
  When he knows that which is higher than the states,
    he enters my realm.

20. A person gains release from the pains
    of birth, old age, and death
  When he goes beyond the three states
    that come through bodily existence.

Arjuna:

21. What marks the existence of man
    when he has gone beyond these three states, Lord?
  How does he behave, and how
    does he transcend the three states?

śrībhagavān uvāca

22. prakāśaṃ ca pravṛttiṃ ca
 moham eva ca pāṇḍava
na dveṣṭi saṃpravṛttāni
 na nivṛttāni kāṅkṣati

23. udāsīnavad āsīno
 guṇair yo na vicālyate
guṇā vartanta ity eva
 yo 'vatiṣṭhati neṅgate

24. samaduḥkhasukhaḥ svasthaḥ
 samaloṣṭāśmakāñcanaḥ
tulyapriyāpriyo dhīras
 tulyanindātmasaṃstutiḥ

25. mānāvamānayos tulyas
 tulyo mitrāripakṣayoḥ
sarvārambhaparityāgī
 guṇātītaḥ sa ucyate

26. māṃ ca yo 'yabhicāreṇa
 bhaktiyogena sevate
sa guṇān samatītyaitān
 brahmabhūyāya kalpate

27. brahmaṇo hi pratiṣṭhāham
 amṛtasyāvyayasya ca
śāśvatasya ca dharmasya
 sukhasyaikāntikasya ca

The Lord:

22. He does not become agitated about
    the light of wisdom,
  Activities, and delusions when they occur,
    nor does he long for them when they are gone.

23. Involved, he seems an onlooker
    The various states of being do not disturb him.
  He knows they are just those states.
    He is firm, unshaken.

24. Self-reliant, steady,
    dispassionate in pleasure and trouble;
  Clods of earth, rocks, pieces of gold are one to him;
    There is no difference between
  Desirable and undesirable;
    Praise for himself and invective are alike;

25. Poised in the face of honor and disgrace,
    allied and opposing parties,
  Able to abandon all undertakings—
    Such a man has transcended the states.

26. Who serves me with
    unfailing, loving devotion
  Goes beyond these states
    and is fit for the divine abode.

27. I am the ground of the divine,
    which is deathless, unchanging,
  And the eternal tradition,
    and unfailing bliss.

XV

śrībhagavān uvāca

1. ūrdhvamūlam adhaḥśākham
   aśvatthaṃ prāhur avyayam
   chandāṃsi yasya parṇāni
   yas taṃ veda sa vedavit

2. adhaś cordhvaṃ prasṛtās tasya śākhā
   guṇapravṛddhā viṣayapravālāḥ
   adhaś ca mūlāny anusaṃtatāni
   karmānubandhīni manuṣyaloke

3. na rūpam asyeha tathopalabhyate
   nānto na cādir na ca saṃpratiṣṭhā
   aśvattham enaṃ suvirūḍhamūlam
   asaṅgaśastreṇa dṛḍhena chittvā

The Lord:

1. They say there is an eternal pipal-tree
   with roots on high and branches downward.
   The verses of Scripture are its leaves.
   Who understands this tree understands the Scriptures.

2. It stretches its branches
   Upward and downward.
   The states of all things
   Nurture the young shoots.
   The young shoots are
   The nourishment of our senses.
   And below,
   The roots go far
   Into the world of men;
   They are the sequences of actions.

3. This understanding
   Of the tree's shape—
   Its end and its beginning,
   And its ground—
   Is not open to
   The ordinary world.
   The roots of that pipal
   Have spread far.
   With the strong ax
   Of detachment
   A man should cut
   That tree.

4. tataḥ padaṃ tat parimārgitavyaṃ
yasmin gatā na nivartanti bhūyaḥ
tam eva cādyaṃ puruṣaṃ prapadye
yataḥ pravṛttiḥ prasṛtā purāṇī

5. nirmānamohā jitasaṅgadoṣā
adhyātmanityā vinivṛttakāmāḥ
dvandvair vimuktāḥ sukhaduḥkhasaṃjñair
gacchanty amūḍhāḥ padam avyayaṃ tat

6. na tad bhāsayate sūryo
na śaśāṅko na pāvakaḥ
yad gatvā na nivartante
tad dhāma paramaṃ mama

7. mamaivāṃśo jīvaloke
jīvabhūtaḥ sanātanaḥ
manaḥṣaṣṭhānīndriyāṇi
prakṛtisthāni karṣati

4. Then he should search
For that place whence
Men who have found it
Do not return.
He should search for it
And reflect:
"I take refuge
In the very first
Divine Being.
The whole world came,
The whole world stretched forth
From Him."

5. Men without delusions
Go to that
Everlasting place.
They are humble,
Sincere people.
They have overcome
The damage
Done by attachments.
They are intent
Uninterruptedly
On that which is Real.
Desires have dwindled away.
From opposites as we know them—
Joy, grief—
They are set free.

6. Neither sun, moon, nor fire
lights up the place they reach,
From which no one returns.
That is my supreme abode.

7. Part of me has become the life of the world.
Everlasting, yet in the world of the living,
This part absorbs the senses and mind,
whose home is in matter.

8. śarīraṃ yad avāpnoti
yac cāpy utkrāmatīśvaraḥ
gṛhītvaitāni saṃyāti
vāyur gandhān ivāśayāt

9. śrotraṃ cakṣuḥ sparśanaṃ ca
rasanaṃ ghrāṇam eva ca
adhiṣṭhāya manaś cāyaṃ
viṣayān upasevate

10. utkrāmantaṃ sthitaṃ vāpi
bhuñjānaṃ vā guṇānvitam
vimūḍhā nānupaśyanti
paśyanti jñānacakṣuṣaḥ

11. yatanto yoginaś cainaṃ
paśyanty ātmany avasthitam
yatanto 'py akṛtātmāno
nainaṃ paśyanty acetasaḥ

12. yad ādityagataṃ tejo
jagad bhāsayate 'khilam
yac candramasi yac cāgnau
tat tejo viddhi māmakam

13. gām āviśya ca bhūtāni
dhārayāmy aham ojasā
puṣṇāmi cauṣadhīḥ sarvāḥ
somo bhūtvā rasātmakaḥ

14. ahaṃ vaiśvānaro bhūtvā
prāṇināṃ deham āśritaḥ
prāṇāpānasamāyuktaḥ
pacāmy annaṃ caturvidham

8. Whatever body the Lord takes on, or, upon death, leaves,
   He grasps and holds those senses and mind
As the wind carries
   fragrances from place to place.

9. The Lord takes his stand upon
   hearing, sight, touch, taste, smell,
And upon the mind.
   He enjoys what mind and senses enjoy.

10. Deluded men cannot trace his course.
   Only the eye of wisdom sees him
Clothed in the states of existence, going forth,
   being in the body, or taking in experience.

11. Disciplined men can also make an effort
   and see his presence in themselves.
Senseless men, far from perfection,
   never see him, in spite of their efforts.

12. The splendor in sun, moon, and fire
   illumines the entire world.
That splendor
   is mine.

13. I enter the earth, and I uphold
   all creatures by my might.
I become Soma, the very sap of life,
   and I nourish all plants.

14. I become the fire of life
   and dwell in the bodies of the living.
Ignited by the breaths
   I digest all the four sorts of food.

15. sarvasya cāhaṃ hṛdi saṃniviṣṭo
 mattaḥ smṛtir jñānam apohanaṃ ca
vedaiś ca sarvair aham eva vedyo
 vedāntakṛd vedavid eva cāham

16. dvāv imau puruṣau loke
 kṣaraś cākṣara eva ca
kṣaraḥ sarvāṇi bhūtāni
 kūṭastho 'kṣara ucyate

17. Uttamaḥ puruṣas tv anyaḥ
 paramātmety udāhṛtaḥ
yo lokatrayam āviśya
 bibharty avyaya īśvaraḥ

18. yasmāt kṣaram atīto 'ham
 aksarād api cottamaḥ
ato 'smi loke vede ca
 prathitaḥ puruṣottamaḥ

19. yo mām evam asaṃmūḍho
 jānāti puruṣottamam
sa sarvavid bhajati māṃ
 sarvabhāvena bhārata

20. iti guhyatamaṃ śāstram
 idam uktaṃ mayānagha
etad buddhvā buddhimān syāt
 kṛtakṛtyaś ca bhārata

15. And in everyone's heart
I am present.
From me come
Knowledge of tradition,
Wisdom
And reasoning.
I am the object
Of all the Scriptures.
I am the knower of the Scriptures.
I have established their purpose.

16. There are two spirits in the world,
one perishable, one imperishable.
All creatures together form the perishable,
the imperishable is that which is on high.

17. Other than these two is the highest being,
known as the supreme reality.
He, the eternal Lord, enters the threefold world—
of gods, men, and the realm between—and carries it.

18. I go beyond the perishable,
and I transcend also the imperishable.
Therefore, the world and Scripture
celebrate me as the Highest Being.

19. Whatever man free from all obsessions
thus knows me as the Highest Being,
Knows all. He loves and worships me
in all ways of worship and love.

20. I have imparted to you, man without blame,
the most secret teachings.
If a man sees their light, he will be enlightened,
and what he should do is done, son of Bharata.

XVI

śrībhagavān uvāca

1. abhayaṃ sattvasaṃśuddhir
   jñānayogavyavasthitiḥ
   dānaṃ damaś ca yajñaś ca
   svādhyāyas tapa ārjavam

2. ahiṃsā satyam akrodhas
   tyāgaḥ śāntir apaiśunaṃ
   dayā bhūteṣv aloluptvaṃ
   mārdavaṃ hrīr acāpalam

3. tejaḥ kṣamā dhṛtiḥ śaucam
   adroho nātimānitā
   bhavanti saṃpadaṃ daivīm
   abhijātasya bhārata

4. dambho darpo 'timānaś ca
   krodhaḥ pāruṣyam eva ca
   adñānaṃ cābhijātasya
   pārtha saṃpadam āsurīm

5. daivī saṃpad vimokṣāya
   nibandhāyāsurī matā
   mā śucaḥ saṃpadaṃ daivīm
   abhijāto 'si pāṇḍava

6. dvau bhūtasargau loke 'smin
   daiva āsura eva ca
   daivo vistaraśaḥ prokta
   āsuraṃ pārtha me śṛṇu

The Lord:

1—3. A man born to divine fortune is brave.
He is inwardly purified.
With determination he cultivates spiritual knowledge.
He is generous and shows self-restraint.
He performs the required sacrifices,
studies the Scriptures,
Practices austerity
and honesty.
He is gentle, truthful, not given to anger,
able to give up possessions.
He has peace
and does not slander anyone.
He has compassion toward all creatures,
and no greed.
He knows mildness and humility,
and is not fickle in his behavior.
There is majesty in him.
He is forbearing, firm, and pure,
Free from all treachery
and conceit.

4. A man born to the demonic lot is
deceitful, arrogant, conceited,
Wrathful, harsh in speech,
and ignorant.

5. Divine fortune leads one to release;
the demonic lot to bondage.
Do not worry, son of Paṇḍu:
You are born to divine fortune.

6. There are two orders of creation:
one divine, the other demonic.
I have spoken at length of the divine.
Now hear what the demonic is like.

7. pravṛttiṃ ca nivṛttiṃ ca
   janā na vidur āsurāḥ
na śaucaṃ nāpi cācāro
   na satyaṃ teṣu vidyate

8. asatyam apratiṣṭhaṃ te
   jagad āhur anīśvaram
aparasparasaṃbhūtaṃ
   kim anyat kāmahaitukam

9. etāṃ dṛṣṭim avaṣṭabhya
   naṣṭātmāno 'lpabuddhayaḥ
prabhavanty ugrakarmāṇaḥ
   kṣayāya jagato 'hitāḥ

10. kāmam āśritya duṣpūraṃ
   dambhamānamadānvitāḥ
mohād gṛhītvāsadgrāhān
   pravartante 'śucivratāḥ

11. cintām aparimeyāṃ ca
   pralayāntām upāśritāḥ
kāmopabhogaparamā
   etāvad iti niścitāḥ

12. āśāpāśaśatair baddhāḥ
   kāmakrodhaparāyaṇāḥ
īhante kāmabhogārtham
   anyāyenārthasaṃcayān

7. Demonic people do not comprehend
   religious acts or search for release.
   Purity as well as liturgy
   are foreign to them, and so is truth.

8. The world is without reality, they say,
   without foundation, without God;
   There is no causality;
   what ground does the world have but desire?

9. Stubbornly adhering to this view,
   these foolish people arise to harm the world.
   Foes of the world, having lost the reality of their lives,
   they wreak havoc.

10. Wholly given to insatiable desire,
    deceitful, haughty, presumptuous,
    They cling to false ideas because of their obsessions
    and go about their lives hugging impurity.

11. They devote themselves to endless fantasies and anxieties,
    though they may die today or tomorrow.
    The enjoyment of desires is uppermost in their minds,
    for they think that that is all there is.

12. Hundreds of expectations ensnare them.
    They are trapped by desires and resentments.
    They have criminal aspirations to amass money
    for the indulgence of their desires.

13. idam adya mayā labdham
   imaṃ prāpsye manoratham
idam astīdam api me
   bhaviṣyati punar dhanam

14. asau mayā hataḥ śatrur
   haniṣye cāparān api
īśvaro 'ham ahaṃ bhogī
   siddho 'haṃ balavān sukhī

15. āḍhyo 'bhijanavān asmi
   ko 'nyo 'sti sadṛśo mayā
yakṣye dāsyāmi modiṣya
   ity ajñānavimohitāḥ

16. anekacittavibhrāntā
   mohajālasamāvṛtāḥ
prasaktāḥ kāmabhogeṣu
   patanti narake 'śucau

17. ātmasaṃbhāvitāḥ stabdhā
   dhanamānamadānvitāḥ
yajante nāmayajñais te
   dambhenāvidhipūrvakam

18. ahaṃkāraṃ balaṃ darpaṃ
   kāmaṃ krodhaṃ ca saṃśritāḥ
mām ātmaparadeheṣu
   pradviṣanto 'bhyasūyakāḥ

19. tān ahaṃ dviṣataḥ krūrān
   saṃsāreṣu narādhamān
kṣipāmy ajasram aśubhān
   āsurīṣv eva yoniṣu

20. āsurīṃ yonim āpannā
   mūḍhā janmani janmani
mām aprāpyaiva kaunteya
   tato yānty adhamāṃ gatim

13–15. Their ignorance beguiles them. They think:
"Today I got this wish fulfilled, tomorrow I'll get that;
This belongs to me, that also;
I shall be rich.

I have slain that enemy,
and I shall slay others too;
I am in control; I enjoy the world;
I am a success; I am strong and happy;

I am wealthy and highborn;
who is my equal?
I shall sacrifice, give proper gifts,
and rejoice at the results."

16. Their many mental waves drive them to distraction.
The net of delusion envelops them.
They are caught in the enjoyment of their lusts.
They fall into a foul hell.

17. Suffering from megalomania, puffed up
with the arrogance and presumption of wealth,
They make a show of sacrificing,
vainly, not in the established liturgy.

18. These men, so full of scorn, rely on their ego, on force,
on pride, on lust and wrath,
And they hate me
in their own body and that of others.

19. Nothing ever prevents me from hurling the wicked
into demonic births in the cycle of existence,
For they are vile, ruthless men,
full of hostilities.

20. In their delusion they come to a demonic womb
birth after birth
Without ever reaching me, son of Kuntī;
they then go to the lowest destination.

21. trividhaṃ narakasyedaṃ
 dvāraṃ nāśanam ātmanaḥ
kāmaḥ krodhas tathā lobhas
 tasmād etat trayaṃ tyajet

22. etair vimuktaḥ kaunteya
 tamodvārais tribhir naraḥ
ācaraty ātmanaḥ śreyas
 tato yāti parāṃ gatim

23. yaḥ śāstravidhim utsṛjya
 vartate kāmakārataḥ
na sa siddhim avāpnoti
 na sukhaṃ na parāṃ gatim

24. tasmāc chāstraṃ pramāṇaṃ te
 kāryākāryavyavasthitau
jñātvā śāstravidhānoktaṃ
 karma kartum ihārhasi

21. The gates of hell destroying the soul
    are threefold:
Desire, anger, and greed.
    Therefore man should avoid these three.

22. Released from these three gates of darkness,
    son of Kuntī, man
Practices what is good for his soul;
    then he attains the highest destiny.

23. If a man neglects the scriptural ordinances
    and lives according to his desires,
He cannot be successful
    or attain happiness or the highest goal.

24. Therefore, let the Scriptures be your criterion
    for distinguishing duties and violations.
You should perform actions and rites
    which you know are enjoined in the Scriptures.

XVII

arjuna uvāca

1. ye śāstravidhim utsṛjya
   yajante śraddhayānvitāḥ
   teṣāṃ niṣṭhā tu kā kṛṣṇa
   sattvam āho rajas tamaḥ

śrībhagavān uvāca

2. trividhā bhavati śraddhā
   dehināṃ sā svabhāvajā
   sāttvikī rājasī caiva
   tāmasī ceti tāṃ śṛṇu

3. sattvānurūpā sarvasya
   śraddhā bhavati bhārata
   śraddhāmayo 'yaṃ puruṣo
   yo yacchraddhaḥ sa eva saḥ

4. yajante sāttvikā devān
   yakṣarakṣāṃsi rājasāḥ
   pretān bhūtagaṇāṃś cānye
   yajante tāmasā janāḥ

5. aśāstravihitaṃ ghoraṃ
   tapyante ye tapo janāḥ
   dambhāhaṃkārasaṃyuktāḥ
   kāmarāgabalānvitāḥ

6. karśayantaḥ śarīrasthaṃ
   bhūtagrāmam acetasaḥ
   māṃ caivāntaḥśarīrasthaṃ
   tān viddhy āsuraniścayān

Arjuna:

1. Some people perform their sacrifices full of trust,
   but they neglect the liturgy given in Scripture.
   What determines their place?
   Is it integrity, passion, or sloth?

The Lord:

2. All living souls have some kind of trust.
   It is part of their nature
   And is determined either by integrity, passion, or sloth.
   Listen to what this trust is:

3. Everyone has a trust
   conforming to his character.
   Man consists in trust:
   What he trusts in, that is what he is.

4. Men of integrity sacrifice to the gods,
   men of passion to sprites and monsters,
   And the others, the men of sloth,
   to the spirits of the dead and hosts of dark creatures.

5. Deceitfulness and ego impel some men.
   Desires and passions fortify them.
   They practice dire austerities
   not enjoined by the Scriptures.

6. These fools starve the elements
   that stay together in the body,
   And they starve me who am in the body.
   People like this are of demonic resolve.

7. āhāras tv api sarvasya
   trividho bhavati priyaḥ
   yajñas tapas tathā dānaṃ
   teṣāṃ bhedam imaṃ śṛṇu

8. āyuḥsattvabalārogya-
   sukhaprītivivardhanāḥ
   rasyāḥ snigdhāḥ sthirā hṛdyā
   āhārāḥ sāttvikapriyāḥ

9. kaṭvamlalavaṇātyuṣṇa-
   tīkṣṇarūkṣavidāhinaḥ
   āhārā rājasasyeṣṭā
   duḥkhaśokāmayapradāḥ

10. yātayāmaṃ gatarasaṃ
    pūti paryuṣitaṃ ca yat
    ucchiṣṭam api cāmedhyaṃ
    bhojanaṃ tāmasapriyam

11. aphalākāṅkṣibhir yajño
    vidhidṛṣṭo ya ijyate
    yaṣṭavyam eveti manaḥ
    samādhāya sa sāttvikaḥ

12. abhisaṃdhāya tu phalaṃ
    dambhārtham api caiva yat
    ijyate bharataśreṣṭha
    taṃ yajñaṃ viddhi rājasam

13. vidhihīnam asṛṣṭānnaṃ
    mantrahīnam adakṣiṇam
    śraddhāvirahitaṃ yajñaṃ
    tāmasaṃ paricakṣate

14. devadvijaguruprājña-
    pūjanaṃ śaucam ārjavam
    brahmacaryam ahiṃsā ca
    śārīraṃ tapa ucyate

7. But the food all men like
is also of three kinds,
And so are their sacrifices, austerities, and gifts.
Hear what the differences are.

8. Men of integrity like food that strengthens life,
courage, stamina, health, bliss, and pleasure,
And that is tasty, substantial,
sustaining, and satisfying.

9. Men of passion desire food
that is pungent, sour, salty, too hot,
Sharp, astringent, or burning.
Such foods cause nausea, misery, sickness.

10. Men of sloth by nature turn to victuals
that are spoiled, tasteless, stale, and rotten,
Even to polluted leftovers
not sanctified by sacrifice.

11. Men who do not build upon the result of rituals
perform sacrifices as they are ordained.
"It is our duty," they know, and they concentrate.
Their sacrifice is one of integrity.

12. A sacrifice is in the order of passion
when it is aimed at results,
Or when it is offered
without honesty.

13. They say a sacrifice is of the nature of sloth
when conducted outside the established liturgy,
When no food is distributed, no sacred verse recited,
no priests rewarded, and when trust is forgotten.

14. To honor the gods, the highest class of men,
spiritual guides, and sages,
To be pure, upright, chaste, and gentle—
such is austerity of the body.

15. anudvegakaraṃ vākyaṃ
    satyaṃ priyahitaṃ ca yat
svādhyāyābhyasanaṃ caiva
    vānmayaṃ tapa ucyate

16. manaḥprasādaḥ saumyatvaṃ
    maunam ātmavinigrahaḥ
bhāvasaṃśuddhir ity etat
    tapo mānasam ucyate

17. śraddhayā parayā taptaṃ
    tapas tat trividhaṃ naraiḥ
aphalākānkṣibhir yuktaiḥ
    sāttvikaṃ paricakṣate

18. satkāramānapūjārthaṃ
    tapo dambhena caiva yat
kriyate tad iha proktaṃ
    rājasaṃ calam adhruvam

19. mūḍhagrāheṇātmano yat
    pīḍayā kriyate tapaḥ
parasyotsādanārthaṃ vā
    tat tāmasam udāhṛtam

20. dātavyam iti yad dānaṃ
    dīyate 'nupakāriṇe
deśe kāle ca pātre ca
    tad dānaṃ sāttvikaṃ smṛtam

21. yat tu pratyupakārārthaṃ
    phalam uddiśya vā punaḥ
dīyate ca parikliṣṭaṃ
    tad dānaṃ rājasaṃ smṛtam

22. adeśakāle yad dānam
    apātrebhyaś ca dīyate
asatkṛtam avajñātaṃ
    tat tāmasam udāhṛtam

15. To speak, without irritating others,
 words that are true, pleasing, and beneficial,
And to recite and study sacred texts—
 that is austerity in speech.

16. To be austere in mind means
 inner peace and joy, a kind disposition,
Stillness, self-control,
 and purifying one's place in the world.

17. These three austerities together,
 performed with the utmost trust
By disciplined men not craving results—
 that is being austere in integrity.

18. When one contrives austerity
 to gain a favor, esteem, or honor,
Then it is austerity of passion.
 It is neither steadfast nor dependable.

19. Obsessions lead some to perform austerity.
 They torture themselves.
Or their purpose is to destroy someone else.
 Such austerity is slothful.

20. A gift is a gift of integrity
 when it is given at the right place and time to
 the proper person,
To one who cannot be expected to return the gift—
 and given merely because it should be given.

21. But what is given to get a gift in return,
 or for the sake of some result,
Or unwillingly,
 that is a gift in the sphere of passion.

22. A gift is called slothful when it is given
 not at the right time and place,
Nor to a worthy person,
 nor with proper ceremony, but with contempt.

23. oṃ tat sad iti nirdeśo
   brahmaṇas trividhaḥ smṛtaḥ
brāhmaṇās tena vedāś ca
   yajñāś ca vihitāḥ purā

24. tasmād om ity udāhṛtya
   yajñadānatapaḥkriyāḥ
pravartante vidhānoktāḥ
   satataṃ brahmavādinām

25. tad ity anabhisaṃdhāya
   phalaṃ yajñatapaḥkriyāḥ
dānakriyāś ca vividhāḥ
   kriyante mokṣakāṅkṣibhiḥ

26. sadbhāve sādhubhāve ca
   sad ity etat prayujyate
praśaste karmaṇi tathā
   sacchabdaḥ pārtha yujyate

27. yajñe tapasi dāne ca
   sthitiḥ sad iti cocyate
karma caiva tadarthīyaṃ
   sad ity evābhidhīyate

28. aśraddhayā hutaṃ dattaṃ
   tapas taptaṃ kṛtaṃ ca yat
asad ity ucyate pārtha
   na ca tat pretya no iha

23. We have the record of a concise instruction
    concerning the Eternal: "OM TAT SAT."
    This threefold instruction of
    OM, THAT, GOOD and REAL
    Established of old
    the people entitled to sacrifice
    And the Scriptures
    and the sacrifices.

24. Therefore those who speak with knowledge of the Eternal
    say "OM" and engage in acts of sacrifice,
    Gift-giving and austerity
    set forth in scriptural statutes.

25. Men aiming for release say "That!"
    and they perform various acts
    Of sacrifice, austerity, and giving
    without concentrating on the results.

26. SAT—good and real—relates to both
    what exists and what is good.
    The word is also fitting
    for celebrated acts.

27. In sacrifice, austerity, and giving
    faithful observance is SAT—good—
    And all rites performed for those purposes
    are likewise called SAT.

28. Whatever deed is done
    in sacrifice, giving or austerity without trust
    Is called ASAT—not good or unreal.
    It is nothing here or in the next world.

XVIII

arjuna uvāca

1. saṃnyāsasya mahābāho
   tattvam icchāmi veditum
   tyāgasya ca hṛṣīkeśa
   pṛthak keśiniṣūdana

śrībhagavān uvāca

2. kāmyānāṃ karmaṇāṃ nyāsaṃ
   saṃnyāsaṃ kavayo viduḥ
   sarvakarmaphalatyāgaṃ
   prāhus tyāgaṃ vicakṣaṇāḥ

3. tyājyaṃ doṣavad ity eke
   karma prāhur manīṣiṇaḥ
   yajñadānatapaḥkarma
   na tyājyam iti cāpare

4. niścayaṃ śṛṇu me tatra
   tyāge bharatasattama
   tyāgo hi puruṣavyāghra
   trividhaḥ saṃprakīrtitaḥ

5. yajñadānatapaḥkarma
   na tyājyaṃ kāryam eva tat
   yajño dānaṃ tapaś caiva
   pāvanāni manīṣiṇām

6. etāny api tu karmāṇi
   saṅgaṃ tyaktvā phalāni ca
   kartavyānīti me pārtha
   niścitaṃ matam uttamam

Arjuna:

1. O warrior, I want to understand
   what renouncing means,
   And also what abandoning possessions means,
   Slayer of Keśin.

The Lord:

2. Some sages hold that abandoning rites performed
   for personal advantage is renunciation.
   Others speak of giving up the effects of all rituals
   as true abandonment.

3. Some wise men say that ritual as such is wrong
   and therefore should be abandoned.
   But others hold that rites
   of sacrifice, gifts, and austerity should be kept.

4. Hear my judgment, best of Bharatas,
   in this matter of abandonments,
   For renunciation is traditionally known
   to be threefold.

5. The work of sacrifice, gifts, and austerity
   should not be given up, but done.
   The wise are purified through
   sacrifice, giving required gifts, and austerity.

6. It is my definitive, supreme judgment
   that these works must be performed,
   But only after giving up attachment
   to them and their effects.

7. niyatasya tu saṃnyāsaḥ
karmaṇo nopapadyate
mohāt tasya parityāgas
tāmasaḥ parikīrtitaḥ

8. duḥkham ity eva yat karma
kāyakleśabhayāt tyajet
sa kṛtvā rājasaṃ tyāgaṃ
naiva tyāgaphalaṃ labhet

9. kāryam ity eva yat karma
niyataṃ kriyate 'rjuna
saṅgaṃ tyaktvā phalaṃ caiva
sa tyāgaḥ sāttviko mataḥ

10. na dveṣṭy akuśalaṃ karma
kuśale nānuṣajjate
tyāgī sattvasamāviṣṭo
medhāvī chinnasaṃśayaḥ

11. na hi dehabhṛtā śakyaṃ
tyaktuṃ karmāṇy aśeṣataḥ
yas tu karmaphalatyāgī
sa tyāgīty abhidhīyate

12. aniṣṭam iṣṭaṃ miśraṃ ca
trividhaṃ karmaṇaḥ phalam
bhavaty atyāginām pretya
na tu saṃnyāsinām kvacit

13. pañcaitāni mahābāho
kāraṇāni nibodha me
sāṃkhye kṛtānte proktāni
siddhaye sarvakarmaṇām

14. adhiṣṭhānaṃ tathā kartā
karaṇaṃ ca pṛthagvidham
vividhāś ca pṛthakceṣṭā
daivaṃ caivātra pañcamam

7. It is not right to abandon
the regular, required sacrifice.
Giving it up out of delusion
is known as an act of sloth.

8. A man will not reap good of any abandonment
that occurs in the sphere of passion,
For then he thinks of the sacrifice as bothersome
and omits it for fear of physical discomfort.

9. Abandonment abides in the sphere of integrity
when a regular, required ritual is done
Merely because it should be done,
without attachment or desire for its effects.

10. The man of integrity practicing abandonment,
who is wise and has vanquished doubt,
Has no loathing for improper ritual
nor has a special love for proper rites,

11. For as long as a man has a body,
he cannot relinquish action altogether,
But he who can give up the effects of actions
is a true renouncer.

12. People unable to renounce have their
triple reward in the next world:
Undesired, desired, or a mixture of both;
but for renouncers there is nothing like that.

13. Learn from me, warrior,
that there are five moments,
Distinguished in the Philosophy of Reason
as the basis of all successful acts:

14. The physical body; the individual self;
the various means by which an act is done;
Various kinds of activities;
and, lastly, providence.

15. śarīravānmanobhir yat
    karma prārabhate naraḥ
nyāyyaṃ vā viparītaṃ vā
    pañcaite tasya hetavaḥ

16. tatraivaṃ sati kartāram
    ātmānaṃ kevalaṃ tu yaḥ
paśyaty akṛtabuddhitvān
    na sa paśyati durmatiḥ

17. yasya nāhaṃkṛto bhāvo
    buddhir yasya na lipyate
hatvāpi sa imāṃl lokān
    na hanti na nibadhyate

18. jñānaṃ jñeyaṃ parijñātā
    trividhā karmacodanā
karaṇaṃ karma karteti
    trividhaḥ karmasaṃgrahaḥ

19. jñānaṃ karma ca kartā ca
    tridhaiva guṇabhedataḥ
procyate guṇasaṃkhyāne
    yathāvac chṛṇu tāny api

20. sarvabhūteṣu yenaikaṃ
    bhāvam avyayam īkṣate
avibhaktaṃ vibhakteṣu
    taj jñānaṃ viddhi sāttvikam

21. pṛthaktvena tu yaj jñānaṃ
    nānābhāvān pṛthagvidhān
vetti sarveṣu bhūteṣu
    taj jñānaṃ viddhi rājasam

15. These five are the grounds of whatever act
    a man engages in
With body, speech, or mind,
    whether the act is enjoined or forbidden.

16. A fool cannot see this, because
    of the imperfection of his intelligence.
In the whole matter, he regards instead
    the self alone as the agent.

17. A man who is not ego-centered
    and whose understanding is not muddled
Does not kill even if he kills these men here,
    and he is not imprisoned by his acts.

18. Our knowledge, what we know, and we the knowers—
    these three together impel us to ritual acts.
A sacrifice consists in three: that which is offered,
    the action, and the performer of the sacrifice.

19. The theory of the three states of being says that
    knowledge, act, and performer are of three kinds,
Each according to the three states.
    Listen also to these three kinds.

***

20. That knowledge, that wisdom, is of integrity
    whereby one sees in all realities
One changeless reality
    undivided in diverseness.

21. But that knowledge which perceives
    many realities, each of a different kind,
In all existing beings—
    that knowledge is in the sphere of passion.

22. yat tu kṛtsnavad ekasmin
    kārye saktam ahaitukam
atattvārthavad alpaṃ ca
    tat tāmasam udāhṛtam

23. niyataṃ saṅgarahitam
    arāgadveṣataḥ kṛtam
aphalaprepsunā karma
    yat tat sāttvikam ucyate

24. yat tu kāmepsunā karma
    sāhaṃkāreṇa vā punaḥ
kriyate bahulāyāsaṃ
    tad rājasam udāhṛtam

25. anubandhaṃ kṣayaṃ hiṃsām
    anapekṣya ca pauruṣam
mohād ārabhyate karma
    yat tat tāmasam ucyate

26. muktasaṅgo 'nahaṃvādī
    dhṛtyutsāhasamanvitaḥ
siddhyasiddhyor nirvikāraḥ
    kartā sāttvika ucyate

27. rāgī karmaphalaprepsur
    lubdho hiṃsātmako 'śuciḥ
harṣaśokānvitaḥ kartā
    rājasaḥ parikīrtitaḥ

28. ayuktaḥ prākṛtaḥ stabdhaḥ
    śaṭho naikṛtiko 'lasaḥ
viṣādī dīrghasūtrī ca
    kartā tāmasa ucyate

22. If one's knowledge attaches itself to one task only,
    as if this task were all-comprehensive,
    While in fact it is groundless, unreal, worthless,
    the knowledge is of sloth.

***

23. When one does the regular rituals without clinging to them,
    neither with passion nor aversion,
    Without anticipating their effects—
    that is acting with integrity.

24. But it is acting in the sphere of passion
    when a man makes strenuous efforts
    And performs the rites to gain his desires
    or out of selfishness.

25. It is an act of sloth when one engages in ritual
    out of delusion, without considering
    What is involved, payments, hurting living beings,
    and one's own ability.

***

26. He who acts demonstrates integrity
    when he is freed from attachments,
    Does not speak of himself, is steady and energetic,
    and is not changed by success or failure.

27. He clearly belongs in the sphere of passion
    when he is excitable,
    Eager for results, greedy, cruel, impure,
    and affected by joy and grief.

28. He who acts is a man of sloth when he is
    undisciplined, uneducated, arrogant,
    Deceitful, dishonest, inert,
    despondent, and boring.

***

29. buddher bhedaṃ dhṛteś caiva
guṇatas trividhaṃ śṛṇu
procyamānam aśeṣeṇa
pṛthaktvena dhanamjaya

30. pravṛttiṃ ca nivṛttiṃ ca
kāryākārye bhayābhaye
bandhaṃ mokṣaṃ ca yā vetti
buddhiḥ sā pārtha sāttvikī

31. yayā dharmam adharmaṃ ca
kāryaṃ cākāryam eva ca
ayathāvat prajānāti
buddhiḥ sā pārtha rājasī

32. adharmaṃ dharmam iti yā
manyate tamasāvṛtā
sarvārthān viparītāṃś ca
buddhiḥ sā pārtha tāmasī

33. dhṛtyā yayā dhārayate
manaḥprāṇendriyakriyāḥ
yogenāvyabhicāriṇyā
dhṛtiḥ sā pārtha sāttvikī

34. yayā tu dharmakāmārthān
dhṛtyā dhārayate 'rjuna
prasaṅgena phalākāṅkṣī
dhṛtiḥ sā pārtha rājasī

35. yayā svapnaṃ bhayaṃ śokaṃ
viṣādaṃ madam eva ca
na vimuñcati durmedhā
dhṛtiḥ sā pārtha tāmasī

29. Let me set forth fully and distinctly,
    Winner of Wealth,
The variety in understanding and in persistence,
    in accordance with the three states.

30. That understanding shows integrity
    which grasps action and its cessation,
Duty and transgression, fear and peace,
    bondage and freedom.

31. That understanding flawed in judging
    what is right, what is prohibited,
What should be done, what not,
    that understanding is in the sphere of passion.

32. When understanding, enveloped by darkness,
    upholds what is wrong as right,
And sees all things perverted,
    it is slothful.

***

33. The persistence whereby one controls
    the activities of mind, breath, and senses,
With unswerving discipline—
    that is persistence of integrity.

34. But the persistence whereby a man,
    with attachment, eager for results,
Holds on to religion, desires, and gains,
    is in the sphere of passion.

35. The stubbornness with which a foolish man
    does not let go of sleep, fear, sorrow,
Despondency, and pride—
    that is persistence of sloth.

***

36. sukhaṃ tv idānīṃ trividhaṃ
 śṛṇu me bharatarṣabha
abhyāsād ramate yatra
 duḥkhāntaṃ ca nigacchati

37. yat tad agre viṣam iva
 pariṇāme 'mṛtopamam
tat sukhaṃ sāttvikaṃ proktam
 ātmabuddhiprasādajam

38. viṣayendriyasaṃyogād
 yat tad agre 'mṛtopamam
pariṇāme viṣam iva
 tat sukhaṃ rājasaṃ smṛtam

39. yad agre cānubandhe ca
 sukhaṃ mohanam ātmanaḥ
nidrālasyapramādotthaṃ
 tat tāmasam udāhṛtam

40. na tad asti pṛthivyāṃ vā
 divi deveṣu vā punaḥ
sattvaṃ prakṛtijair muktaṃ
 yad ebhiḥ syāt tribhir guṇaiḥ

41. brāhmaṇakṣatriyaviśāṃ
 śūdrāṇāṃ ca paraṃtapa
karmāṇi pravibhaktāni
 svabhāvaprabhavair guṇaiḥ

42. śamo damas tapaḥ śaucaṃ
 kṣāntir ārjavam eva ca
jñānaṃ vijñānam āstikyaṃ
 brahmakarma svabhāvajam

36. And now, Strongest of Bharatas, hear from me
    what the threefold happiness is,
In which a man delights through training
    and where he reaches the end of unpleasantness.

37. Happiness of integrity springs
    from clearly understanding the reality of the self.
This happiness seems like poison in the beginning;
    in the end it is like ambrosia.

38. That which comes from the confusion
    of senses and sense-objects and tastes first like nectar
But like poison in the end,
    is happiness in the sphere of passion.

39. That happiness which at its beginning
    and in its wake is a delusion
And which arises from sleep, idleness, or negligence,
    that is happiness of sloth.

***

40. There is no being on earth or
    among the gods in heaven
That can be free from these
    three states of matter.

41. Spiritual guides, warriors, producers of wealth,
    and the servant class, O Conqueror,
Have tasks and rites which differ
    according to the state natural to each class.

42. The acts of spiritual leaders by nature express
    serenity, self-control, austerity,
Purity, forbearance, uprightness,
    wisdom, discernment, the proper teachings.

43. śauryaṃ tejo dhṛtir dākṣyaṃ
    yuddhe cāpy apalāyanam
dānam īśvarabhāvaś ca
    kṣatrakarma svabhāvajam

44. kṛṣigorakṣyavāṇijyam
    vaiśyakarma svabhāvajam
paricaryātmakaṃ karma
    śūdrasyāpi svabhāvajam

45. sve sve karmaṇy abhirataḥ
    saṃsiddhiṃ labhate naraḥ
svakarmanirataḥ siddhiṃ
    yathā vindati tac chṛṇu

46. yataḥ pravṛttir bhūtānāṃ
    yena sarvam idaṃ tatam
svakarmaṇā tam abhyarcya
    siddhiṃ vindati mānavaḥ

47. śreyān svadharmo viguṇaḥ
    paradharmāt svanuṣṭhitāt
svabhāvaniyataṃ karma
    kurvan nāpnoti kilbiṣam

48. sahajaṃ karma kaunteya
    sadoṣam api na tyajet
sarvārambhā hi doṣeṇa
    dhūmenāgnir ivāvṛtāḥ

49. asaktabuddhiḥ sarvatra
    jitātmā vigataspṛhaḥ
naiṣkarmyasiddhiṃ paramāṃ
    saṃnyāsenādhigacchati

50. siddhiṃ prāpto yathā brahma
    tathāpnoti nibodha me
samāsenaiva kaunteya
    niṣṭhā jñānasya yā parā

43. Valor, majesty, perseverance, skill,
    and endurance in battle,
  Generosity, and authority are inherent
    in the acts of warriors.

44. The work of those who produce wealth is by nature
    agricultural, pastoral, and commercial.
  The servant class by nature has work
    consisting in service.

45. If a man is engaged in his proper work,
    he attains the highest end.
  Hear how this engagement to his own work
    is crowned with success.

46. He reaches success when he worships
    with his own work him
  From whom all beings emanate
    and who stretched forth the world.

47. One's own duty in its imperfection
    is better than someone else's duty well performed.
  A man doing work proper to his own station
    does not incur demerit.

48. Man should not give up work natural to him,
    even though it is imperfect;
  Imperfection mars *all* undertakings,
    as smoke beclouds the fire.

49. In the end, he does reach perfection beyond acts
    through renunciation,
  When his meditation is not tied down to anything,
    he has conquered himself, and is free from desires.

50. Learn from me, concisely,
    how upon this success he can reach the Divine.
  It is the absolute
    culmination of wisdom.

51. buddhyā viśuddhayā yukto
dhṛtyātmānaṃ niyamya ca
śabdādīn viṣayāṃs tyaktvā
rāgadveṣau vyudasya ca

52. viviktasevī laghvāśī
yatavākkāyamānasaḥ
dhyānayogaparo nityaṃ
vairāgyaṃ samupāśritaḥ

53. ahaṃkāraṃ balaṃ darpaṃ
kāmaṃ krodhaṃ parigraham
vimucya nirmamaḥ śānto
brahmabhūyāya kalpate

54. brahmabhūtaḥ prasannātmā
na śocati na kāṅkṣati
samaḥ sarveṣu bhūteṣu
madbhaktiṃ labhate parām

55. bhaktyā mām abhijānāti
yāvān yaś cāsmi tattvataḥ
tato māṃ tattvato jñātvā
viśate tadanantaram

56. sarvakarmāṇy api sadā
kurvāṇo madvyapāśrayaḥ
matprasādād avāpnoti
śāśvataṃ padam avyayam

57. cetasā sarvakarmāṇi
mayi saṃnyasya matparaḥ
buddhiyogam upāśritya
maccittaḥ satataṃ bhava

58. maccittaḥ sarvadurgāṇi
matprasādāt tariṣyasi
atha cet tvam ahaṃkārān
na śroṣyasi vinaṅkṣyasi

51–53. Man is qualified for reaching the Divine
when his meditation is pure and properly directed,
When he controls himself steadily, when he has done away
with sound and other nourishment of the senses, cast off
Desire and aversion, learned to observe solitude,
eat moderately, control speech, body, and mind;
When he is always intent on the practice of meditation,
devoted to equanimity,
No longer centered in his ego,
freed from reliance on force; from pride,
Desire, anger, attachment to possessions;
when he is unselfish, at peace.

54. Having reached the Divine, and perfectly peaceful,
he knows no sadness and has no cravings.
Equal-minded to all creatures,
he reaches the supreme devotion to me.

55. Through love and worship he recognizes me,
how great I am and who I am.
Then, knowing me as I am,
at once he enters into me.

56. Still he performs all actions, all rites,
but, relying on me,
He attains by my grace
the eternal, changeless abode.

57. Having turned to training in meditation,
makine me your goal,
Keep your thoughts directed to me, always,
while inwardly resigning all you do to me.

58. Directing your thought to me, by my grace, you will
overcome all obstacles.
But if you are centered in yourself and hence unable to listen,
you will perish.

59. yad ahaṃkāram āśritya
na yotsya iti manyase
mithyaiṣa vyavasāyas te
prakṛtis tvāṃ niyokṣyati

60. svabhāvajena kaunteya
nibaddhaḥ svena karmaṇā
kartum necchasi yan mohāt
kariṣyasy avaśo 'pi tat

61. īśvaraḥ sarvabhūtānāṃ
hṛddeśe 'rjuna tiṣṭhati
bhrāmayan sarvabhūtāni
yantrārūḍhāni māyayā

62. tam eva śaraṇaṃ gaccha
sarvabhāvena bhārata
tatprasādāt parāṃ śāntiṃ
sthānaṃ prāpsyasi śāśvatam

63. iti te jñānam ākhyātaṃ
guhyād guhyataraṃ mayā
vimṛśyaitad aśeṣeṇa
yathecchasi tathā kuru

64. sarvaguhyatamaṃ bhūyaḥ
śṛṇu me paramaṃ vacaḥ
iṣṭo 'si me dṛḍham iti
tato vakṣyāmi te hitam

65. manmanā bhava madbhakto
madyājī māṃ namaskuru
mām evaiṣyasi satyaṃ te
pratijāne priyo 'si me

66. sarvadharmān parityajya
mām ekaṃ śaraṇaṃ vraja
ahaṃ tvā sarvapāpebhyo
mokṣayiṣyāmi mā śucaḥ

59. If you decide not to fight
    out of sheer self-centeredness,
  Your decision will be worthless.
    Nature herself will compel you.

60. Whatever you do not wish to do
    because of your delusions,
  You will do even against your will,
    bound by your natural duty.

61. The Lord, Arjuna, is present
    inside all beings,
  Moving all of them like puppets
    by his magic power.

62. Seek refuge with him alone
    with your whole being, Bhārata.
  By His grace, you will reach
    supreme peace, an everlasting estate.

63. Thus have I made known to you the wisdom
    of ultimate secrecy.
  Reflect on it in full.
    Then, as you will, so act.

64. Listen again to my supreme word,
    to the highest of mysteries.
  I truly love you.
    Therefore I shall tell you what is best for you.

65. Turn you mind to me, devoted to me.
    Doing your rituals for me, bow to me.
  You will come to me.
    I promise it to you surely. I love you.

66. Passing beyond appearances,
    come for refuge to me alone.
  I shall set you free from evil.
    Do not be anxious.

67. idaṃ te nātapaskāya
    nābhaktāya kadācana
na cāśuśrūṣave vācyaṃ
    na ca māṃ yo 'bhyasūyati

68. ya idaṃ paramaṃ guhyaṃ
    madbhakteṣv abhidhāsyati
bhaktiṃ mayi parāṃ kṛtvā
    mām evaiṣyaty asaṃśayaḥ

69. na ca tasmān manuṣyeṣu
    kaścin me priyakṛttamaḥ
bhavitā na ca me tasmād
    anyaḥ priyataro bhuvi

70. adhyeṣyate ca ya imaṃ
    dharmyaṃ saṃvādam āvayoḥ
jñānayajñena tenāham
    iṣṭaḥ syām iti me matiḥ

71. śraddhāvān anasūyaś ca
    śṛṇuyād api yo naraḥ
so 'pi muktaḥ śubhāṃl lokān
    prāpnuyāt puṇyakarmaṇām

72. kaccid etac chrutaṃ pārtha
    tvayaikāgreṇa cetasā
kaccid ajñānasaṃmohaḥ
    praṇaṣṭas te dhanaṃjaya

arjuna uvāca

73. naṣṭo mohaḥ smṛtir labdhā
    tvatprasādān mayācyuta
sthito 'smi gatasaṃdehaḥ
    kariṣye vacanaṃ tava

67. You must never tell this to a man who is
    devoid of religious zeal, or love,
Or to one who cannot listen to instruction,
    or one who shows indignation.

68. Whoever in supreme love and worship for me
    makes this highest mystery known
Among my worshipers
    shall certainly come to me.

69. No one renders me service
    more precious than this man's,
Nor will there ever be anyone
    whom I love more on earth.

70. I also hold that whoever recites
    this discourse of ours about the way to be followed
Sacrifices to me
    by his thirst for wisdom.

71. The man who merely listens to it,
    trustful and with an open mind,
He also, set free, will reach
    the fair worlds of the meritorious.

72. Have you truly heard this, son of Pṛthā,
    with singleness of heart?
Has the delusion of your ignorance
    come to an end, Winner of Wealth?

Arjuna:

73. My delusion is cast out; I have gained understanding
    by your grace, Unshakable One.
I stand firm; my doubts are dispelled.
    I shall act according to your word.

saṃjaya uvāca

74. ity ahaṃ vāsudevasya
pārthasya ca mahātmanaḥ
saṃvādam imam aśrauṣam
adbhutaṃ romaharṣaṇam

75. vyāsaprasādāc chrutavān
etad guhyam ahaṃ param
yogaṃ yogeśvarāt kṛṣṇāt
sākṣāt kathayataḥ svayam

76. rājan saṃsmṛtya saṃsmṛtya
saṃvādam imam adbhutam
keśavārjunayoḥ puṇyaṃ
hṛṣyāmi ca muhur muhuḥ

77. tac ca saṃsmṛtya saṃsmṛtya
rūpam atyadbhutaṃ hareḥ
vismayo me mahān rājan
hṛṣyāmi ca punaḥ punaḥ

78. yatra yogeśvaraḥ kṛṣṇo
yatra pārtho dhanurdharaḥ
tatra śrīr vijayo bhūtir
dhruvā nītir matir mama

Samjaya:

74. This is the exciting and wonderful
 discourse I heard
Between the son of Vasudeva
 and that great man, the son of Pṛthā.

75. Through Vyāsa's favor I heard
 this supreme mystery
From Kṛṣṇa, the Lord of mystic power,
 who revealed his discipline himself.

76. O King, as often as I recall
 this wonderful and holy discourse
Between Keśava and Arjuna,
 I rejoice, every time again.

77. And as often as I recall
 that marvelous form of Hari,
I am filled with astonishment
 and delight, every time.

78. Wherever the Lord of mystic power, Kṛṣṇa,
 and the Bowman, the son of Pṛthā, are present,
There happiness, victory, prosperity,
 and unswerving morality are found, I am certain.

PART TWO

ON TRANSLATING THE BHAGAVADGĪTĀ

On Translating the Bhagavadgītā

The Bhagavadgītā and Its Setting

The Bhagavadgītā, the "Song of the Lord," has been presented so many times to Western audiences, and in so many garbs, that almost everyone is familiar with its main tenets. The text is an episode in the great epic of India, the Mahābhārata, and forms a part of the sixth book (*Bhīṣmaparvan*, chaps. 23–40 in the critical edition).

The war between the Pāṇḍavas and the Kauravas, two great opposing parties, is about to ensue. Arjuna, one of the Pāṇḍava brothers, develops second thoughts about the purpose and justness of this war. He conveys his doubts to Kṛṣṇa, his charioteer. Kṛṣṇa answers; but he does so not merely as a fellow warrior and friend but as a spiritual preceptor instructing his pupil. Still more: Kṛṣṇa is none other than God, Viṣṇu himself, and in chapter 11 he reveals himself in his full divine glory to Arjuna.

The Bhagavadgītā has eighteen chapters. Its teachings are not systematically arranged and are not presented for the first time here. Yet the text presents several of the principal subjects that most Indians recognize as part of the *sanātanadharma*, the eternal lore, Hinduism. The text is more "catholic" in its embrace of various views, and at the same time more concise than other texts.

The Bhagavadgītā makes a case for the importance of action. Arjuna, dejected at the beginning, regains his strength, accepts Kṛṣṇa's instructions and his admonitions to stand up and fight. At the same time, the text sings the praises of renunciation, of meditation and (physical) *yoga* exercises, and advocates the way of love and devotion (*bhakti*), and all discipline that leads to wisdom or knowledge. The ancient Vedic-Brahmanic ritual ways are not at all discarded, but also have their place, and in fact provide some of the conceptual tools to bring the principal teachings to the listener's attention. A summary of the instructions to Arjuna seems to offer mutually exclusive items, but this impression is not quite right. The *Bhagavadgītā* is characteristic of the Hindu tradition precisely in this respect: that an instruction is not supreme because it excludes all others, but because it is perfect in itself. Hence the ritual, asceticism, and other ways as well, can be depicted as superior.

It is true that the author has often been credited with conscious attempts to harmonize diverse traditions. It is possible that this was the case, but it is also possible that many of those traditions were not always conceived of as mutually exclusive, even before the text was composed. Some traditions named in the text had certainly not yet taken on the rigid, standardized form they were given later. Next to the bodily and psycho-mental techniques of yoga, *sāṃkhya* should be mentioned: the lucid, analytical training of the mind to achieve liberation, which at this early date does not show signs of the atheism characterizing its later, classical form. The text does not mention Buddhism by name, but the author is certainly acquainted with Buddhist tenets.[1]

The text may have been composed in the third or second century B.C. It resumes the discussion on a number of ideas and images of the Upaniṣads (especially the Kaṭha and Śvetāsvatara).[2] As to its verse form, most of the text, like most of the Mahābhārata, employs the so-called *anuṣṭubh*, but in some parts (as in chap. 2.5–8, and in most of chap. 11) longer verse forms are employed. My translation has tried to do justice to the poetry of the text without imitating it. Imitation of Sanskrit verse forms would be highly artificial in English. The Indian traditions require chanting. I certainly hope that my translation is such as to invite reading aloud, but the regularity of Sanskrit chanting cannot be reproduced any more than the original poetry.

The Fascination of Translating

A translation should speak for itself.

This is certain, even though the demand that a mere human effort must speak for itself may often be inappropriate, misplaced, or

[1]R. C. Zaehner, *The Bhagavad-Gītā, with a Commentary based on the Original Sources* (London: Oxford University Press, 1969), cites many instances, passim.

[2]See for recurrences and parallels the list by George C. O. Haas in R. E. Hume, *The Thirteen Principal Upanishads* (London: Oxford University Press, 1971), pp. 560–562.

extravagant. After all, we are aware that the family of man has always spoken in a particular context. How can we understand any human statement without understanding the social life in which it occurred and the period when it was said?

All this is true, and translators should take note of it. Still I maintain that a *translation* should speak for itself. If it does not do that, it will not stand.

The infallibility of this rule is especially obvious when classical texts are involved. The rule is also practical, for a good translation creates the illusion that the text, this text, could have been composed in the modern tongue of the reader. No matter how many problems have vexed the translator, the reader can recognize a good translation fairly well. Arthur Waley's translations from classical Chinese have justly become famous among readers devoid of all knowledge of Chinese. Anyone can take up *The Book of Songs* and read

> I went to the eastern hills;
> Long, long was it till I came back.
> When I came from the east,
> How the drizzling rain did pour!
> "The oriole is in flight,
> Oh, the glint of its wings!
> A girl is going to be married.
> Bay and white, sorrel and white are her steeds.
> Her mother has tied the strings of her girdle;
> All things proper have been done for her."
> This new marriage is very festive;
> But the old marriage, what of that?[3]

These lines conclude the song of a soldier returning home to find his sweetheart marrying another man. The song is footnoted in good scholarly fashion, but the outstanding quality here and elsewhere in Waley's work is that it seems to be said for the first time in English. And Arthur Waley is able to create that marvelous illusion even in songs that speak of sacrifices and other religious customs foreign to the reader.

Another such master of translation is Robert Graves. If it were not for the betrayal by proper names, it would seem that Apuleius had composed his famous *Golden Ass* in English rather than Latin.

[3]Arthur Waley, trans., *The Book of Songs* (New York: Grove Press, 1960 [original 1937]), p. 117.

> Then in came Venus, smiling sweetly and greeted with a roar of welcome by the audience. She advanced to the centre of the stage, with a whole school of happy little boys crowding around her, so chubby and white-skinned that you might have taken them to be real cupids flown down from Heaven or in from the sea. They had little wings and little archery sets and (this was a nice touch) all carried lighted torches as if they were conducting their mistress to her wedding breakfast. In came a great crowd of beautiful girls: the most graceful Graces, the loveliest Seasons, who strewed the path before Venus with bouquets and loose flowers, propitiating her, as Queen of all pleasures, with the shorn locks of spring.[4]

I realize that ordinary mortals cannot attain the heights reached by scholars-and-poets-in-one, such as Waley and Graves, but more prosaic examples can easily be found to validate the basic rule of translation. I am an ardent admirer of W. H. D. Rouse's translations of Homer, although many might consider them trivializing here and there. The scholar is entitled to ask questions such as: Do we really meet with Homer's world in these translations? But wherever the ensuing debate may lead, the basic rule is clearly applicable. Rouse renders Homer as if the story were originally English.

When Calypso has received word from the gods that she should at last let Odysseus return to his homeland, Rouse has her say:

> Poor old fellow! please don't sit here lamenting anymore, don't let yourself pine away like this. I'm going to send you off at once, and glad to do it. Come along, cut down trees, hew them into shape, make a good broad raft; you can lay planks across it and it shall carry you over the misty sea! I will provide you with bread, water, red wine, as much as you like, you need not starve. I'll give you plenty of clothes and send a fair wind behind you to bring you home safe and sound—if it so please the gods who rule the broad heavens, who are stronger than I am both to will and to do.[5]

Among the outstanding translations from Sanskrit we have *The Panchatantra* of Arthur W. Ryder, who succeeds magnificently in rendering this most famous and down-to-earth, witty and instructive cycle of stories, and who succeeds even in reproducing the terse

[4]Apuleius, *The Transformations of Lucius, Otherwise Known as The Golden Ass*, trans. Robert Graves (New York: Farrar, 1971 [orig. 1951]), p. 258.

[5]W. H. D. Rouse, trans., *Homer, The Odyssey* (New York: Mentor, 1962 [orig. 1937]), p. 65.

metric morals of the tales in laconic little rhymes—as if they were meant that way:

After money has departed,
  If the wit is frail,
Then, like rills in summer weather,
  Undertakings fail.

Forest-sesame, crow-barley,
  Men who have no cash,
Owning names but lacking substance,
  Are accounted trash.[6]

We are very fortunate in the English-speaking world to have *Buddhism in Translations* by Henry Clarke Warren. It is a model for all translators of Indian religious texts in the scrupulousness of its scholarship. At the same time, it is a model in the fascination of its English form. It is virtually impossible for the reader to close the book. How often can one say that of a translated religious text?

> On this same day the happy and delighted hosts of the Heaven of the Thirty-three held a celebration, waving their cloaks and giving other signs of joy, because to king Suddhodana in Kapilavatthu had been born a son who should sit at the foot of the Bo-tree, and become a Buddha.
>
> Now it came to pass at that time that an ascetic named Kāladevala, who was an intimate friend of king Suddhodana, and practised in the eight stages of meditation, went, after his daily meal, to the Heaven of the Thirty-three to take his noon-day rest. And as he was sitting there resting, he noticed these gods, and said,—
>
> "Why do you frolic so joyously? Let me too know the reason." "Sir," replied the gods, "it is because a son has been born to king Suddhodana, who shall sit at the foot of the Bo-tree, and become a Buddha, and cause the Wheel of the Doctrine to roll; in him we shall be permitted to behold the infinite and masterful ease of a Buddha, and shall hear the Doctrine."[7]

If translations must be adorned by footnotes, let them. If they must be accompanied by long prefaces or postscripts, let them. But the translation of the text should be readable by itself. Most great texts lasted long not because they forced their hearers or readers

[6]Arthur W. Ryder, trans., *The Panchatantra* (Chicago: Phoenix, 1964 [orig. 1956]), p. 242.

[7]Henry Clarke Warren, trans., *Buddhism in Translations* (Cambridge, Mass.: Harvard University Press, 1953), pp. 48–49.

into erudite explanations, but because they were clear and immediate.

Some Reasons for this Translation

Translators of classical texts, imprinted on the memory of numerous generations, and certainly translators of texts with religious authority, owe the reader an account of their own understanding of their task, of their tools and principles, to the point of providing the reader with means for incisive criticism. It is certainly with this in mind that I compiled the indices at the end of this work, for they will enable the reader to see at a glance in what manner any word or expression of any significance in the Gītā has been rendered.

Many a well-read person, even before glancing at either index, is bound to raise the question: Why do we need another translation of the Bhagavadgītā?

It is proper to confront this objection at the outset. The bafflement of reviewers can best be met with an obvious counterquestion: How could we possibly have enough translations of a classical religious text of overwhelming importance? This century has seen dozens of translations into Western languages alone of the Bible, and no one would suggest that the "final" translation has been arrived at or ever will be. All interpreters of Hinduism would agree that the Bhagavadgītā can be compared in importance to the New Testament in the History of the West.[8] New translations are the only clear sign that we want to understand. The consideration that the Gītā scholarship behind our translations has not attained the age and maturity of New Testament scholarship is a stimulus rather than an impediment.

As for this particular translation, it is not facetious to begin by saying that the many translations we need of an important text should be *good* translations and that the present one is intended as one of those good translations. W. Douglas P. Hill, who in 1928 gave us the most outstanding English rendering of the text, was quite conscious of the difference between good and bad translations.[9] He noted in his "Bibliographical Notes" that in the eighteen

[8]No one less than Franklin Edgerton made this comparison. See Part II of his *The Bhagavadgītā* (Cambridge, Mass.: Harvard University Press, 1946), p. 3.

[9]W. Douglas P. Hill, *The Bhagavadgītā* (London: Oxford University Press, 1928), pp. 276, 277.

eighties and nineties the Bhagavadgītā had become "the playground of western pseudo-mystics." He did not appreciate the attempts that he grouped together as "Theosophical Versions"; he referred to the greater part of other works on the Gītā as "comparatively worthless," and he added: "Hundreds of vernacular editions have found a home in the Indian Office Library, and still continue to encumber its reluctant shelves."

The number of "comparatively worthless" works has increased enormously since the days of Hill. To review all of them would be not only impossible but not worth the trouble. It will be more useful to reflect for a moment on the causes of such inadequacy.

Serious endeavors to translate the Bhagavadgītā began in the eighteenth century, when Sir Charles Wilkins published *The Bhagvat Geeta, or Dialogues of Kreeshna and Arjoon in Eighteen Lectures, with notes* (London, 1785). Western scholarship in Sanskrit, and historical linguistics generally, were still in their infancy. In the following decades historical linguistics became a full-fledged science, and many other serious translations of our text were published in various Western languages. Among these was a Latin translation by A. W. Schlegel in 1823, and an improved and enlarged version of the same by the famous Indologist C. Lassen in 1846. From the beginning of Western Sanskrit studies, all serious translations addressed themselves principally to an erudite audience, and I think that we should place this fact among the unintentional causes for the production of so many mediocre or bad versions of the text. Many scholarly translations were undertaken for the very simple reason that the Bhagavadgītā is among the most accessible poems for students of Sanskrit literature; after a year of Sanskrit grammar everyone can find his way through the text somehow, while at the same time receiving the satisfaction of dealing with a significant piece of literature.

As a rule it is not necessary in serious translations for Sanskrit students to find English equivalents for crucial terms; the student is already aware that *mokṣa* means something like "salvation" or "liberation," that *yoga* refers to techniques to attain *mokṣa*, that *brahman* is something like "the Absolute" in Indian metaphysics, and so on. As a result, most translators, to this very day, leave several of those words untranslated.

This procedure would not necessarily have contributed to mediocrity, if the Western learned occupation with the Gītā had not coincided with peculiar waves of enthusiasm for "things oriental" during and since the Romantic movement. Serious scholars, like A. W. Schlegel, who in 1818 became the first professor of Indology at the University of Bonn, and his famous brother Friedrich Schlegel, who also studied Sanskrit; Franz Bopp, one of the founders of historical and comparative linguistics; Eugène Burnouf, who initiated modern Buddhist studies in Paris, and other pivotal figures, were read avidly by many not-so-serious and not-so-competent students. These scholars provided food for the hungry romantic epigons and hangers-on who longed for evidence that there truly was *ex oriente lux*. Possibly, if anyone had suggested to these hangers-on that *Gulliver's Travels* was an adaptation from the Sanskrit, they would have found within it a mystical authority unparalleled in the West. This observation is not so exaggerated, for we should remember that it was not much more than a coincidence of grammatical predilection that made the Bhagavadgītā so very available; and we know for certain that the English translations of the Gītā helped the text to attain a greater fame, or at least a vogue, more tremendous than the text had enjoyed in India.[10]

The situation today is not drastically different. We have serious Sanskritists, and we have a good many hangers-on, many a self-styled *guru* who uses his second-hand knowledge of the Gītā and his degree in psychology to find employment and teach an extension course in some permissive university.

Of course, one could not reproach serious Sanskritists for allowing questionable spiritual guides and sundry faddish dreamers to use or abuse their work, but it is true that *real* translations should leave less space for misinterpretation.

Translating means making the first and basic step in interpreting. What would have happened to the Bible if translators had decided to leave crucial words untranslated? The word *God* itself is a choice, and so are righteousness, justification, hope, faith, and many more. Translators should not shirk from making these choices, which must be made if the translation is to mean anything. For the Gītā, words like *yoga, mokṣa,* and *brahman* must be translated.

[10]Srī Aurobindo and Mahātma Gandhi read the text for the first time in English. This fact may cause some surprise, but there is no doubt that countless Indians gained access to the text in the same manner. The new vogue for the Bhagavadgītā in translation is well described in Gerald James Larson's "The Bhagavad Gītā as as Cross-Cultural Process: Toward an Analysis of the Social Locations of a Religious Text," *Journal of the American Academy of Religion,* XLIII (1975), 651–669.

But could we not avoid mistakes by leaving seminal terms in Indian texts untranslated? The question can be asked, and ought to be answered firmly in the negative. We have a classical example of traditional scholarly misunderstanding in the untranslated Buddhist term *nirvāṇa*. Untranslated and misunderstood, the term found its way into Western learned discussions.[11] Schopenhauer, although not as far off the mark as others, understood the term mainly as a negative notion, the denial of the will, and the untranslated term continued to function in Western scholarly life, with a confused meaning unsupported by any actual Buddhist text. As late as 1948, the Swiss theologian Karl Barth could refer to the Buddhist *nirvāṇa* in an offhand manner as a *harmless, neutral and even enjoyable nothing,*[12] and could do so without evoking so much as a question among his readers. The theologian Hans Urs von Balthasar, in his elucidation of prayer, unnecessarily equated *nirvāṇa* with *absolute void.*[13] In theological treatises, as well as anywhere else, contrasts between misunderstood or misjudged, or misappropriated notions of Indian religions and the Christian verities do not serve any purpose. But is it not the modesty, the undue self-limitation, of translators that brings on such misunderstandings? If translators had taken the trouble to translate the word *nirvāṇa* even in different ways in different contexts, much less confusion would have been engendered. "Freedom," or "ultimate freedom," or "total bliss" would definitely be among those translations, and glib references like those of Karl Barth and Urs von Balthasar would have been as impossible as they were unnecessary.

With respect to the Gītā, I believe it is possible to indicate precisely which confusions and deficiencies in vocabulary are not necessary anymore.

It certainly is no longer necessary to deal with the Gītā only as a simple exercise in grammar and vocabulary. Saying this is not meant as a criticism of the tradition of Sanskrit instruction in which

[11]See Guy R. Welbon, *The Buddhist Nirvāṇa and its Western Interpreters* (Chicago: University of Chicago Press, 1968); see especially chapter V.

[12]See K. Barth, *Kirchliche Dogmatik* (Zurich: Zollikon, 1948), Vol. III, pt. 2, p. 739. For a discussion of the problem, see my "History of Religions with a Hermeneutic Oriented toward Christian Theology?" in J. M. Kitagawa, ed., *The History of Religions. Essays on the Problem of Understanding* (Chicago: University of Chicago Press, 1967), p. 112.

[13]Hans Urs von Balthasar, *Prayer,* trans. A. V. Littledale (New York: Paulist Press, 1967), pp. 44–45 (orig. *Das betrachtende Gebet,* 1957).

the Gītā served eminently. In Sanskrit courses the tradition will no doubt continue to flourish. The most glorious attempt to present the Bhagavadgītā to Sanskrit students is the one by Franklin Edgerton.[14] In the first volume, just as in the present edition, text and translation face each other. The Sanskrit text consists for the most part of a simple verse form (the so-called *anuṣṭubh śloka*) which has two lines, a caesura dividing each line into two halves of eight syllables each. Edgerton's translation is unique in rendering the text word for word when that is at all possible. Throughout, he follows the Sanskrit order of lines and half lines. The result is marvelous for students trying to plow their way through the text, but, naturally, whatever beauty there is in the English is purely coincidental. Moreover, the clarity is lost on an audience without knowledge of Sanskrit. This is how the text begins in Edgerton:

> Dhṛtarāṣṭra said:
> 1. In the Field of Right, the Kuru-field,
>   Assembled ready to fight,
> My men and the sons of Pāṇḍu as well,
>   What did they do, Saṃjaya?

This may not sound too bad, and everyone already familiar with the general outline of the story sees the old blind king (Dhṛtarāṣṭra) inquiring from his vizier (Saṃjaya), who has the gift of seeing things at a distance, how the war is proceeding. The lines that follow jolt us:

> Saṃjaya said:
> 2. Seeing however the host of the sons of Pāṇḍu
>   Arrayed, Duryodhana then
> Approached the teacher (Droṇa)
>   And spoke a word, the prince:
> 3. Behold of Pāṇḍu's sons this
>   Great host, O Teacher!

The "however" in verse 2 makes no sense, but Edgerton inserts it to point out to the Sanskrit student that he did not overlook the particle *tu*, of which the student has learned that as a rule it indicates an opposition of a sentence to the preceding one. "The prince," dangling in the end of a line, qualifies Duryodhana; and by

[14]Franklin Edgerton, *The Bhagavadgītā, Translated and Interpreted*, 2 vols. (Cambridge, Mass.: Harvard University Press, 1946; Harvard Oriental Series, vols. 38 and 39).

placing it in that peculiar position, Edgerton remains faithful to the word order in the last half line in the Sanskrit.

The same lines in my translation run, without submission to the Sanskrit syntax:

> Dhṛtarāṣṭra:
> 1. In the land of the right tradition, the land of the Kurus,
> my men and the men of Pāṇḍu met,
> Ready to fight.
> What did they do, Saṃjaya?
>
> Saṃjaya:
> 2. The king, Duryodhana, surveyed
> the Pāṇḍava army drawn up for battle.
> Then he went to his mentor
> and said:
> 3. "Master, see that mighty army
> of Pāṇḍu's men.

I have no intention of belittling the serious works that have made the Gītā available, and least of all Edgerton's useful version.[15] His translation aimed for consistency, rendering the same Sanskrit terms by the same English terms to the farthest extent possible. The particle *tu* might have been rendered by "for his part," but Edgerton, virtually eliminating exceptions, insisted on being of service to the learner of Sanskrit. What is remarkable, however, is that so many translators, without any of the pedagogical purposes of Edgerton, decided to follow Sanskrit grammar and syntax scrupulously in English, and thus made comprehension needlessly difficult.

Sanskrit has a special liking for passive verb forms, which in English come across in a very stilted way. For instance, in 1905 L. D. Barnett translated BhG. 4.14, 15 as follows:

> Works defile me not; in me is no longing for fruit of works. He who recognizes me as such is not fettered by works. With such knowledge works were done by former seekers after deliverance . . .[16]

[15]The only blame rests on the publisher, who some years ago decided to republish Edgerton's translation by itself, without the Sanskrit, thereby depriving the work of its reason for existence.

[16]L. D. Barnett, trans., *The Bhagavadgītā* (London, 1905), reprinted in Nicol MacNicol, *Hindu Scriptures* (New York: Dutton, 1963 [Everyman's Library, no. 944]), pp. 223–287.

Not all translators who aimed for a literal translation were as consistent as Barnett, but most serious translations are marred by an overdose of passive forms. Active verb forms make the text much livelier.

What I wish to focus on is the conspicuous fact that the genius of English is reflected in its active, finite verbs. This makes English, no matter how Indo-European it may be, very different from Sanskrit with its love for prefixes, past participles, compounds, and verbal nouns. English, like our other Western languages, was given a decisive turn toward active religious expressions when Hebrew texts were translated and divulged in the vernacular. We have not only a great many verbs to express variations in very ordinary acts but also for acts of a more "spiritual" character (venerate, render honor, look up to, pay homage to, worship, revere, adore, pray, supplicate, beseech, invoke, etc.). It seems extraordinary to me that in our history of translating from Sanskrit we have generally followed a course of unjustifiable literalism.

Examples can easily be multiplied to show that the intention of the text comes across much better if we make use of the natural abilities of our language. Thus in Bhagavadgītā 4.13, where a couple of agent nouns occur (*kartṛ*, "doer," and *akartṛ*, "non-doer"), we do violence to the text by insisting on agent nouns in English. Hill has:

> The order of the four castes was created by me, with due distribution of Strands and works; I did that work indeed; yet know me as *no worker* and immutable.

And Zaehner:

> The four-caste system did I generate with categories of "constituents" and works; of this I am *the doer* [the agent]—this know—[and yet I am] the Changeless One, who does not do [or act].[17]

Each of the translations avoids one of the two agent nouns, yet nothing would seem more natural and more precise than to avoid both. Without for the moment elaborating on other terms (such as "caste") I propose

> I brought forth the four great divisions of men
> according to their qualities and rituals.
> Although I made all this,
> know that I never act at all.

[17]My italics in both examples.

(See for a comparable example 13.7–11, where I used verbs to translate a series of nouns and nominal compounds.)

I want to mention one more peculiarity of modern English that a translator should bear in mind. Modern English is more direct than other Germanic languages. We not only tend to center our sentences on finite verb forms but, especially in comparison to German, English has a strong inclination to say whatever is most important at the beginning of a passage or sentence. As a rule, English does not slowly work its way up to the principal thought but comes right out with it. Sanskrit is comparable to German speech customs in that it tends to hold the most important thing for the end. Since this is principally a simple matter of syntax, we do not do any harm by English rephrasing. On the contrary, the strength of a sentence can best be maintained that way. A passage in the sixteenth chapter of the Bhagavadgītā speaks of "demonic people." Three verses tell us what is going on in these people's minds. The information that they think thus and so is conveyed only in v. 15 in Sanskrit, and virtually all translators wait equally long to reveal it. One translation runs like this:

12. They are bound by hundreds of vain hopes. Anger and lust is their refuge; and they strive by unjust means to amass wealth for their own cravings.
13. "I have gained this today, and I shall attain this desire. This wealth is mine and that shall also be mine."
14. "I have slain that enemy and others also shall I slay. I am a lord, I enjoy life, I am successful, powerful and happy."
15. I am wealthy and of noble birth: who else is there like me? I shall pay for religious rituals, I shall make benefactions, I shall enjoy myself." Thus they say in their darkness of delusion.[18]

The translation is all right, but listening to the text is made more difficult than it need be, for we cannot hear at once *who* thinks these thoughts; thus the flow of the song is interrupted. I think we can preserve the flow by following rather than ignoring English speech patterns:

12. Hundreds of expectations ensnare them.
    They are trapped by desires and resentments.
They have criminal aspirations to amass money
    for the indulgence of their desires.

[18]Juan Mascaró, *The Bhagavad Gita* (Baltimore: Penguin, 1966 [first printed 1962]).

15. Their ignorance beguiles them. They think:
"Today I got this wish fulfilled, tomorrow I'll get that;
This belongs to me, that also;
I shall be rich.
I have slain that enemy,
and I shall slay the others too;
I am in control; I enjoy the world;
I am a success; I am strong and happy;
I am wealthy and high-born;
who is my equal?
I shall sacrifice, give proper gifts,
and rejoice at the results."

So far we have dealt only with external questions of translating. The most important questions concern the translator's attitude and the meaning of the text.

Attitudes and Translations

The faultiness of so many translations is often simply a matter of shallow attitudes. Cravings to romanticize India are satisfied by masters with an attitude of certainty that has nothing to do with the text of the Bhagavadgītā. Orientalizing comforters of souls merrily translate and comment unencumbered by things the text actually says.

Bhagavadgītā 18.26 uses the word *dhṛtyutsāhasamanvita,* which I translated as "steady and energetic." The word, a compound, is not problematic. Zaehner has "steadfast and resolute." Most other translators follow the common custom of rendering the formation of the compound in its entirety: "filled with constancy and zeal" (Hill); "full of steadfastness and energy" (Edgerton); "possessed of constancy and vigour" (Barnett); "who has determination and zeal" (Mascaró); "mit Standhaftigkeit und Energie begabt" (Deussen);[19] "capable de volonté et d'énergie" (Sénart).[20] All in all, the meaning is perfectly clear. Only Swami Bhaktivedanta comes out of the blue with "with great enthusiasm." Such disregard for the text can seem

[19]Paul Deussen, *Der Gesang des Heiligen* (Leipzig: Brockhaus, 1911).

[20]Emile Sénart, *La Bhagavad-Gîtâ* (Paris: Société d'Edition "Les Belles Lettres," 1944).

comical, as when the same translator renders the Lord's words in 15.6 as:

> That abode of Mine is not illumined by the sun or moon, nor by electricity. And anyone who reaches It never comes back to this material world.[21]

The translation of *pāvaka* (fire) as "electricity" is certainly a surprise. The only comparable effect I know was achieved by the Bible translator Goodspeed in Matthew 17. It is the story where Jesus takes an unusual course to pay his temple tax. He orders Peter to go catch a fish, open its mouth, and find what according to translators so far had been a shekel or a silver coin. According to Goodspeed however, it was a dollar. However, it is only the unexpected comical effect which is comparable to Bhaktivedanta's "electricity," for Goodspeed was a conscientious translator, and there are no serious objections to the word dollar,[22] even for Jesus' taxes. The word electricity instead of fire is a trivial distortion. It is more than a triviality that Bhaktivedanta's translation glosses over the last half line (*tad dhāma paramam mama*), in which occurs the only choice in this verse: "This [is] My supreme abode," or—with Rāmānuja—: "That place is My own supreme light."

The translation by Swami Prabhavananda and Christopher Isherwood[23] is probably the most "flowing" of all English renditions. Unfortunately, it distorts the text considerably. For example, one could hardly guess in some lines that the subject of ritual is under discussion. Obviously, this subject had little meaning for the translators. The lines of 3.8:

> Activity is better than inertia. Act, but with self-control. If you are lazy, you cannot even sustain your own body.

sound nice. At most, the unsuspecting reader might think of them as rather trite moral advice. What the text actually says in this verse is clearly stated in the first half line, which Prabhavananda and

[21]His Divine Grace A. C. Bhaktivedanta Swami Prabhupāda, *Bhagavad-gītā As It Is* (New York: Collier Books, 1972).

[22]Fewer and fewer people have a clear recollection of the dollar as a *coin*, and hence Goodspeed's dollar is almost as archaic as the shekel.

[23]Swami Prabhavananda and Christopher Isherwood, trans., *The Song of God. Bhagavad-Gita*. Introduction by Aldous Huxley (New York: Mentor, 1951 [orig. 1944]).

Isherwood omitted; the following lines do not refer to activity in general, and have nothing to say on the subject of laziness:

> Perform the required ritual work.
> Action is better than inaction
> Without action, the body would stop functioning.

The text is a matter-of-fact statement about the necessity of required ritual. The subject of ritual and sacrifice is generally among the most neglected subjects in Bhagavadgītā translations; we shall return to it in discussing crucial terms of the text.

It sometimes seems as if unconsciously the majority of translators, and some of the best translators part of the time, tried to make the Hindu look odd. Although it was not always done in the same spirit, the Hindus were depicted as members of another world—perhaps higher, perhaps lower than "ours," but certainly different. I can think of the endeavors only as unconscious, for who would willfully mutilate meanings? If the translator's object was not to show his own superior erudition (in contrast to the uneducated Hindu's), it was to show the sublime message of the text all too instantly.

Prabhavananda and Isherwood, and likewise Bhaktivedanta, did their best to present "the message" of the Gītā, but their certainty of possessing the truth led them to make the text look "modern" and "relevant," and the result was a good many distortions making a mockery of a venerable Hindu document.

Scholarly seriousness by itself is not necessarily a better guide than the zeal of proselytism. There is a considerable tradition of scholarship looking down upon Hinduism. Monier Monier Williams, the indefatigable compiler of Sanskrit dictionaries which we still use, is on record as saying that one of his reasons for learning Sanskrit well was to translate the Bible and convert the natives to Christianity.[24] Whatever one thinks of this idea, it is not likely to foster a sympathetic attitude toward Hindu texts.

In our own century Edgerton, who did not show any eagerness to convert the natives, nevertheless at times could not hide his disdain

[24]Monier Monier Williams, *A Sanskrit English Dictionary* (Oxford, 1956 [first edition, 1899]). See his preface, pp. ix, x. Monier Williams elaborates on his agreement with the founder of the Boden Chair for Sanskrit in Oxford. The stated purpose of Colonel Boden was "to enable his countrymen to proceed in the conversion of the natives of India to the Christian Religion."

for Indian tradition. A few remarks in the notes to his translation of the Bhagavadgītā are startling. One note concerns the meaning of the word *puruṣa* in 8.4 (which he translated as "the spirit"). It reads thus:

> *Puruṣa* can only be a practical synonym of *ātman*. All the terms used here are somewhat loose and vague; the language is grandiloquent.[25]

Granted that the term *puruṣa* and three other terms in this verse (*adhibhūta, adhidaivata,* and *adhiyajña*) have generally constituted a problem for translators, it certainly takes a special scholarly cockiness to finish the subject by deciding to call them loose and vague and the language grandiloquent. Only the *translation* becomes loose, vague and grandiloquent if Edgerton and others render the three terms beginning with adhi- as "over-being," "over-divinity," and "overworship."[26] There are several such examples of scholarly pretentiousness in Edgerton's notes. Commenting on 15.3 he summarily dismisses Śaṅkara and Rāmānuja, the most prestigious Hindu commentators (in their interpretation of Īśvara); in 18.3 he berates the author of the Gītā for using the word *karman* instead of *kārya*. I am not proposing an uncritical acceptance of learned commentaries, whether European and American, or Indian, but it would seem fitting from a strictly academic point of view to pay attention to what the author of the text said, and to what Indian thinkers had to say, especially if no reasons are adduced for alternative views.

A modicum of respect for the tradition through which the Bhagavadgītā has come to us does not seem an excessive demand. Before leaving the topic of attitudes, I want to look for a moment at the translation of Arthur W. Ryder. Ryder, as I have already noted,

[25]Edgerton, Part I, p. 184.

[26]There is, however, no necessity for that. *Adhi* can be understood as an archaic preposition, meaning "bearing on" or "relating to." This is how, among recent translators, Zaehner interpreted it. Cf. V. Raghavan, *The Indian Heritage* (Bangalore, 1956), p. xxxvi. Trying to follow the sense of the enumeration in the verse as well as possible, I translated the first of the three with the help of a finite verb (. . . make for . . .):

> Historical circumstances make for
> the principles of existence.
> Man's spirit relates to the gods.
> Indeed, I myself,
> Here in the body, relate to sacrifice,
> o you, supreme mortal!

showed himself a genius in translating the *Pañcatantra* from the Sanskrit. His translation of the Bhagavadgītā, first published in 1929 and reprinted one year later,[27] is less well known. This is fortunate, in spite of the fact that Ryder made a consistent effort to translate every Sanskrit term with English (and thereby aimed for an ideal that I also hold to). It is fortunate because of the form his translation took. The "cute" expressions and phrases that served Ryder so well in the popular, entertaining, and edifying tales of the *Pañcatantra* led to total disaster in this case. Indeed, it is hard to believe that anyone could have taken the work seriously at the time and that a reprint was called for within a year. Ryder maintained rhyme throughout, thereby arriving at such crambo as this (in chapter 4.16 ff.):

To work? or not to work? Such are
  The questions that perplex

Even the poets. Therefore I
  Will solve the doubts that vex,
Imparting knowledge apt to save
  Your soul from sinful flecks.
True work, perverted work, non-work
  Must all be understood:
For this mysterious path of work
  Winds through a tangled wood.

Who sees non-working lurk in work,
  Working in non-work lurk,
Is wise, is disciplined, a man
  Successful in all work.

Obviously, this work was no improvement on the—still impressive—old poetic rendering by Sir Edwin Arnold.[28] It is not enough, however, to observe the poor taste displayed in Ryder's rendering. The attitude of a Sanskritist who could commit such a travesty on the *Gītā* text was not one man's problem, but a problem shared in various ways by many. At that time no one was surprised, amused, or irritated, by reading Ryder's dedication page:

[27]Arthur W. Ryder, *The Bhagavad-Gita* (Chicago: University of Chicago Press, 1929).

[28]*The Song Celestial.* First published in 1885 and reproduced in Part 2 of Edgerton's work.

To my dear sister
WINIFRED
This version of a most noble poem is
Appropriately dedicated

If there is any value in comparing the function of the Bhagavadgītā in India with that of the New Testament in the West, it would seem not a very appropriate dedication anymore. It is not likely that a New Testament translator would dream of adorning his version of the text with a comparable personal dedication, or, for that matter, of designating it as "most noble," on the verge of condescension.

This is not the place to write a history of political ideologies; it will be enough to remember that a good deal of Western work on the Bhagavadgītā was done during the period of European colonialism. Was not another English-speaking poet of the day the creator of the winged phrase: "the white man's burden?" The time did not foster an attentiveness, a willingness to listen to what Hindu texts said.

The Bhagavadgītā; Terms, Meanings, Choices

Perhaps some day, someone will publish a variety of Gītā translations side by side in one volume. Any translator could only hope that his work would be deemed worthy of publication next to Edgerton's, for there is no doubt that Edgerton's would be included in any future synopsis. The comparison of translations is part of any serious study, and Edgerton's work will remain indispensable. His fixed translations of Sanskrit terms throughout the text force the reader back to the original. "Reason method" stands for *sāṃkhya*, "worship" for *yajña*, and words like *brahman* and *nirvāṇa* remain untranslated.

I cannot force my readers to the Sanskrit; at most, I can *urge* students to turn back to the text constantly. The terms I chose for *brahman, aksara, avyaya, mahat, ātman, buddhi*, the *guṇas* and so on, are meant only as a ground for further study for Sanskrit students, and perhaps in some instances no more than a starting point.

The choice of words to render the meanings of Sanskrit terms is a delicate matter to discuss. I want to go back to my first maxim, that a translation should speak for itself. This implies that the general discussion here should not be given undue attention; it is "theory."

Translating is a practical exercise in hermeneutics; even more accurately, it precedes hermeneutics. Hermeneutics is the theory of understanding. It is the continuous reflection engaged in by all those who want to interpret human beings and their documents. Translators must engage in hermeneutics; they must be as aware as possible of what it is to understand human beings. But unlike philosophers, who can speak of hermeneutics interminably, the translator or historian has to terminate the discourse somewhere and make his choices of words. He knows from experience as well as from reflection that understanding is a primordial human occupation. Joachim Wach wrote on the first page of his great work on hermeneutics: "Understanding existed even before there was communication."[29] Translators might well add: translating, being fundamentally human, always exists before any theory of hermeneutics is designed. Theory does not become superfluous, but it is easy to see how translators can become impatient with hermeneuticizing philosophers who have never translated anything.

It is high time to emphasize the primordial practicality of translation and to insist on its right of primogeniture in all matters of hermeneutics. Our time has seen the gradual decrease of language requirements in institutions of higher education. One can only hope that this decrease is temporary, for there is no substitute for language study. Substitutes that have been suggested have been makeshift. It is sad to note too that at the very time when sociologists criticize their own discipline for its theoretical inadequacy, church dignitaries expect to obtain an understanding of foreign religious traditions from sociological analyses. Sociology, psychology, various quantifying methods of ethnography, and even of linguistics cannot serve us in place of the study of specific languages and literatures, no matter how useful all those methods may be in addition to that study. The unique act of translating remains basic, in spite of its own limits and its stupendous problems in the actual choice of words.

All of us have learned from teachers of literature that poetry, and good literature generally, cannot really be translated. This cliché is correct, if by translation is meant a reproduction through another language of exactly the same effect the original had on its listeners. In the case of classical languages we can at most guess what that

[29]Joachim Wach, *Das Verstehen* (Hildesheim: George Olms, 1966 [orig. 1926]), I, 1.

original effect might have been. The point was made very well by Matthew Arnold in his beautiful essay "On Translating Homer:"

> No one can tell him [the translator] how Homer affected the Greeks; but there are those who can tell him how Homer affects *them*. These are scholars; who possess, at the same time with knowledge of Greek, adequate poetical taste and feeling. No translation will seem to them of much worth compared with the original; but they alone can say whether the translation produces more or less the same effect upon them as the original.[30]

There are many scholars in India, and some in the West, who might help us here. The Bhagavadgītā is a text with religious authority, and of texts of that character, more than of worldly poetry, it can be said that they are meant to be understood. We cannot make the mistake of narrow, postromantic literary criticism and revel in our personal experience, or of socioanalytic scholarship and consider our task finished when we relate the text to its limited setting of one concept of beauty or one form of society. Indian traditions of interpretation should be our principal key. These traditions emphatically include the language of the text itself, Sanskrit, its Vedic roots, and the commentaries of Śaṅkara and of Rāmānuja. The Indian scholarly interpretations of Śaṅkara and Rāmānuja are endowed with a developed sensitivity for religious terms. We cannot slight Śaṅkara and Rāmānuja except at our own peril. Not only Rāmānuja, but Śaṅkara too, no matter how renowned for deemphasizing the ritual, had a much more immediate understanding of sacrificial procedures and meanings than any modern scholar, however well versed in Sanskrit and steeped in historical criticism.

A general difficulty in translating the ritual connotations of many words exists for most modern Westerners (as well as for many modern, advaitacally inclined Indians). This difficulty springs from the fact that our secularization has no doubt hit us hardest in our religious behavior. We may hold certain things, places and, above all, ideas to be sacred; but our manners of acting, the style of life, the etiquette of our experienced and enacted existence, seem to have lost touch with tradition. Here the world presupposed and depicted in the Gītā is altogether different.

[30]Matthew Arnold, *On the Classical Tradition*, ed. R. H. Super (Ann Arbor: The University of Michigan Press, 1960), pp. 98, 99.

Over and over the text speaks of the tradition, the age-old customs (*dharma*) that should be *followed, practiced*. Ritual work, cult (*karma*) is to be performed, and specific sacrifices (*yajña*) are to be brought, all in accordance with the established liturgy (*vidhi*). It is quite obvious from the existing translations that most scholars had a hard time evaluating all those references positively. Their sloppiness in choosing terms to render the terms in the text speaks an unmistakable disdain for "primitive" and fortunately bygone customs, for magical and superstitious beliefs. In fact, this sloppiness and this disdain are quite wrong, for the cultic topics in the text are articulate, carefully expressed, and coherent. In fact, without an understanding of them, a good deal of the teachings of the Bhagavadgītā is lost on its listeners.

In the description of "demonic people" in chapter 16, from which I quoted before, Edgerton translates v. 17 as follows:

> Self-conceited, haughty,
> Full of pride and arrogance of wealth,
> They do acts of religious worship in name alone,
> Hypocritically, not according to the (Vedic) injunctions.

Not all, but most translators see "hypocrites" in the people here described; one gets the impression that the translators remembered Sunday school versions of Jesus rebuking the Pharisees. However, the text never loses sight of the importance of the ritual itself, even though it scorns those demonic people who make a wrong use of it. The word *dambhena* is not so much "hypocritically" as "ostentatiously" (Radhakrishnan); the activity of the "demonic people" is ultimately a matter of self-deception; *dambhena* refers more to wrong goings-on and harmful results than to inner intentions. The emphasis in the last two half-lines is clearly on the fact that these people's engagement in the ritual is *in vain* and not in harmony with the ancient, trustworthy *vidhi* (liturgy):

> Suffering from megalomania, puffed up
> with the arrogance and presumption of wealth,
> They make a show of sacrificing,
> vainly, not in the established liturgy.

The statement that it is "not in the established liturgy" is not an extra barb in a series of denouncements. The ritual *counts;* here and in many other contexts, understanding the ritual is the condition for understanding the sense of the instructions, which are never angry (anger is in conflict with all Hindu ideals), but always descriptive and to the point. One should perform cultic action without counting on a reward; this is a cornerstone of Kṛṣṇa's teachings (See, for example, the references in the Sanskrit index under *karmaphala; karmaphalahetu; karmaphalāsaṅga; karmaphalatyāga*). Throughout, knowledge of the elements and function of the ritual is assumed, and exhortations that to many of us would seem unrelated to ritual (such as those of self-discipline; asceticism; devotion) are clarified in the text on the basis of that knowledge.

The beginning of chapter 6 reveals the living soul of a ritual religiosity, although the principal topic is renunciation.

1. That man knows renunciation and is disciplined
   who does the required cultic acts not counting on their results,
   Not he whose sacrificial fire is extinct
   and who avoids all liturgy.

The vocabulary is quite clear. In the Vedic and Brahmanic tradition, *agni*, fire, is not just fire in general, but the fire used for sacrifice; the verb *kṛ* (from which *akriya*, "who avoids all liturgy" in the text is derived) means not only "to do" or "make" in general but "to perform ritual acts." The next verse explains further what renunciation means, and it does so in terms of the ritual tradition:

2. What people call renunciation
   is really liturgical discipline,
   For a man acquires no discipline whatever
   without detaching himself from the purpose of the ritual.

The text is again quite clear, and I found it difficult to make the translation any clearer without making the lines too long. The text simply states that we cannot become renouncers or ascetics (*saṃnyāsins*) or disciplined men (*yogins*) of any sort without prior involvement in ritual. Accordingly, Śaṅkara comments that *karmayoga* (the discipline of ritual action) leads the practitioner to *dhyānayoga* (the discipline of meditation). Neither he nor Rāmānuja had to belabor the point, although Rāmānuja is convinced that the devotee never "overcomes" the ritual but should continue it even after reaching the pinnacle of meditation.

Many a modern reader may have his difficulties with this, which all go back to the unfamiliarity in his conscious life with anything cultic. How can renunciation really be liturgical discipline? What do the two have to do with each other? And how should detaching oneself from the purpose of the ritual lead to discipline? The verse is one of the more difficult ones for us to translate meaningfully. Nevertheless, I believe that my version can be taken at face value. Granted that every translation is only a pale shadow of the original, I think my translation here has some of the simplicity of the original. The word *saṃkalpa* is generally translated as "purpose." That is correct, but it is essential to keep in mind that it is in the first place the purpose *of the ritual*. The term occurs significantly in the ritual tradition. L. Renou, in his *Vocabulaire du rituel védique*[31] defines *saṃkalpa* as "intention annoncée par le *yajamāna* d'exécuter un sacrifice" (the stated purpose of a sacrificer to perform a sacrifice). This stated purpose has its natural place at the beginning of a ritual; it is an official announcement: I am going to perform such and such a sacrifice. The ritual is man's true involvement in the universe. Without such real involvement, it makes no sense to think of him as really giving up, renouncing anything. The officially stated purpose confirms this involvement. He is not asked to abandon the ritual (Rāmānuja insists on this point throughout his commentary), but he should be able to detach himself from it. Thus the verse makes quite explicit what is said in verse 1 and in various other places in the Gītā: one should perform the required cultic acts without pinning one's faith upon the results. The verse actually means what it says:

> What people call renunciation
> is really liturgical discipline,
> For a man acquires no discipline whatever
> without detaching himself from the purpose of the ritual.

Throughout the text, *karman* is a positive notion. It differs sharply from *karman* in Buddhism, where it becomes the inevitable law governing the infinity of existences, opposing the liberation one should strive for. It could be argued that Arjuna finds himself close to Buddhism in his complaints at the beginning of the Gītā and lays out what seems a suitable counterposition to the *dharma-varṇa* system of Hindu tradition. If it is not called Buddhist, it seems implicitly Buddhist in that Arjuna, by abstaining from his duty as a warrior, thinks he opts for a "higher" *dharma* than the tradition calls for.

> And he concluded: "I shall not fight!"
> Then he was silent. [2.9]

[31]Paris: Klincksieck, 1954.

An absolute contrast between tradition-sanctioned activity and an ultimate purpose of life beyond activity is suggested. A good deal of the ensuing instruction intends to set Arjuna right on this point.

Ritualism and the question of Vedic authority are interwoven. Among my learned friends, one who is unwilling to grant the importance of ritual in the text also wants to play down the Bhagavadgītā's concern for *śruti*, that is, the Vedic scriptures; his views are shared by many. However, the crucial verses under discussion (2.42—47; 9.20—21) in this matter point to the poet's distaste for men obsessed with ritual or who unduly cling to ritual, rather than for ritual. These thoughts are in line with the well-known and recurrent advice that one should never anticipate the results of rituals and never act as if sacrificers were entitled to divine gifts or guarantees, for all this would amount to a wrong invocation of Vedic authority. If we can speak of hostility on the part of the author, it is hostility toward certain ritualists and their speculations.

Dharma is a transparent term in most instances. Translators have understood it as "duty," "law," "traditional rules," "(right) tradition," and "religion," and I have not deviated from these specific interpretations. "Hinduism" is the name outsiders assigned to the entire collection of Indian religious customs and institutions, and it is interesting to recall again that from within Hinduism the only name that qualifies to sum up this collection is *sanātanadharma*, the eternal *dharma*.

The most disputed and difficult passage in which the term *dharma* occurs in the Bhagavadgītā is 18.66. This is where Kṛṣṇa invites his pupil to leave or abandon all *dharmas* and to go for refuge to him alone. There is no doubt that the context wants us to understand that we are at the high point of the Gītā's teachings. In the following verses Kṛṣṇa speaks about their secret nature and about the "highest mystery" for his worshipers. How should we interpret "all *dharmas*" that are to be abandoned here? It is possible to think again of duties (Edgerton and others). It is also possible to broaden our understanding a bit and think of all rules (*règles*, says Sénart). In either case, the implication is that commonly accepted coherences and norms of life are somehow transcended.

At first sight, the old glosses by Śaṅkara and Rāmānuja seem to add to the confusion. Śaṅkara claims that one should abandon both *dharma* and its opposite, *adharma*. Thus he seems to understand the word *dharma* in the text as something exceedingly flexible: it refers to the right duty as well as the mistaken duty. Rāmānuja's interpretation is more complex, but his view is principally—and predictably—that all religious forms and acts (of *karman*, *jñana*, and *bhakti*) leading to God should be continued. He also states that nonessential rites, and, of course, obsessions with the results and agency of religious acts should be abandoned. Śaṅkara and Rāmānuja are obviously not in agreement, but both come out with interpretations assigning a wide spectrum of meaning to the *dharmas* in the text—too wide to be comfortably covered by any of our terms: duty, law, and the rest.

Something else should be added. While the Bhagavadgītā never clearly addresses a specific school of thought, it is clear from the many subjects treated that the writer was familiar with many discussions. Proof in detail and concerning "influences" is lacking in each instance, but the cumulation of subjects and vocabulary makes it hard to see it otherwise. The author was familiar with early *sāṃkhya* ideas and *yoga* techniques, but—as said before—it is not only possible but virtually certain that he was familiar with Buddhist patterns of thought. *Sāṃkhya, yoga,* and Buddhism are all part of a pan-Indian pattern; all employ endeavors to penetrate or transcend the appearances of the world toward a reality beyond them. This does not necessarily mean that the reality we perceive now is unreal, but the freedom that is the only proper goal of man is situated beyond those appearances. It so happens that one of the senses in which Buddhism uses the word *dharma* (*dhamma* in Pāli) refers to the coherences present in the phenomenal world, although that world is obviously not the "ultimate reality" the Buddhist monk strives for.[32]

Now, in the present context of Bhagavadgītā 18.66 an "influence" from Buddhism is as difficult to demonstrate with irrefutable proofs as anywhere else in the text. Nevertheless, the idea of coherences in things seen, thought, and done, that are given, and can even be important—but never of ultimate importance—in our phenomenal world is part of the early, pan-Indian tradition, including *sāṃkhya*, *yoga*, and the Buddha's teachings. Rather than translate the word *dharmas* in our verse once more in too confined a manner that does not quite fit, I decided for "appearances." Of course, this decision will not close the debate. All discussions induced by our verse on

[32]See Surendranath Dasgupta, *A History of Indian Philosophy*, Vol. I (Cambridge: University Press, 1951), p. 84, and E. J. Thomas, *The History of Buddhist Thought* (London: Routledge, 1959; first print 1933), passim.

the question whether or not *adharma* or *dharma* was really meant, or both, or the question whether *dharma* here should be understood exclusively in a ritual sense or in a more general legal or moral sense, are of significance. However—the point is almost too obvious to make—Śaṅkara and Rāmānuja did agree on one point: that the relationship between Arjuna and God, or man's ultimate destiny was the crucial issue in the context. For the translator that should be an extra stimulus to try out a "catholic," all-encompassing translation which, like the original, will allow various interpretations.

A brief remark will suffice on the subject of proper names. With proper names and standard epithets I have not made many attempts at translation. When I did translate any, it was not for erudite reasons, but either to make the translation flow better, or to meet non-Sanskritists more than halfway. After all, no matter how much Indologists may deplore it, names from Indian legends and myths are not as widely known among us as those from Greek mythology. Thus in chapter 10, in the chant of Kṛṣṇa's many "I am . . ." statements, I translated

> Know me among horses as charger of Indra. . . . Among elephants as the elephant of Indra. . . . Of weapons, I am Indra's thunderbolt. . . . Regarding procreation, I am the God of Love. . . . Of serpents, I am Vāsuki [their prince]. . . . I am the primeval watersnake. . . . [10.27—29]

Reading becomes easier for nonspecialists, and it will be obvious at once to Sanskritists that the descriptions refer to Uccaiḥśravas, Airāvata, Indra's *vajra*, Kandarpa, Vāsuki, and Ananta. In some instances (as in this passage with Vāsuki), I have added elucidations in square brackets. These elucidations, I believe, can be read without breaking the flow of the translation. The square brackets will avoid confusion for the student who turns to the text.

The Confrontation of Languages

Two things are indispensable for translating religious documents. It is obvious that knowledge of the text in its tradition is required. But a second requirement is knowledge of the religious heritage we ourselves carry in our hearts; it is knowledge of the religious meanings and overtones of terms we have to choose from in our renderings. Such knowledge is indeed necessary if we do not want to confuse the text we translate with half-digested clichés. In the framework of cultic expressions we just discussed, it should be clear that a word meaning "sacrifice" cannot be rendered as "worship." An elementary sensitivity to our own language traditions tells us in this case that sacrifice can be a form of worship, but that worship hardly ever includes the bringing of a sacrifice.

"Activity" in the Bhagavadgītā, as in the entire Vedic-Brahmanic tradition it inherited, can best be seen as a series of concentric circles. The center is the paradigmatic detached activity of God Himself. He says (in 3.22, 23):

> There is nothing at all I need to do
> in the worlds, heaven, air, and earth.
> There is nothing I need that I do not have.
> And yet I am engaged in work.
>
> For if I did not engage in action,
> tirelessly,
> People everywhere
> would follow my example.

And in 4.13, 14

> I brought forth the four great divisions of men
> according to their qualities and rituals.
> Although I made all this,
> know that I never act at all.
>
> Actions do not pollute me;
> desire for results is unknown to me.
> He who understands me thus
> is not ensnared by ritual acts.

The circle around this center, God, is the ritual of men, each group characterized by its function: the spiritual leaders (*brāhmaṇas*); the defenders of society (*kṣatriyas*); the people producing the wealth on which society rests (*vaiśyas*); and the servant class (*śūdras*).

The "ordinary," "worldly" activity of people makes up the next circle. It is obviously different from the prescribed, ritual acts. Nevertheless, the "ordinary" tasks of man derive from the cultic duty, and the Sanskrit language makes it possible to extend the discussion from one to the other smoothly. The Gītā, after all, is that episode in the great epic in which Arjuna, the warrior, commences with his doubts as to his "ordinary" duty; and the episode ends—after long instruction concerning ritual, renunciation, meditation, bodily yoga-techniques, love, and worship of God—with Arjuna taking up arms and performing his duty as a warrior.

An elaborate essay on the Bhagavadgītā cannot take the place of the reader's curiosity and exploratory spirit. In 2.50 we are told in the translation that "discipline is skill in works and rites." What are "works" and "rites"? All the book can do is invite the reader to the English guide. There both "work" and "rite" lead to *karman*, and the reader can find in the concordance that the chapter he had been reading uses the same word in verses 47 (rituals), 48 (rites), 51—cultic works). Thus a beginning is made in understanding the text.

We might speak of a radiation from divine activity to other activities farther and farther toward the fringes of the world. Indeed, we do have to select our words carefully in the work of translating, for the basic ideas of the Indian text and of the language in our own religious heritage hardly ever cover each other completely. The imagery of concentric circles or radiation toward the fringes is helpful as a reminder that the Indian world does not make the sort of radical separation between "the sacred" and "the profane" that we usually take for granted. The divine sphere and the human sphere are not contrasted after the manner of the biblical imagery of potter and pot (Isa. 45.9; Jer. 18.19).

Specialists in the Bible are quick to point out that the biblical languages do not use the philosophical notions"transcendent" and "immanent." However, the theological traditions that took the biblical world as their starting point unanimously used the word "transcendent" in discussing the doctrine of God, they were not stopped by the fact that this word came from classical, pagan philosophical terminology. And certainly, the word "transcendent" fits the "unpredictability" of God in the biblical accounts. He does not act in conformance with any worldly calculations and forecasts. At the same time, however, his acts concern the world, take place in the world, and hence there is some ground to speak of God's "immanence" as well, although it would seem logically excluded by his "transcendence."

Would it be extravagant to urge theologians and philosophers in the West who think about religious issues to listen carefully to Indian words, to look at Indian imageries, and to try out Indian conceptions? The genius of Christianity is to turn toward the world around it, not to turn in toward itself for fear of becoming polluted. The commandment to go and make disciples of all the heathen, to baptize all nations, is part of the very structure of Christianity.[33] Christianity "pushed to the extreme the formula of proselytism and turned resolutely toward the Gentiles, substituting a circumcision of the heart for circumcision of the flesh."[34] The commandment is not an order to subjugate the world, but rather to be involved in it. From the beginning the gospel needed *translation*, because this involvement concerned the hearts of people, the source of human speech, of all confession. Therefore, discussions in Greek and Latin terms became necessary and natural, for those languages were part of the world that was to be met. Similarly, in our world, the vocabulary, the teachings, the heart of Indian traditions should not be ignored, but received, encountered, reflected on.

No reader will find that Sanskrit terms suddenly fill the gaps hitherto unfilled in his spiritual or intellectual articulation. But then, we shall do well to remember that in the past, terms like *transcendence, immanence,* and a great many others of Latin or Greek origin (absoluteness, aseity, mediator, eternity, trinity, adiaphora, apokatastasis, synergia) were not handed to anyone on a silver platter. The confrontation with Sanskrit terms will often demand a struggle. This struggle will have a special fascination, for most of the Indian terms arise out of religious experience and out of the actual practice of spiritual discipline, while most of the technical theological, religious, and philosophical terms the West inherited from our classics *nolens volens* by comparison are quite abstract.

Sometimes, we should economize on the use of terms that have acquired specific meanings in Jewish and Christian traditions. Two words I have avoided consistently are *sin* and *faith*. They figure heavily in most Gītā translations, but they are blatant examples of the erosion in our religious articulateness. Sin and faith are not only terms discussed extensively by Western theologians but also embedded in the vocabulary of laymen. Whatever variety in interpretation may exist through the ages in Judaism and Christianity, faith always has to do with the divinely inspired certainty of man's salvation, sin with the inconceivable, more-than-human force that tempts man to turn away from his Lord.

[33]Matthew 28.19.

[34]Henry Duméry, *Phenomenology and Religion* (Berkeley, Los Angeles, and London: University of California Press, 1975), p. 67.

Strangely, the erosion of religious terminology, the ignorance of religious meanings, has made it possible not only for college freshmen but even for specialists in historical studies in our time to use the words *faith* and *religion* as if they were synonyms.[35] Perhaps, after a period of Western colonialism, including superiority feelings of Western Christians, some intellectuals would wish to embrace a new fad of proving that nothing is unique in Western religion. But such fads have no role in serious work on religious documents. Sloppy misstating of our own spiritual traditions leads inevitably to a misunderstanding of others.

The Sanskrit word *śraddhā*, which is the word most often translated as "faith," is usually much more down-to-earth than the notion of faith, *Glaube, foi, fides* in the discussions of Saint Augustine, Pelagius, and Luther. *Śraddhā* is almost always trust in general, as a necessary item in the human psyche. It is like the confidence with which a man who has broken his leg entrusts himself to a surgeon. It is important, but not "ultimate" in the sense of "faith" for Luther and others. Hence Arjuna, perfectly naturally, can ask Kṛṣṇa (in 6.37):

> If a man is full of trust, yet makes no effort,
> and his mind strays from discipline,
> And he achieves no enduring success—
> where does he end up, Kṛṣṇa?

Whatever may be said about the history of religion in India (and one might argue that everything fits into it somewhere and sometime), one could not conceive of a *sola fide* argument on the basis of the Gītā.

The crucial notion of *bhakti* has no equivalent in our Western languages. It comes close to devotion, love, offer of love, or love and worship in one. I have translated the term accordingly, depending on the context. "Love" may seem the most concrete experience in our religious tradition, but the term *love* lacks the stylization, the self-evident accompanying liturgical form, that surrounds it in Indian religion. For that reason, I preferred the double expression "love and worship," for instance in 18.68, 69:

[35]An example is the collection of scholarly treatises on the major religions of the world edited by R. C. Zaehner with the title *The Concise Encyclopedia of Living Faiths* (New York: Hawthorn Books, 1959).

Whoever in supreme love and worship for me.
  makes the highest mystery known
Among my worshipers
  shall certainly come to me
No one renders me service
  more precious than this man's.

The word *pūjā* does not occur in the Bhagavadgītā. It is the term comprising all devout forms of worship, in the temple and at home. The *idea* of *pūjā*, however, is virtually identical with *bhakti* in some lines:

When you offer with love a leaf,
  a flower, or water to me,
I accept that offer of love
  from the giver who gives himself. [9.26]

Terms bearing on ritual have been the most neglected by translators of Sanskrit texts. The problem of languages confronting each other here takes on the dimensions of caricature. Western scholars and laymen alike developed an image of themselves as dynamic, full of responsibility for their fellowmen, morally concerned. By contrast, "the Eastern mind" was seen as not active, but passive, or meditative, or impervious to ethical concerns, or oblivious to the needs of a fellow man, and in general, uninterested in activity. Whether this sort of cartoon, this ludicrous dichotomy of the world had its strongest impetus in Hegel's description of the Oriental nations, or in any other particular author, is not as important as the fact that its development was another by-product of nineteenth-century Western expansionism, political and religious.

As late as 1935, Albert Schweitzer published his *Indian Thought and Its Development*,[36] in which the thesis is precisely this: that what is lacking in Hinduism is a genuine sense of moral concern and activity. In popular textbooks related ideas have appeared throughout our century. R. E. Hume, to whom we owe the best translation of the principal Upaniṣads,[37] also published a general work, *The World's Living Religions*.[38] In this simplistic book, the treatment of

[36]Published in English in 1936; Boston: Beacon, 1957.

[37]*The Thirteen Principal Upanishads* (London: Oxford University Press, 1931 [2d. rev. ed.]).

[38]First published in 1924, revised in 1959. I have before me the edition of 1959 containing the author's Preface to the fourteenth (!) printing (New York: Scribner).

every religion concludes with a list of pros and cons. Among the points against Hinduism we find:

> No personal character or moral responsibility in the Supreme Being. . . .
>
> No universal moral standard, except social distinctions. No possible improvement in a person's social status, except after death. No possible improvement in the general arrangements of society, except in the teachings of a few unheeded reformers. The excessive general ceremonialism of worship, or else the extreme of empty meditation.[39]

The problem is: How are we to do justice to a religious tradition that is *dynamic* in structure with the help of an ideology that we have inherited which is comparatively static, conceptualistic, and disinclined to see anything dynamic in an archaic culture? The general studies of early and classical India which we have are not very helpful, for they do not quite know what to make of ritual. Even though serious students of man no longer use terms like "primitive mentality" to explain customs of the ancients, sacred acts continue to be more perplexing to our understanding than do myths and religious symbols.[40] Our perplexedness before religious acts no doubt accounts for the tenacity of Sir James Frazer's hypothesis of magic as the soil from which religion and science derived their nourishment.[41] Students of Indian ritual generally associated ritual with magical manipulation and have generally relegated the subject

[39]P. 42.

[40]See, e.g., the following passages to realize how little progress has been made in understanding Vedic and Brahmanic ritual: Hermann Oldenberg, *Die Religion des Veda* (Berlin, 1894), pp. 302–317; A. Hillebrandt, *Ritual-Litteratur. Vedische Opfer und Zauber* (Strassburg, 1897), pp. 1–2, 167–168; A. B. Keith, *The Religion and Philosophy of the Veda and Upanishads* (Cambridge, Mass.: Harvard University Press, 1925), chap. 18 and passim; Vincent Smith, *The Oxford History of India*, 3d ed. rev. by Sir Mortimer Wheeler, A. L. Basham, et al. (Oxford: Clarendon Press, 1958), p. 47; Franklin Edgerton, *The Beginnings of Indian Philosophy* (Cambridge: Harvard University Press, 1965), p. 28; R. C. Zaehner, *Hindu Scriptures* (London: Dent, 1966), p. v.

I do not suggest that all work on Indian ritual, or on cult in general, is worthless. Hillebrandt is still invaluable. See also J. C. Heesterman, *The Ancient Indian Royal Consecration* ('s Gravenhage: Mouton, 1957), and its bibliography (p. 228). A recent magnificent study on the problem of sacrifice, a history of interpretations and a promising beginning to a solid interpretation is Richard D. Hecht, *Sacrifice, Comparative Study and Interpretation* (Ph.D. diss. University of California, Los Angeles, 1976).

[41]See for a summary and critique of Frazer's views J. de Vries, *Perspectives in the History of Religions* (Berkeley, Los Angeles, London: University of California Press, 1977), chap. 22.

to mankind's dim past, left behind by the evolution of Indian culture.

A reader who is willing to grant that the Bhagavadgītā contains teachings of great importance may take the opportunity of a renewed study of the text to rectify traditional errors concerning ritual in early Hinduism. The vocabulary itself of the text cannot be spiritualized away. A quick look in the index at the many instances of the terms *yajña* (sacrifice) and *karma* (ritual, act) and their compounds makes clear that we cannot relegate cultic matters to an inaccessible prehistory of man. In addition, many other terms function as they do because of the ritual structures in Hinduism. No act is peripheral. All acts have results. Results can be good, *puṇya* (a word that occurs in the Gītā in the compounds *puṇyakarman* or *puṇyakṛt*, meritorious). Results can also be negative: *kilbiṣa*, "demerit." All evil, *pāpa*, is a matter of acting, doing, performing. It is therefore untranslatable as "sin."

Sin in the mainstream of Christian tradition cannot cover the Hindu terms for evil. In Christian tradition sin relates to the very condition of man. It is, as a writer of a very influential Christian theological work in this century has written:

> that by which man as we know him is defined, for we know nothing of sinless men. . . . Particular sins do not alter the status of a man; they merely show how heavily the general dominion of sin presses upon him.[42]

The history of Christian thought that has had such an impact on our vocabulary has by and large been theoretically inclined; it has tended to go into an ontological direction. By contrast, the Indian emphasis in teaching has been much more practical. *Pāpa* is above all the evil of an evil*doer*. Pāpa refers to an evil that is committed, or to something that clings to one as a result of an evil *act*. (Similarly, the word *kilbiṣa* means in the main a harmful or faulty act committed, or the resulting stain on the evildoer.) Its fundamental function is not to describe man's nature, and therefore it is less than correct to translate the word as *sin*.

I should also say that quite often I have felt at ease in using words with a biblical ring when they rendered this or that verse in the Gītā most perfectly. I have used the word *creature* several times, though

[42]Karl Barth, *The Epistle to the Romans* (London: Oxford University Press, 1972; trans. from the 6th rev. ed. [orig. ed. 1918]), p. 167.

strictly speaking the Gītā knows only "beings" (*bhūtas*), as do all Hindu texts. The many beings emerge, or are born, rather than being created after the manner of Adam and Eve. However, in many passages the manifoldness or transitoriness or lowliness or finiteness of those many beings is expressed so poignantly that our word *creature* seems more appropriate than the lofty *being*.

The words *God* and *Lord* I have also used freely. Not only are these words general by nature, but they may have the advantage at times that specific associations with the biblical religions have become vague. I have occasionally seen fit to use the word God not only for Viṣṇu but also for *brahman* (n.), the "supreme principle."

I realize that interpreting our own language can easily become a matter of controversy. Nevertheless, here again the translator cannot wait until all hermeneutical disputations have led to universally acceptable conclusions. I decided that the word *God* as we use it nowadays, no matter how vaguely, still refers to whatever is felt as highest. The loosening of conscious ties with Christianity and Judaism, which has increased the undefined quality in the word, makes it a perfect translation for *brahman* in some verses.

The word *brahman* (n.) remains poly-interpretable, but that does not imply ambiguity or obscurity. It is a religious symbol, and Professor Gonda has pointed out that in its earliest attested use, in the Vedas, it relates especially to the power inherent in the *mantras*, the Vedic verses.[43] The word never separates itself completely from this earlier significance, and I have tried to be as careful as possible in selecting terms to translate it. I think I am justified in having used the word *God* for *brahman* in several verses where it occurs by itself (4.24, 32; 5.6, 10, 19; 6.38; 8.24; 10.12; 13.12), and also in rendering some compounds with *brahman*: *brahmavid*, "knower of God" (5.20; see also 8.24); and *brahmanirvāna*, "the freedom that is God's" (2.72; 5.24, 25; see also 5.26). In other instances, however, I have used more "neutral" terms: the Divine, godhead, the Eternal. In three cases (7.29; 8.1, 3) where the context encouraged it, I chose as translation "the divine secret." This choice is in harmony not only with the early use pointing to the power in the *mantras* but also with the Upaniṣadic discussions which are continued in the Gītā concerning "the highest" and the instruction a pupil receives from his *guru*, his spiritual preceptor, concerning it.

[43]J. Gonda, *Die Religionen Indiens* (Stuttgart: Kohlhammer, 1960), I, 32.

Perhaps someone will cringe when I translate *Vedas* as "Scriptures" or "sacred texts." However, the translation makes sense. "The scriptures" are authoritative, the only writings beyond questioning; that is the manner the word is used among us, and not only in the "Bible belt." Of course, there are differences between the Indian conception of the Vedas and our term, and they will continue to exist, but I do not think they are sufficient to prevent us from using our term in translating. In terms of comparative history, the Vedas are far more authoritative and comprehensive than other sacred scriptures: they tell us things that we have no other way of knowing, such as what sacrifices to perform and how.

But how to deal with the word *Vedānta*? *Vedānta* is also Veda; it is another name for the Upaniṣads, the concluding part of the Vedic texts. No doubt, this is in the poet's mind in Bhagavadgītā 15.15. In translating the verse, however, another consideration enters also. The Veda or the Vedas are always named as *the* scriptural authority. Vedānta, on the other hand, while referring to the Upaniṣads, refers at the same time to the study of the essence of *śruti*, the Vedic revelation. Hence Vedānta next to completion of the Vedas means also the purpose of vedic study. The consequences are clear: not only is it possible to interpret the word *vedāntakṛt* in 15.15 as "I have established their [the Scriptures'] purpose," but in the context it is the obvious sense. Immediately before, in the same verse, we read: "From me come knowledge of tradition, wisdom, and reasoning. I am the object of all the scriptures," and thus the verse concludes, quite consistently with its theme: "I am the knower of the Scriptures. I have established their purpose."

There is one single word that I have left untranslated. It is the ancient sacred syllable of the Vedic tradition, *Om*. Fortunately, the text of the Gītā using the term is very helpful in explaining it. In chapter 8 we are instructed about the man who meditates and studies Scripture properly and who controls himself. Verse 13 states:

> He goes to the highest goal
>   who leaves the body,
> Meditating on me, saying the divine secret,
>   one syllable, OM.

The other verses mentioning the syllable are equally helpful (17.23, 24; 9.17). Similarly, the ancient expression *"om tat sat,"* introduced in 17.23 is immediately elucidated in subsequent stanzas.

In view of fashions that have become popular in the West, I may point to two more problems: yoga, and the problem of class and caste. The term *yoga* does not merely refer to bodily techniques or even mental techniques to attain freedom. Yoga in principle is any manner of attaining any goal and hence in our text we see a wide variety of meanings. In 13.24 the expression *sāṃkhyena yogena* occurs, which simply means "through reason," or "by way of reason." The word *discipline*, although it is quite general, which was used quite consistently by Edgerton in his translation, covers the meaning in many verses. The word *yoga* can also be used to refer to the way of ritual or liturgical discipline (6.2). It even refers to God's methods, his "mystic power" (as in 10.18). Arjuna begs the Lord:

> Tell me more, and in detail,
> of your mystic power, and mighty forms,
> For I cannot listen enough, o Stirrer of Men,
> to your immortal word.

The problem of class and caste can be summarized in a few words. Virtually all translators of Sanskrit texts have translated *varṇa* as "caste." A far more accurate translation is "class," while "caste" is best reserved for *jāti*, literally "birth." The Indian texts do not confuse the two, and it is high time we stopped the confusion also. There are only three (or, including the "servants," four) classes that together make up society as a totality. The number of castes, however, is virtually limitless. They are the concrete groups in society, divided from one another by birth (as the word *jāti* itself indicates), and by profession, customs, rights, privileges, and obligations. The meaning of the word *jāti*, caste, is always determined by its empirical reference to groups in society. The *varṇas* relate in the first place to the *ideal* divisions of society as a whole.

In the first chapter of the Gītā, Arjuna worries about the possible results of the internecine war about to ensue. The climax of his worries evokes the most down-to-earth catastrophes (verse 43):

> The crimes of those who destroy the race
> cause promiscuity;
> They overturn the rules governing caste
> and the eternal family traditions.

In the Sanskrit text the order is obvious: the illegitimate mixture of *varṇas* is the basic promiscuity; the result in the empirical world of human existence will be the destruction of the rules of *jāti*, caste.

The ideal meaning for society as a whole of the concept of *varṇa* is clear from a verse such as 4.13. God speaks of the world as he brought it forth, his *cāturvarṇya* (literally, "what has four *varṇas*"):

> I brought forth the four great divisions of men
> according to their qualities and rituals.

This world at its birth is "the ideal structure" of the cosmos. It is elaborated and proliferated in man's empirical reality, with its subgroups and castes, families, and traditions. Thus, class and caste are related to each other, even complementary, but never identical.[44]

Meditation and Redundance

The Bhagavadgītā is officially *smṛti*, a part of the venerable tradition; it is not *śruti*, Revelation, as are only the Vedas. However, the text takes up and continues teachings found in the Upaniṣads, the most widely memorized and cherished texts of the Vedas. Like the Upaniṣads, the Bhagavadgītā has always been a text of meditation in India. Scholarly exposition should not obscure this fact. Rather, it should lead to a rendering that makes meditation possible. This is a goal that I have had in mind with this work.

The Gītā's beauty is not at once obvious to the reader who was not nurtured in Hinduism. The reader without a background in Sanskrit and its literary styles may become aware of a certain redundancy. By the time he reaches chapter 12 and reads

> I love my devotee—the unperturbed
> onlooker, carefree, pure, intelligent,
> Able to give up
> all he undertakes.
> I love that man of devotion who shows
> neither exhilaration nor disgust,
> Neither regret nor desire, and who can
> give up good as well as evil things.

he will remember earlier statements, admonishments, praises, given in much the same terms in the text.

[44]See Kees W. Bolle, "The Idea of Mankind in Indian Thought," in W. W. Wagar, ed., *History and the Idea of Mankind* (Albuquerque: University of New Mexico Press, 1971), pp. 3–26; "Views of Class, Caste, and Mankind," *Studia Missionalia*, XIX (1970), 165–175.

And in chapter 11, Arjuna's vision of God, the reader may have registered a redundancy of a rather different kind: the abundant repetition of God's powers and acts in an ecstatic description. Redundancies can be pruned a bit in translation, but they cannot be removed. They belong to the meditational function of the book.

In comparison with the Sanskrit of the Gītā, the English language is a puritanical straitjacket. It makes some pruning inevitable, for it does not allow for constant superlatives. But the activity of meditation requires repetitions with only slight variations in emphasis and point of view. And as to the superabundant descriptions of Arjuna's visions in chapter 11, their redundancies—if that is truly what they are—overwhelm the reader and create a dreamlike trance, setting the meditative faculty in motion.

The redundancy has a purpose, exactly because it is a matter of "rubbing things in" and therefore repeating them. Wisdom is not something to be *attained* at a certain moment. It is not bestowed on Arjuna like an academic degree. It is a thing practiced continually. And the good pupil, Arjuna, wants to be exposed to it continually. A verse I have quoted before and which I like most in the Gītā is the one in chapter 10 where Arjuna addresses Kṛṣṇa, after having been taught concerning the highest:

> Tell me more, and in detail
>   of your mystic power and mighty forms,
> For I cannot listen enough, o Stirrer of Men,
>   to your immortal word.

Note on the Text

The present work is based on the critical edition established by S. K. Belvalkar (Poona, 1947). However, one exception was made for Bhagavadgītā 1.10. This verse in the critical edition reads:

> aparyāptaṃ tad asmākam
>   balam Bhīṣmābhirakṣitam
> paryāptaṃ tv idam eteṣām
>   balaṃ Bhīmābhirakṣitam.

The most obvious difficulty with this version is that it suggests that the Pāndava army is larger in size than the Kaurava army, while we know from the rest of the Mahābhārata that the reverse was true. Also syntactically the pronouns *tad* (that) and *idam*

Bibliography

Āpte, V. G. *Rāmānuja's Gītābhāṣya, edited with the Tātparyacandrikā of Veṅkatanāṭha*. Bombay: Ānandāśram Press, 1923 [Ānandāśrama Sanskrit Series, vol. 92.]

———. *Śaṅkara's Gītābhāṣya, with Ánandagiri's Gloss*. Bombay: Ānandāśrama Press, 1936. [Ānandāśrama Sanskrit Series, vol. 34, 3d. ed.]

Barnett, L. D. *Bhagavadgītā, The Lord's Song*. London, 1905. Reprinted in Nicol MacNicol, ed. *Hindu Scriptures*. London: Dent, 1963 [Everyman's Library, no. 944], pp. 223–287.

Arnold, Sir Edwin, *The Song Celestial*. London, 1885. Reprinted in Vol. II of Edgerton, *The Bhagavad Gītā*.

Belvalkar, Shripad Krishna. ed. *The Bhīṣmaparvan, being the Sixth book of the Mahābhārata, the Great Epic of India, for the first time critically edited*. Poona: Bhandarkar Oriental Research Institute, 1947.

van Buitenen, J. A. B. "A Contribution to the Critical Edition of the Bhagavadgītā," *Journal of the American* Oriental Society, 85 (1965), 99–109.

van Buitenen, J. A. B. *Rāmānuja on the Bhagavadgītā. A Condensed Rendering of his Gītābhāṣya, with Copious Notes and an Introduction*. Delhi: Motilal Banarsidass, 1968 (orig. 1953).

Dasgupta, Surendranath. *A History of Indian Philosophy*, vols. II and III. Cambridge: University Press, 1952 (orig. 1932, 1940).

Deussen, Paul. *Der Gesang des Heiligen, eine philosophische Episode des Mahābhāratam, aus dem Sanskrit übersetzt*. Leipzig: Brockhaus, 1911.

Edgerton, Franklin. *The Bhagavad Gītā, Translated and Interpreted*. 2 vols. Cambridge, Mass.: Harvard University Press, 1946. [Harvard Oriental Series, vols. 38, 39.]

Eliade, Mircea. *Yoga, Immortality and Freedom*. New York: Pantheon, 1958. [Bollingen Series, Vol. LVI.]

Garbe, Richard. *Die Bhagavadgītā aus dem Sanskrit übersetzt, mit einer Einleitung über ihre ursprüngliche Gestalt, ihre Lehren und ihr Alter*. Leipzig: H. Haessel Verlag, 1905.

Gonda, J. *Notes on Brahman*. Utrecht: Oosthoek, 1950.

———. *Die Religionen Indiens:* Vol. I, *Veda und älterer Hinduismus;* Vol. II, *Der jüngere Hinduismus*. Stuttgart: Kohlhammer, 1960–1963. [Die Religionen der Menschheit, vols. 11–12.]

———. "Some Notes on the Study of Ancient Indian Religious Terminology." *History of Religions*, Vol. I (1962).

Hill, W. D. P. *The Bhagavadgītā*. London: Oxford University Press, 1928.

Hume, R. E. *The Thirteen Principal Upanishads, Translated from the Sanskrit, with an Outline of the Philosophy of the Upanishads*. 2d rev. ed. London: Oxford University Press, 1931 (orig. 1921).

Jacob, Colonel J. A. *A Concordance to the Principal Upanishads and the Bhagavadgītā*. Delhi: Motilal Banarsidass, 1963 (orig. 1891).

Lamotte, Etienne. *Notes sur la Bhagavadgītā*. Paris: Geuthner, 1929.

Mascaró, Juan. *The Bhagavad Gita, Translated from the Sanskrit with an Introduction*. Baltimore: Penguin, 1962.

Otto, Rudolf. *Die Lehr-Traktate der Bhagavad-Gītā*. Tübingen: Mohr, 1935.

———. *Die Urgestalt der Bhagavad-Gītā*. Tübingen: Mohr, 1934.

Radhakrishnan, S. *The Bhagavadgītā, with an Introductory Essay, Sanskrit Text, English Translation and Notes*. New York: Harper, 1973 (orig. 1948).

Renou, L. "Sur la notion de 'Brahman,' " *Journal Asiatique* (1949).

———. *Vocabulaire du rituel védique*. Paris: Klincksieck, 1954.

Renou L., and J. Filliozat, *L'Inde Classique*. Vol. I. Paris: Payot, 1947.

Roy, Anilbaran. *The Gita, with Text, Translation and Notes, Compiled from Aurobindo's Essays on the Gita*. Pondicherry: Sri Aurobindo Ashram, 1954.

Sastry, A. Mahadeva. *The Bhagavad-Gita, with the Commentary of Sri Sankaracharya, translated from Sanskrit into English*. Madras: V. Ramaswamy Sastrulu and Sons, 1972 (orig. 1897).

Sénart, Emile. *La Bhagavad-Gîtâ traduite du Sanskrit*. 2d ed., with the text. Paris: Société d'édition "Les Belles Lettres," 1944 (orig. 1922).

Stanford, Ann. *The Bhagavad Gita, A New Verse Translation*. New York: Herder and Herder, 1970.

Telang, K. T. *The Bhagavadgītā with the Sanatsujātīya and the Anugītā*. Delhi: Motilal Banarsidass, 1965 (orig. 1882). [Sacred Books of the East, vol. 8.]

Zaehner, R. C. *The Bhagavad-Gītā, with a Commentary based on the Original Sources*. London: Oxford University Press, 1969.

Indices

The following two indices, the Sanskrit Concordance and the English Guide to the Concordance, have been compiled primarily for the use of readers without knowledge of Sanskrit. The Sanskrit index is more elaborate than the English one, but neither one is exhaustive. Only the words whose significance in the framework of the Gītā teachings seems obvious (and some that are not quite so obvious) have been included. The English Guide does not give equivalents of the English entries, but is only meant to lead the reader back to the Sanskrit Concordance. Thus, with the English translation as a starting point, the second index will make it easier to find cross references.

SANSKRIT CONCORDANCE TO THE BHAGAVADGĪTĀ AND GENERAL INDEX

Numbers refer to chapters and verses of the text. Numbers in square brackets [ ] refer to pages in Part II.

abhakta
  18.67 man who is devoid of . . . love
abhāva
  2.16 (nā 'bhāvo vidyate sataḥ) what is has no end
  10.4 [the] passing away of things
  See also bhāva
abhaya
  10.4 courage
  16.1 (abhayam . . . abhijātasya) a man born to . . . is brave . . .
  See also bhaya; bhayābhaya
abhijñā
  4.14 understand
  7.13, 25; 9.24; 18.55 recognize
abhikramanāśa
  2.40 (nehābhikramanāśo 'sti) in Discipline no observance is lost
abhirata
  18.45 engaged in
abhyāsa
  6.35; 12.10, 12; 18.36 training
  See also pūrvābhyāsa
  cf. svādhyāyābhyasana
abhyāsayoga
  12.9 training
abhyāsayogayukta
  8.8 practiced
abuddhi
  7.24 man without understanding
acalapratiṣṭha
  2.70 its equilibrium is undisturbed
ācārya
  1.2, 26 mentor
  1.3 Master!
  1.34 teacher
  13.7 spiritual guide
acetas
  3.32; 17.6 fool
  15.11 senseless man
acintya
  2.25 unthinkable
  12.3 passing beyond understanding
acintyarūpa
  8.9 Whom thought cannot fathom
acyuta
  1.21; 18.73 Unshakable One
  11.42 imperishable Lord
adharma
  1.40 chaos
  1.41 (adharmābhibhavāt . . .) such predominance of chaos leads to . . .
  4.7 unright
  18.31 what is prohibited
  18.32 what is wrong
  [243, 245]
adhibhūta
  8.1 what can be said of the principles of existence

8.4 . . . make for the principles of existence
See also sādhibhūtādhidaiva
[235]
adhidaiva
8.1 (adhidaivaṃ kim ucyate) what relates to the gods?
See also sādhibhūtādhidaiva
adhidaivata
8.4 (puruṣaś cādhidaivatam) man's spirit relates to the gods
[235]
adhiyajña
8.2 related to the sacrifice
8.4 (adhiyajño 'ham . . .) I Myself . . . relate to sacrifice
See also sādhiyajña; yajña
[235]
adhyātma
3.30 (adhyātmacetasā) directing your thought to the reality of your self
7.29 bearing on the self
8.1 (kim adhyātmam) what affects the self?
8.3 . . . affects the self
See also adhyātmanitya; adhyātmajñānanityatva
adhyātmacetas
3.30 directing your thought to the reality of your self
adhyātmajñānanityatva
13.11 . . . cultivate knowledge pertaining to the self . . .
adhyātmanitya
15.5 intent uninterruptedly on that which is Real
adhyātmasaṃjñita
11.1 (guhyam adhyātmasaṃjñitam) secret, concerning the self
adhyātmavidyā
10.32 (adhyātmavidyā vidyānām) [I am] that knowledge that affects the self
See also vid
ādideva
10.12 [divine being] who existed before the gods
11.38 the very first god
ādikartṛ
11.37 (garīyase brahmaṇo 'py ādikartre) you impelled even the creator
āditya
5.16 (singular) the sun
10.21; 11.6, 22 the Gods of Heaven
ādityavarṇa
8.9 whose luster is like the sun's
See also anekavarṇa; nānāvarṇakṛtin; varṇa
adṛṣṭapūrva
11.6 never seen before
11.45 what no one saw before
advaita [239]
adveṣṭṛ
12.13 (adveṣṭā sarvabhūtānām) accepting all creatures
agha
3.13 evil
aghāyu
3.16 of evil intent
agni [241]
ahaṃkāra
3.27 self-consciousness
7.4; 13.5 self-awareness
16.18 [they rely on their] ego
17.5 [deceitfulness and] ego [impel some men]
18.53 (ahaṃkāram . . . vimucya) no longer centered in his ego
18.58 (ahaṃkārāt . . .) centered in yourself and hence . . .
18.59 (yad ahaṃkāram āśritya) if . . . out of sheer self-centeredness
See also sāhaṃkāra
cf. anahaṃkāra; ahaṃkṛta; nirahaṃkāra (*see* nirmama)
ahaṃkṛta
18.17 (yasya nāhaṃkṛto bhāvaḥ) a man who is not ego-centered
ahorātravid
8.17 [he] truly knows day and night
See also vid
aiśvara
9.5 (yogam aiśvaram) sovereign technique
11.3 (te rūpam aiśvaram) your form as Lord
11.8 (yogam aiśvaram) absolute power
11.9 absolute
aiśvarya
See bhogaiśvarya-
aja
2.20, 21; 4.6; 7.25; 10.3 unborn
10.12 (ajaṃ vibhum) Lord without birth
ajānat
7.24 (plural) they do not know

9.11 (plural) because they do not know
11.41 unaware of
13.25 (anye tv evam ajānantaḥ śrutvā-nyebhyaḥ . . .) but others have a different understanding. They hear the word from others . . .

ajña
3.26 unwise man
4.40 lacking understanding

ajñāna
5.16; 13.11; 14.16, 17 ignorance
16.4 (ajñānam . . . abhijātasya . . .) a man born to . . . is ignorant

ajñānaja
10.11 which comes from ignorance
14.8 born from ignorance

ajñānasaṃbhūta
4.42 [the] product of [your] ignorance

ajñānasaṃmoha
18.72 the delusion of [your] ignorance

ajñānavimohita
16.15 (plural) their ignorance beguiles them
See also muh

ajñānāvṛtta
5.15 (ajñānāvṛttam jñānam) ignorance veils wisdom

akarmakṛt
3.5 inactive

akarman
2.47 (. . . mā te sango 'stv akarmani) . . . nor should you abstain from ritual
3.8; 4.18 inaction
4.16 "inactive"
4.17 nonaction

akartṛ
4.13 *See* kartṛ
13.29 not engaged in acts
[230]

akārya
18.31 what is prohibited
See also kāryākarya

akriya
6.1 he who avoids all liturgy
[241]

akrodha
16.2 (. . . akrodha . . . abhijātasya . . .) a man born to . . . is . . . not given to anger

akṛta
3.18 inaction

akṛtabuddhitva
18.16 the imperfection of his intelligence

akṛtātman
15.11 far from perfection

akṛtsnavid
3.29 who know only part
See also kṛtsnavid; vid

akṣara
3.15; 10.25 the one supreme, subtle sound
8.3 the supreme, subtle sound behind the sacred texts
8.11 the imperishable, the subtle sound
8.21; 10.33; 12.3; 15.16a, 16b, 18 imperishable
11.18 (akṣaraṃ veditavyam) the imperishable, necessary core of knowledge
11.37 the imperishable beginning
12.1 (akṣaram avyaktam) the invisible nucleus of all things
See also ekākṣara; kṣara
[237]

ālasya
See nidrālasyapramādottha

alpabuddhi
16.9 (plural) foolish people

amṛta
9.19 deathlessness
10.18 [your] immortal word
13.12 the immortal
14.27 deathless
See also amṛto-; dharmyāmṛta; mṛ; yajñaśiṣṭāmṛtabhuj

amṛtatva
2.15 immortality
See also mṛ

amṛtodbhava
10.27 sprung from immortality
See also mṛ

amṛtopama
18.37 like ambrosia
18.38 like nectar
See also mṛ

amūḍha
15.5 man without delusions
See also muh

anagha
3.3; 14.6 Blameless One
15.20 man without blame

anahaṃkāra
13.8 (anahaṃkāra . . . etaj jñānam iti

proktam) to be wise, . . . stop seeing yourself in the center
anāmaya
2.51 blissful
14.6 (sattvam anāmayam) [integrity is] health
ananyabhāj
9.30 (bhajate mām ananyabhāk) [he] worships, loving none but me
ananyacetas
8.14 who thinks of nothing . . . but of me
anapekṣa
12.16 carefree
anāśin
2.18 who does not perish
anātman
6.6 if he rejects his own reality
anekacittavibhrānta
16.16 (plural) their many mental waves drive them to distraction
anekadivyābharaṇa
11.10 with many divine ornaments
anekajanmasaṃsiddha
6.45 after a number of births, perfected
See also sidh
anekavarṇa
11.24 (nabhaḥspṛśaṃ dīptam anekavarṇam) [seeing you] ablaze with all the colors of the rainbow, touching the sky . . .
See also adityavarṇa; nānāvarṇakṛtin; varṇa
anirviṇṇacetas
6.23 without losing heart
anīśvara
16.8 without God
antahsukha
5.24 with joy . . . within
See also sukha
antarātman
6.47 his inmost self
See also pravyathitāntarātman
anubandha
18.25 [without considering] what is involved
18.39 wake
See also bandh
anucint
8.8 meditate
anurañj
11.36 (tava prakīrtyā jagat prahṛṣyaty anurajyate ca) the world revels in your glory
anusañj
6.4 (na . . . anusajjate) he is no longer obsessed with . . .
18.10 have a special love for
See also saṅga
anuṣṭubh [220, 228]
anyadevatā
7.20 (plural) other gods [than me]
9.23 (plural) [they] have other gods and . . .
apahṛtacetas
2.44 (plural) they are fooled [by their own discourses]
apāna
4.29a, 29b exhalation
See also prāṇa
aphalākānkṣin
17.11 men who do not build upon the results of rituals
aphalaprepsu
18.23 without anticipating their effects
aprameya
2.18 who . . . cannot be measured
11.17, 42 immeasurable
See also pramāṇa
arāgadveṣataḥ
18.23 neither with passion nor aversion
ārjava
13.7(-11) (. . . ārjavam . . . etaj jñānam iti proktam) [to be wise . . .] you should be just [. . . all this together constitutes wisdom]
16.1 honesty
17.14 to be . . . upright [. . . such is austerity of the body]
18.42 uprightness
arpaṇa
4.24 dedication [of the sacrifice]
9.27 (madarpaṇam) an offering to me
arthakāma
2.5 (plural) even if they were greedy
asadgrāha
16.10 false idea
asakta
3.7 not anxious for results [of ritual work]

3.19 [acting] in that freedom . . .
3.25; 13.14 unattached
9.9 detached
āsakta
See āsaktamanas; āsaṅga; avyaktāsaktacetas; karmaphalāsaṅga; saṅga; tṛṣṇāsaṅgasamudbhava
asaktabuddhi
18.49 (asaktabuddhih sarvatra) when his meditation is not tied down to anything
āsaktamanas
7.1 when your thought clings [to me]
See also saṅga
asaktātman
5.21 wholly free from
See also saṅga
asakti
13.9 [to be wise . . .] do not be attached
aśama
14.12 uneasiness
See also śānti
asaṃmoha
10.4 clarity
See also moha; muh
asaṃmūḍha
5.20 wide awake
10.3; 15.19 free from all obsessions
See also muh
asaṃnyastasaṃkalpa
6.2 without detaching himself from the purpose of the ritual
asaṃśaya
6.35 (asaṃśayam) surely
7.1 (asaṃśayam) there is no doubt that . . .
8.7 no doubt
18.68 (asaṃśayaḥ) certainly
See also saṃśaya
asaṃyatātman
6.36 man without self-control
āsaṅga
See karmaphalāsaṅga; saṅga; tṛṣṇāsaṅgasamudbhava
asaṅgaśastra
15.3 the ax of detachment
aśānta
2.66 without peace
See also śānti
aśāśvata
8.15 fleeting
See also śāśvata
asat
2.16 what is not
9.19 (sad asac cāham) I am the entire world
11.37 what does not exist
13.12 inexistent
17.28 not good or unreal
See also asadgrāha; sadasad-; sat
āścaryavat
2.29 (as) by (a) miracle
asiddhi
4.22 failure
See also siddhyasiddhi; sidh
aśraddadhāna
4.40 lacking . . . trust
9.3 (plural) who do not trust in . . .
See also śraddhā
aśraddhā
17.28 (aśraddhayā) without trust
See also aśraddadhāna; śraddhā
āstikyam
18.42 the proper teachings
aśubha
9.1 (mokṣyase 'subhāt) nothing will stand in your way
4.16 (jaj jñātvā mokṣyase 'subhāt) knowing this will free you from evil
asukha
9.33 joyless
See also sukha
asura
11.22 demon
āsura
7.15 infernal
9.12 such as belongs to . . . demons
16.4, 5, 6, 7, 19 demonic
āsuraniścaya
17.6 of demonic resolve
asvargya
2.2 (asvargyam) it does not lead to heaven
See also svarga
aśvin
11.6 the Kind Celestial Twins
11.22 the Celestial Twins
atapaska
18.67 a man who is devoid of religious zeal

bhāva
2.16 (nā 'sato vidyate bhāvaḥ) what is not cannot come into being
7.12 state of mind
7.13, 15 state
7.24 being
8.4 (kṣaro bhāvaḥ) historical circumstances
8.6a, 6b estate
8.20 (paras tasmāt tu bhāvo 'nyo 'vyaktaḥ) beyond that unmanifest is another . . . unmanifest
10.5 (bhavanti bhāvā bhūtānām) whatever exists is disposed to such states of mind
10.17 state of being
18.17 (yasya nāhaṃkṛto bhāvaḥ) a man who is not ego-centered
18.20 reality
See also abhāva; bhūtapṛthagbhāva; madbhāva; sarvabhāva; svabhāva
cf. sthāna
bhāvasaṃśuddhi
17.16 purifying one's place in the world
bhaya
2.35; 11.45; 18.35 fear
2.40 danger
10.4 anxiety
See also abhaya; bhīmakarman; bhītabhīta; harṣāmarṣabhayodvega; kāyakleśabhaya; vigatabhī; vigatecchābhayakrodha; vītarāgabhayakrodha; vyapetabhi
bhayābhaya
18.30 (bhayābhaye) fear and peace
bhayāvaha
3.35 perilous
bhīmakarman
1.15 the Worker of Terror (= Bhīma, also known as Vṛkodara, Wolf-Belly)
See also bhaya
bhīmārjunasama
1.4 matching Bhīma and Arjuna [in battle]
See also sama
Bhīṣmaparvan
[219]
bhītabhīta
11.35 overcome by fear
See also under bhaya
bhogaiśvaryagati
2.43 (bhogaiśvaryagatiṃ prati) [their words] aim at pleasure and power
bhogaiśvaryaprasakta
2.44 (plural) they cling to pleasures and power
See also īśvara; prasakta; saṅga
bhuj
2.5a (bhoktum) to live on . . .
2.5b (bhuñjīya bhogān rudhirapradigdhān) my food . . . would taste of blood
2.37 (bhokṣyase) you will enjoy
3.12 (bhuṅkte) [he] enjoys
3.13 (bhuñjate . . . aghaṃ pāpāḥ) the wicked partake of evil
9.21 (bhuktvā) after they have enjoyed
11.33 (bhuṅkṣva) enjoy!
13.21 (bhuṅkte) it enjoys
15.10 (bhuñjāna) taking in experience
bhūta (included are only those occurrences where bhūta can be understood as a noun)
2.28 thing
2.34 (bhūtāni) the world
2.69 (bhūtāni) they [all creatures]
3.14; 8.22; 13.15, 16, 27; 15.16; 18.54 creature
3.33; 15.13 (bhūtāni) all creatures
4.35 (bhūtāny aśeṣeṇa) all [exists]
7.11 living being
7.26 (bhūtāni) existences
8.20 (sarveṣu bhūteṣu naśyatsu) although every creature perish
9.5 (bhūtabhṛt) supporting beings
9.25 demon
10.5 (bhūtānām) whatever exists
10.20 (bhūtānām) all creatures
10.22 (bhūtānām) all that evolved
13.30 (bhūtapṛthagbhāvam) *See* bhāva
16.2 (dayā bhūteṣu) he does not slander anyone
18.21 existing being
18.46 (bhūtānām) all beings
See also sarvabhūta
[253]
bhūtabhṛt
See bhūta
bhūtamaheśvara
9.11 (bhāvam . . . mama bhūtamaheśvaram) my . . . state as Lord of Beings

bhūtaprakṛtimokṣa
13.34 freedom from existence and matter
bhūtapṛthagbhāva
13.30 (yadā bhūtapṛthagbhāvam ekastham anupaśyati . . .) when he sees that creatures different in state and habitat are really in one place
bhūteśa
10.15 Lord of life
brāhma
2.72 divine
brahmabhūta
5.24 [he] becomes one with God and . . .
6.27 [he] has become one with God
18.54 having reached the Divine
brahmabhūya
14.26 (brahmabhūyāya kalpate) he is fit for the divine abode
18.53 (brahmabhūyāya kalpate) [he] is qualified for reaching the Divine
brahmacārivrata
6.14 (brahmacārivrate sthitaḥ) faithful to the vow of his sacred study
brahmacarya
8.11 life of chastity
17.14 to be . . . chaste
brahmakarman
18.42 act of spiritual leaders
brahmakarmasamādhi
4.24 who concentrates on God's cultic work
See also samādhi
brahman (n)
3.15; 14.3, 4, 27; 18.50 the Divine
4.24, 32; 5.6, 10, 19; 6.38; 8.24; 10.12 (paraṃ brahma); 13.12 God
4.31 godhead
7.29; 8.1, 3 the divine secret
8.17; 13.30; 17.23 the Eternal
[225–226, 237, 253]
brahman (m)
11.15 the creator
11.37 (garīyase brahmaṇo 'py ādikartre) for you are most worthy of honor, you impelled even the creator
See also brāhma; śabdabrahman
brāhmaṇa
2.46 spiritual man
5.18 man of purest birth
9.33 (brāhmaṇāḥ puṇyāḥ) who have merit by birth
17.23 the people entitled to sacrifice
[246]
brāhmaṇakṣatriyaviś
18.41 (plural) spiritual guides, warriors, producers of wealth
brahmanirvāṇa
2.72; 5.24, 25 the freedom that is God's
5.26 God's freedom
[253]
brahmavid
5.20 knower of God
8.24 (plural) who know God
See also vid
[253]
brahmayogayuktātman
5.21 fully trained in God's discipline
bṛhatsāman
10.35 (bṛhatsāma tathā sāmnām . . . aham) in ritual I am the perfect chant
See also sāmaveda; ṛg
Buddha, Buddhism [220, 223, 244]
buddhi
2.39a; 7.10; 10.4; 18.17, 29, 30, 31, 32 understanding
2.39b, 49 meditative knowledge
2.41 the knowledge meditation attains
2.44 knowledge
2.52; 5.11; 12.8; 18.51 meditation
2.53 meditating mind
2.65 judgment
2.66 (nāsti buddhir ayuktasya) the undisciplined does not meditate
3.1 meditative knowledge or right judgment
3.2 (buddhiṃ mohayasīva me) you confuse me
3.40 our concentration
3.42 the power of concentration
3.43 concentration
6.25 meditative power
7.4 the faculty of meditation
13.5 the Great Principle (= mahat, concept in Sāṃkhya enumeration of elements)
See also abuddhi; akṛtabuddhitva; alpabuddhi; asaktabuddhi; budha;

budh; durbuddhi; nibudh; samabuddhi; sthirabuddhi; tadbuddhi
[237]
buddhibheda
3.26 (na buddhibhedaṃ janayet) he should not unsettle [their] minds
buddhigrāhya
6.21 which meditation can grasp
buddhimat
4.18 understanding
7.10 (plural) those who understand
15.20 enlightened
buddhināśa
2.63 (smṛtibhraṃśād buddhināśo buddhināśāt praṇaśyati) distortion of memory distorts consciousness, and then a man perishes
buddhisaṃyoga
6.43 inclination
buddhiyoga
2.49 the Discipline of Meditation
10.10 the right mind
18.57 training in meditation
buddhiyukta
2.50, 51 man with meditative knowledge
budh
3.43; 4.17a understand
4.17b know
10.9 (bodhayantaḥ parasparam) instructing one another
15.20 (etad buddhvā) if a man sees their [the teachings'] light . . .
See buddhi
budha
4.19 (plural) those with understanding
5.22 wise man
10.8 intelligent man

calitamānasa
6.37 (yogāc calitamānasaḥ) [if] his mind strays from discipline
car
2.64 (viṣayān . . . caran) roaming the sensual world
2.67 (indriyāṇāṃ hi caratām yan mano 'nuvidhīyate) for when a man allows his mind to obey the whims of the senses . . .
2.71 moves about
3.36 (kena prayukto 'yam pāpaṃ carati) what or who makes man do wrong?
cāturvarṇya
4.13 (cāturvarṇyaṃ mayā sṛṣṭaṃ guṇakarmavibhāgaśaḥ) I brought forth the four great divisions of men according to their qualities and rituals
See also varṇa
[256]
cetanā
10.22 awareness
13.6 consciousness
cetas
8.8 mind
18.57 (cetasā) inwardly
18.72 heart
See also acetas; adhyātmacetas; ananyacetas; anirviṇṇacetas apahṛtacetas; aveśitacetas; avyaktāsaktacetas; dharmasaṃmūḍhacetas; jñānavasthitacetas; lobhopahatacetas; prasannacetas; sacetas; vicetas; yatacetas; yuktacetas
cf. cetanā; cint; citta
chinnasaṃśaya
18.10 who . . . has vanquished doubt
See also saṃśaya
cikīrṣu
See lokasaṃgraha
cint
6.25 think of
9.22 think on
10.17 envisage
See also acintya; anucint; cintā; paricint
cintā
16.11 fantasies and anxieties
citta
6.18,20 thought
12.9 (cittaṃ samādhātum) to concentrate
See also acetas; anekacittavibhrānta; cetas; maccitta; sacetas; samacittatva; yatacitta; yatacittātman; yatacittendriyakriya
cf. cetanā; cint; cintā

daiva
4.25 (daivamevā 'pare yajñaṃ yoginaḥ paryupāsate) the discipline of some is to revere the sacrifice itself
7.14; 9.13; 16.3, 5a, 5b, 6a, 6b divine

18.14 (noun) providence
cf. deva
dama
10.4 inner control
16.1 self-restraint
18.42 self-control
dambha
16.4 (dambho . . . 'bhijātasya sampadam āsurīm) a man born to the demonic lot is deceitful
16.17 (dambhena) vainly
17.18 (tapo dambhena caiva yat kriyate) when one contrives austerity
[240]
dambhāhaṃkārasaṃyukta
17.5 (plural) deceitfulness and ego impel some men . . .
dambhamānamadānvita
16.10 deceitful, haughty, presumptuous
dambhārtha
17.12 (dambhārtham) without honesty
dāna
8.28 (plural) alms giving
10.5 (sing.); 11.53 (sing.); 18.43 (sing.) generosity
11.48 (plural) acts of generosity
16.1 (dānam . . . bhavanti saṃpadaṃ daivīm abhijatasya) a man born to divine fortune . . . is generous
17.7 (sing.) gifts
17.20a, 20b, 21, 22 (sing.) gift
17.25 (dānakriyāḥ) acts of giving
17.27 (sing.) giving
dānakriyā
17.25 act of giving
darpa
16.4 (darpo . . . 'bhijātasya sampadam āsurīm) a man born to the demonic lot is . . . arrogant
16.18 pride
daurbalya
2.3 faintheartedness
deha
2.13, 18, 30; 8.2, 4, 13; 11.7; 13.32; 14.5, 11; 15.14 body
4.9 (tyaktvā dehaṃ) after this life
11.15 (tava . . . dehe) within you
13.22 (dehe 'smin . . .) with respect to the human body
See also ātmaparadeha; dehin; paurvadehika
dehabhṛt
8.4 (dehabhṛtām vara) supreme mortal
14.14 person
18.11 (na hi dehabhrtā śakyam . . .) for as long as a man has a body, he cannot . . .
dehasamudbhava
14.20 (plural) . . . that come through bodily existence
dehavad
12.5 souls in their human form
dehin
2.13, 30, 59; 14.20 person
2.22 the embodied
3.40 a man
14.5, 7 soul
17.2 living soul
See also deha
deva
3.11, 12; 9.25; 10.2, 14; 11.11, 14, 15, 52; 17.4; 18.40 god
7.23 (plural) other gods
10.22 (plural) the celestial race
11.44 God!
11.45 o God!
See also adhidaiva; adhidaivata; ādideva; daiva; div; divya; sādhibhūtādhidaiva
devabhoga
9.20 (plural) the gods' . . . enjoyments
devadeva
10.15; 11.13 God of gods
devadvijaguruprājñapūjana
17.14 to honor the gods, the highest class of men, spiritual guides, and sages
devayaj
7.23 (plural) making offerings to other gods [they go to other gods]
See also yaj
devarṣi
10.13, 26 divine seer
devatā
4.12 (plural); 9.23 gods
See also anyadevatā
devavara
11.31 supreme God
deveśa
11.25, 45 Lord of gods

11.37 Lord of the gods
dhāman
8.21; 10.12; 15.6 abode
11.38 estate
[233]
dhanaṃjaya
1.15; 10.37 Arjuna
2.48 Pursuer of Wealth
2.49; 4.41 (omitted)
7.7 Conqueror of Wealth
9.9 Fighter for Wealth
11.14 Arjuna, the Pursuer of Wealth
12.9; 18.29, 72 Winner of Wealth
dharma
1.40; 14.27 tradition
2.40 (svalpam apy asya dharmasya) even the least practice on this path
4.7; 9.3; 18.31, 32 right
18.34 religion
See also adharma; dharmya; jātidharma; kuladharma; paradharma; sarvadharma; svadharma; trayīdharma
[219, 240, 242–245]
dharmakāmārtha
18.34 religion, desires, and gains
dharmakṣetra
1.1 the land of the right tradition
dharmasaṃmūḍhacetas
2.7 [I am] confused. What should be done?
dharmasaṃsthāpanārtha
4.8 to establish the right and true
dharmātman
9.31 completely righteous
dharmya
2.31, 33 just
9.2 right
18.70 (dharmyaṃ saṃvādam) discourse about the way to be followed
See also sādharmya
dharmyāmṛta
12.20 true immortality
See also mṛ
dhīra
2.13, 15 composed man
14.24 steady
dhṛti
10.34 Constancy
11.24 certainty
13.6 mental steadiness
16.3 (dhṛtiḥ . . . bhavanti sampadam daivīm abhijātasya) he who is born to divine fortune is firm . . .
18.29, 33, 34, 35b persistence
18.35a (yayā [dhṛtyā]) stubbornness
18.43 perseverance
18.51 (dhṛtyā) steadily
dhṛtigṛhīta
6.25 (buddhyā dhṛtigṛhītayā) through his firm meditative power
dhṛtyutsāhasamanvita
18.26 steady and energetic
[232]
dhyā
2.62 (dhyāyato viṣayān puṃsaḥ sangas teṣū 'pajāyate) a man gets attached to what the senses tell him if he does not turn his mind away
12.6 meditate
dhyāna
12.12; 13.24 meditation
[241]
dhyānayogapara
18.52 intent on the practice of meditation
div
9.20 the divine world
11.12 (omitted)
18.40 heaven
divya
1.14; 4.9; 9.20; 10.12, 16, 19, 40; 11.8, 15 divine
8.8, 10 the Divine [Being]
11.5 [my . . . forms] in their heavenly splendor
See also anekadivyabharaṇa; deva
divyagandhānulepana
See divyamālyāmbaradhara
divyamālyāmbaradhara
11.11 (divyamālyāmbaradharaṃ divyagandhānulepanam . . .) He wore garlands and robes and ointments of divine fragrance
divyānekodyatāyudha
11.10 with divine, unsheathed weapons
See also udyam
doṣa
1.38, 39 wickedness
18.48 imperfection
See also duṣ; janmamṛtyu-; jitasanga-

doṣa; kārpaṇyadoṣopahata-; nirdoṣa; praduṣ; sadoṣa
doṣavat
18.3 wrong
dravyayajña
4.28 (plural) those who sacrifice things
See also yajña
dṛḍha
6.34 set in its ways
12.14 (dṛḍhaniścaya) firm of will
15.3 strong
18.64 (dṛḍham) truly
dṛś; paśyati
1.2 survey
1.3, 20 look
1.25, 26, 28, 31, 38; 2.29, 59; 4.18; 5.5, 8; 6.30, 32, 33; 9.5; 11.3, 4a, 5, 6b, 8; 11.13, 15, 16a, 16b, 17, 19, 23, 24, 45a, 46, 48, 49, 51, 52, 53, 54; 15.10, 11a, 11b; 18.16b see
2.16; 6.20; 13.24 perceive
2.69 (paśyato muneḥ) seer
4.35 (. . . yena . . . drakṣyasi) [this] will show you
11.4b (darśyaya); 11.45b (darśyaya) show
11.6a look upon
11.7a (omitted)
11.9 (darśayām āsa) [He] gave the vision
11.20 (dṛṣṭvā 'dbhutaṃ rūpam ugraṃ) at the awesome sight . . .
11.25 look at
11.47 (darśitam) [I have] shown
11.50 (darśayām āsa) [He] showed
13.28 have the right vision
13.29 have true insight
18.16a regard
dṛṣṭapūrva
11.47 (rūpam . . . yan me tvadanyena na dṛṣṭapūrvam) It is my . . . form . . . No one but you has ever seen it
dṛṣṭi
16.9 view
duḥkha
2.56 unpleasant things
5.6 difficult
6.22 sorrow
6.32 unpleasant
10.4 grief
12.5 (gatir duḥkham . . . avāpyate) [they have] difficulty reaching a goal
13.6 unpleasantness
14.16 pain
17.9 nausea
18.8 bothersome
See also janmamṛtyujarāvyādhiduḥkhadoṣānudarśanam; samaduḥkhasukha
duḥkhahan
6.17 that ends sorrow
duḥkhālaya
8.15 miserable
duḥkhānta
18.36 the end of unpleasantness
duḥkhasaṃyogaviyoga
6.23 loosening of sorrowful ties
duḥkhatara
2.36 worse
duḥkhayoni
5.22 source of unpleasantness
durbuddhi
1.23 perverse
durgati
6.40 (na . . . kaścid durgatiṃ . . . gacchati) no one . . . ends up badly
durnigraha
6.35 hard to control
duṣ
1.41 (duṣṭa) corrupted
See also doṣa
duṣkṛtin
7.15 worker of evil
dvandva
10.33 (dvandvaḥ sāmāsikasya) [I am] in grammar the compound of perfect balance
15.5 (plural) opposites
See also nirdvandva
dvandvamoha
See icchādveṣasamuttha
dvandvamohanirmukta
7.28 set free from the delusion of opposites
See also dvandva; moha; muc
dvandvātīta
4.22 outside the realm of opposites
dveṣa
13.6 hate

See also adveṣṭṛ; arāgadveṣataḥ; dviṣ; icchādveṣasamuttha; rāgadveṣau; rāgadveṣaviyukta
dvija
17.14 the highest class of men
dvijottama
1.7 most venerable nobleman
dviṣ
2.57 hate
5.3 know disgust
9.29 (na me dveṣyo 'sti na priyaḥ) they neither enrapture me nor enrage me
12.17 show disgust
14.22 become agitated
16.19 (dviṣant) full of hostilities
18.10 have loathing for
See also adveṣṭṛ, suhṛnmitrāryudāsīna-; pradviṣ

ekabhakti
7.17 devoted to me alone
ekākṣara
8.13 one syllable, OM
See also akṣara

gandharvayakṣāsurasiddhasaṃgha
11.22 (plural) multitudes of heavenly musicians, good sprites, demons, and perfect sages
gatasaṅga
4.23 he has no attachment anymore
See saṅga
gatavyatha
12.16 unperturbed
gati
4.17 (karmaṇo gatiḥ) the nature of action
4.29 (prāṇāpānagatī) the course of their breath up and down
6.37 (kām gatiṃ . . . gacchati) where does he end up
6.45; 8.13, 21; 9.32; 12.5; 13.28; 16.23 goal
7.18 way
8.26 course
9.18 your way and goal
16.20 destination
16.22 destiny
See also bhogaiśvaryagati; durgati; svargati

grah
6.35 control
See also ātmavinigraha; dhṛtigṛhīta; durnigraha; nigrah; nigraha
guṇa
3.5 (prakṛtijair guṇaiḥ) the states of all existence
3.27 (prakṛteḥ guṇaiḥ) the states arising in primal matter
3.28 (guṇā guṇeṣu vartante) nature's forces always move one another
13.19 the underlying states in all things
13.21 (prakṛtijān guṇān) the states matter brings about
13.23 (prakṛtiṃ guṇaiḥ saha) primal matter with its states
14.5 (guṇāḥ prakṛtisaṃbhavaḥ) the states arising in primal matter
14.19a, 19b, 20, 26 states
14.21 state
14.23a the various states of being
14.23b just those states
18.40 (prakṛtijaiḥ . . . tribhir guṇaiḥ) three states of matter
18.41 (svabhāvaprabhavair guṇaiḥ) according to the state natural to each class
[237]
guṇabhoktṛ
13.14 immanent
guṇakarma
3.29 (sajjante guṇakarmasu) [they are] entranced by their motions [viz. of the guṇas]
guṇakarmavibhāga
3.28 (guṇakarmavibhāgayoḥ tattvavit) he who knows how the forces of nature and cultic work are really divided
guṇamaya
7.13 (tribhir guṇamayair bhāvair ebhiḥ sarvam idam jagat mohitam) these three states, made up of integrity, passion, and sloth, mislead the world
7.14 (. . . eṣā guṇamayī mama māyā) my veil, woven of these three strands
guṇānvita
15.10 clothed in the states of existence

guṇasaṃkhyāna
18.19 the theory of the three states of being
See also sāṃkhya
guṇasaṃmūḍha
3.29 (prakṛter guṇasaṃmūḍhāḥ) obsessed by the forces of nature
guṇasaṅga
13.21 attachment to those states which matter brings about
See saṅga
guṇatas
18.29 (guṇatas trividhaṃ) in accordance with the three states
guṇātīta
14.25 [he] has transcended the states
guru
[226, 253]

harṣāmarṣabhayodvega
12.15 (plural) the turmoil of joy, impatience, and fear
See also bhaya
hiṃsātmaka
18.27 cruel
hitakāmyā
10.1 for I desire what is best

icchā
13.6 desire
See also vigatecchābhayakrodha
icchādveṣasamuttha
7.27 (icchādveṣasamutthena dvandvamohena . . . sarvabhūtāni saṃmoham . . . yānti) all creatures enter delusion . . . for they are obsessed by the opposites, haunted by likes and dislikes
ijyā
11.53 sacrifice
See also yaj
indriya
2.8 (śokam ucchosaṇaṃ indriyāṇām) . . . this sorrow which lames me
2.58, 60, 61, 64, 67, 68; 3.7, 34, 40, 41, 42; 4.26, 39; 5.7, 9, 11, 28; 10.22; 15.7 (all plural) senses
13.5 (plural) senses of action and perception; with these, thought
See also atīndriya; karmendriya; prāṇendriyakriya; sarvendriyaguṇābhāsa; sarvendriyavivarjita; vijitendriya; viṣayendriyasaṃyoga; yatacittendriyakriya
indriyagocara
13.5 (plural) ranges of the senses
indriyagrāma
6.24 the horde of the senses
12.4 (saṃniyamye 'ndriyagrāmam) [they have] restrained their senses
indriyakarman
4.27 sensual act
indriyārāma
3.16 engrossed in the senses
indriyārtha
2.58 (plural) the sensual world
2.68 (plural) the world of the senses
3.6 (plural); 5.9 (plural) the objects of sense
6.4 (plural) sense objects
13.8 (plural) what the senses tell you
iṣ
1.35; 11.3; 18.60 wish
7.21 (yo-yo . . . arcitum icchati) any devotee may draw near . . .
8.11 seek
11.7, 31; 18.1 want
11.46 (icchāmi) I would like to . . .
12.9 try
18.63 will
See also icchā
īśa
11.15 (brahmāṇam īśam) the Creator
11.44 Lord
See also bhūteśa; deveśa
cf. īśvara
īśvara
4.6 Lord
13.28; 15.8; 18.61 the Lord
15.17 the . . . Lord
16.14 (īśvaro 'ham ahaṃ bhogī) I am in control; I enjoy the world
See also aiśvara; aiśvarya; anīśvara; mahāyogeśvara; maheśvara; parameśvara; viśveśvara
cf. īśa
[235]
īśvarabhāva
18.43 authority

jñānāgnidagdhakarman
4.19 his actions are consumed in the fire of wisdom
jñānasaṃchinnasaṃśaya
4.41 understanding has dissolved his doubts
See also saṃśaya
jñānatapas
4.10 the fire of wisdom
jñānavasthitacetas
4.23 his mind is held steady in wisdom
jñānavat
3.33; 7.19 wise man
10.38 the wise
jñānavijñānanāśana
3.41 destroyer of wisdom and discrimination
jñānavijñānatṛptātman
6.8 abundantly endowed with wisdom and sense
jñānayajña
4.33 sacrifice carried out through understanding
9.15 (jñānayajñena . . . yajanto mām upāsate) [they] know Me in reverence, when thirsting for wisdom they bring their sacrifices
18.70 (jñānayajñena tenā 'ham iṣṭaḥ syām) [he] sacrifices to Me by his thirst for wisdom
See also yajña
jñānayoga
3.3 the way of knowledge
jñānayogavyavasthiti
16.1–3 (jñānayogavyavasthitiḥ . . . bhavanti saṃpadam daivīm abhijātasya) a man born to divine fortune . . . with determination he cultivates spiritual knowledge
jñānin
3.39 the wise
4.34 (plural) those who have understanding
6.46 man of wisdom
7.16 wise
7.17, 18 the wise man

kalyāṇakṛt
6.40 (na . . . kalyāṇakṛt kaścit) no one who has done anything salutary

kāma
2.55, 62, 70, 71; 3.37; 6.24; 7.11, 20, 22; 16.10, 21; 18.53 desire
16.18 lust
See also arthakāma; dharmakāmārtha; hitakāmya; kāmya; yoddhukāma
kāmabhoga
16.16 enjoyment of lusts
kāmaduh
3.10 source of abundance
10.28 Kāmaduh, the Cow of Plenty
kāmahaituka
16.8 (kim anyat kāmahaitukam) what ground does the world have but desire?
kāmakāma
9.21 they lust and desire
kāmakāmin
2.70 he who goes after desires
kāmakāra
5.12 [the undisciplined man] acts out of desire
kāmakārataḥ
16.23 according to his desires
kāmakrodhaparāyaṇa
16.12 trapped by desires and resentments
kāmakrodhaviyukta
5.26 who release themselves from desire and anger
kāmarāgabalānvita
17.5 (plural) desires and passions fortify them
kāmarāgavivarjita
7.11 free from lust and passion
kāmarūpa
3.39 it appears as desire
3.43 in the form of desire
kāmasaṅkalpavarjita
4.19 [whose undertakings] have lost desire and calculation
kāmātman
2.43 full of desire
kāmepsu
18.24 to gain his desires
kāmopabhogaparama
16.11 enjoyment of desires [is] uppermost in their minds
kāmya
18.2 (kāmyānāṃ karmaṇāṃ nyāsam)

abandoning rites performed for personal advantage
kāṅkṣ
1.32 have desire for
1.33 desire
4.12 want
5.3 know desire
12.17 show desire
14.22 long for
18.54 have cravings
karaṇa
18.14 means by which an act is done
18.18 that which is offered
kāraṇa
6.3 way
13.21 (. . . kāraṇam guṇasaṅgo 'sya sadasadyonijanmasu) its attachment to those states effects good and evil births
18.13 moment
See also kāryakāraṇakartṛtva
karmabandha
2.39 imprisonment by actions
See also bandh
karmabandhana
3.9 enslaved by activity
9.28 (plural) the prison of deeds
See also bandh
karmacodanā
18.18 (jñānaṃ jñeyaṃ parijñātā trividhā karmacodanā) our knowledge, what we know, and we the knowers—these three together impel us to ritual acts
karman
2.47, 49; 3.4; 18.3, 9, 10, 23 ritual
2.48; 17.27; 18.2 rite
2.50 (karmasu) works and rites
3.8a; 6.4 ritual work
3.1b, 22, 24, 30; 4.9; 9.9b; 18.6, 44, 45, 47, 48 work
3.1a, 8b, 23; 4.14a, 16, 17a, 17b, 20, 23, 33, 41; 14.9, 12; 18.11, 18 action
3.5 (kāryate . . . karma sarvaḥ . . . guṇaiḥ) the states . . . make everyone act
3.9a (yajñārthāt karmaṇaḥ) work for the sake of sacrifice
3.9b (tadarthaṃ karma . . . samācara) act for that purpose
3.15, 20, 25 cultic work
3.19a (kāryaṃ karma) the work that is required
3.19b (ācaram karma) acting
3.27, 31; 5.1, 10, 14; 6.17; 17.26; 18.15, 19, 25, 43 act
4.12, 15a; 6.1 cultic act
4.14b ritual act
4.15b (omitted)
4.18a prescribed cultic act
4.18b effective act
4.21; 9.9a activity
5.11 (karma kurvanti [they] act
6.3 cult
7.29 ordained work
8.1 (kiṃ karma) what work is ordained?
12.6 (sarvāṇi karmāṇi) all their rituals and doings
12.10 cultic acts
13.29 (karmāṇi . . . sarvaśaḥ) all that is done
14.16 (karma) works or cultic acts
16.24 (karma) actions and rites
18.7, 8 sacrifice
18.12 (karmaṇaḥ phalam) reward
18.24 acting . . . rites
18.41 (karmāṇi) tasks and rites
18.60 duty
See also akarmakṛt; akarman; bhīmakarman; brahmakarman; brahmakarmasamādhi; jñānāgnidagdhakarman; karma-; kṛ; kṣatrakarma; kriyā; matkarmakṛt; matkarmaparama; moghakarman; naiṣkarmya; puṇyakarman; sarvakarmaphalatyāga; ugrakarman; vikarman; yogasaṃnyastakarman
[233–236, 239–240, 242, 244, 246–247, 252]
karmānubandhin
15.2 (plural) [the roots are] the sequences of actions
See also bandh
karmaphala
4.14 results [of actions]
5.12 results of acts
6.1 results [of required cultic acts]
karmaphalahetu
2.47 (mā karmaphalahetur bhūḥ) the results of rituals should not be your motive
[241]

2.38 (. . . samekṛtvā) realizing that . . . and . . . are the same
2.48; 3.8; 16.24; 17.19, 25; 18.24, 56 perform
3.5 (kāryate . . . sarvaḥ . . . guṇaiḥ) the states . . . make everyone act
3.18 (kṛta) action
3.20, 25b; 4.22; 5.7, 10, 13a; 13.31; 18.63, 73 act
3.21 (sa yat pramāṇam kurute) the standard he sets for himself
3.33 accomplish
4.21 (śārīraṃ kevalam karma kūrvan) involved in no activity other than that of the body alone
4.37a (bhasmasāt kurute) reduce to ashes
4.37b (bhasmasāt kurute) consume
5.11 (karma kurvanti) [they] do act
5.13b (kārayan) causing action
5.27 (. . . kṛtvā bahir . . .) . . . who dispels . . .
6.12 (ekāgraṃ manaḥ kṛtvā) he fixes his mind on one point . . .
6.25 (ātmasaṃsthaṃ manaḥ kṛtvā) he fixes his mind on the self, and . . .
12.11b *See* sarvakarmaphalatyāga
17.18 contrive
18.8 *See* tyāgaphala
18.68 (bhaktiṃ mayi parāṃ kṛtvā) in supreme love and worship for Me
See also akarmakṛt; akartṛ; akārya; akriya; akṛta; akṛta-; cikīrṣu; duṣkṛtin; kalyāṇakṛt; karaṇa; kāraṇa; karma-; karman; kartṛ; kriyā; kṛta-; kṛtsnakarmakṛt; lokakṣayakṛt; matkarmakṛt; pāpakṛttama; priyacikīrṣu; priyakṛttama; puṇyakṛt; sarvakarmaphalatyāga; sukṛta; sukṛtin; tyāgaphala; vedāntakṛt
[241]

kriyā
11.48 ritual
See also danakriyā; luptapiṇḍodakakriyā; manaḥpraṇendriyakriyā; yajñadānatapaḥkriyā; yajñatapaḥkriyā; yatacittendriyakriya

kriyāviśeṣabahula
2.43 (vācam pravadanti . . . kriyāviśeṣabahulām) their words . . . dwell at length on various rites

krodha
2.62, 63; 3.37; 16.21; 18.53 anger
16.4 (. . . krodhah . . . abhijātasya . . .) a man born to . . . is wrathful . . .
16.18 wrath
See also akrodha; kāmakrodhaparāyaṇa; kāmakrodhaviyukta; kāmakrodhodbhava; vigatecchābhayakrodha; vītarāgabhayakrodha

kṛta
See kṛ

kṛtakṛtya
15.20 (buddhimān syāt kṛtakṛtyaś ca) he will be enlightened and what he should do is done

kṛtaniścaya
2.37 (. . . uttiṣṭha . . . yuddhāya kṛtaniścayaḥ) stand up . . . determined to fight

kṛtāñjali
11.14 . . . joined his palms, and . . .
11.35 joining his palms

kṛtānta
18.13 (sāṃkhye kṛtānte) in the Philosophy of Reason

kṛtsnakarmakṛt
4.18 doing all right acts

kṛtsnavid
3.29 man of full knowledge
See also vid

krūra
16.19 ruthless

kṣamā
10.4 forbearance
10.34 Patience
16.3 (. . . kṣamā . . . bhavanti saṃpadaṃ daivīm abhijātasya) a man born to divine fortune . . . is forbearing . . .

kṣara
8.4 (kṣaro bhāvaḥ) historical circumstances
15.16a, 16b, 18 perishable

kṣatrakarma
18.43 (śauryaṃ . . . īsvarabhāvaśca kṣatrakarma svabhāvajam) valor . . . and authority are inherent in the acts of warriors

kṣatriya
2.31, 32; 18.41 warrior

See also brāhmaṇakṣatriyaviś [246]
kṣetra
13.1, 3, 6, 18, 33 field
See also dharmakṣetra; kṣetrin; sarvakṣetra
kṣetrajña
13.1, 2 knower of the field
See also kṣetrakṣetrajña; kṣetrakṣetrajñasaṃyoga
kṣetrakṣetrajña
13.34 (dual) field and master of the field
kṣetrakṣetrajñasaṃyoga
13.26 the joining of the field and the master who knows the field
kṣetrin
13.33 master of the field
kuladharma
1.40, 43, 44 family tradition
kūṭastha
6.8 solitary
12.3 the highest
15.16 on high

lip
4.14 pollute
5.7 stain
5.10 (lipyate na sa pāpena) evil clings to him no more . . .
13.31 (paramātmā . . . na karoti na lipyate) the . . . supreme self . . . does not act and is not affected by action
18.17 (buddhir yasya na lipyate) whose understanding is not muddled
See also upalip
lobha
14.12, 17; 16.21 greed
See also lobhopahatacetas; lubdha; rājyasukhalobha
lobhopahatacetas
1.38 (plural) since greed has clouded their wits
loka
3.3, 9, 21; 4.12, 31, 40; 7.25; 8.16; 9.33; 11.23, 43; 12.15a, 15b; 13.33; 14.14; 15.16, 18; 18.71 world
3.22 (triṣu lokeṣu) in the worlds, heaven, air, and earth
3.24 (ime lokāḥ) these worlds
5.14 (lokasya . . . prabhuḥ) the Lord
6.41 region
6.42; 10.6 earth
10.16 (lokān imān) this multiple world
11.29 (lokāḥ) men
11.30 (grasamānaḥ . . . lokān samagrān) devouring all
11.32 (lokān samāhartum) to gather in the people
16.6 (dvau bhūtasargau loke 'smin) there are two orders of creation
18.17 (imāṃl lokān) these men here
See also trailokya-
lokakṣayakṛt
11.32 who destroys man's world
lokamaheśvara
10.3 Lord of worlds and peoples
lokasaṃgraha
3.20 the upholding of the world
3.25 (kuryād . . . cikīrṣur lokasaṃgraham) [he] should act . . . envisaging the totality of the world
lokatraya
11.20 the world above, man's world, and the world in between
11.43 the world above, . . . man's world, and . . . the realm between the two
15.17 the threefold world—of gods, men, and the realm between—
See also trailokyarājya
lubdha
18.27 greedy
See also lobha
luptapiṇḍodakakriya
1.42 (plural) [they end up in hell] because the ancestral rites are discontinued

maccitta
6.14 his thought set on me
10.9 thinking of me
18.57 (maccittaḥ . . . bhava) keep your thought directed to me
18.58 directing your thought to me
madbhakta
9.34 devoted to me
18.68 my worshiper
madbhakti
18.54 devotion to me

See also mṛ
martyaloka
9.21 mortal life
See also mṛ
matkarmakṛt
11.55 who does his rites for me
matkarmaparama
12.10 (matkarmaparamo bhava) give yourself wholly to rites for Me
matpara
2.61; 12.6 intent on me
18.57 making me your goal
matparama
11.55 (śraddhadhānā matparamāḥ) they trust me beyond all the world
12.20 (matparamāḥ) they hold me supreme
18.55 intent on me
matprasāda
18.56, 58 my grace
māyā
7.14, 15 wizardry
18.61 his magic power
See also ātmamāyā; yogamāyāsamāvṛta
moghakarman
9.12 (plural) vain . . . are their rituals
moha
4.35 (moham . . . yāsyasi) you will . . . be confused
4.11 darkness of mind
14.13; 18.7, 25, 73 delusion
14.22 (moha) delusions
16.10 (mohāt) because of their obsessions
18.60 (mohāt) because of your delusions
See also asaṃmoha; mohana; mohin; muh; pramādamoha
mohajālasamāvṛta
16.16 the net of delusion envelops them
mohana
14.8 (mohanaṃ sarvadehinām) it deludes all souls
18.39 (yad . . . sukhaṃ mohanam ātmanaḥ) happiness which is a delusion
See also muh
mohin
9.12 (mohinī prakṛti) beguiling nature
mokṣa
18.30 freedom
See also bhūtaprakṛtimokṣa; jarāmaraṇamokṣa; muc
[225–226]
mokṣakāṅkṣin
17.25 aiming for release
mokṣaparāyaṇa
5.28 intent on freedom
mṛ
2.20 die
2.26 (nityam . . . manyase mṛtam) you think He . . . dies continually
2.27 (dhruvaṃ janma mṛtasya) whoever dies will certainly be born
See also amṛta; maraṇa; martya; mṛtyu
mṛtyu
2.27 (jātasya . . . dhruvo mṛtyuḥ) whoever is born will certainly die
9.19; 10.34 death
13.25 the ocean of death
See also janmamṛtyujarāduḥkha; janmamṛtyujarāvyādhi-; mṛ
mṛtyusaṃsārasāgara
12.7 the ocean of the round of deaths
See also mṛ
mṛtyusaṃsāravartman
9.3 the endless round of deaths
See also mṛ
muc
3.13 cleanse
3.31 (mucyante te 'pi karmābhiḥ) [they] are no longer imprisoned by their acts
4.16; 9.28 free
4.23 (muktasya) he is free
5.28 (muktaḥ) set free
8.5 leave [the body]
9.1 (. . . yaj jñātvā mokṣyase 'śubhāt) then nothing will stand in your way
12.15 (mukta) free from . . .
18.40 (muktam) free from . . .
18.66 (mokṣayiṣyāmi) I shall set . . . free
See also dvandvamohanirmukta; janmabandhavinirmukta; muktasaṅga; mumukṣu; pramuc
mūḍhayoni
14.15 (mūḍhayoniṣu jāyate) he is

bound for an inert, misguided existence
muh
2.13 (dhīras tatra na muhyati) this does not upset the composed man
3.2 (mohayasi) you confuse
4.16 (mohita) confused
5.15 (tena muhyanti jantavaḥ) [it] misleads people
7.13 (ebhiḥ . . . jagat mohitaṃ) these mislead the world
7.15 (mūḍha) man with obsessions
7.25 (mūḍha) perplexed
8.27 (muhyati) [he] becomes lost
9.11 (mūḍha) fool
16.20 (mūḍha) in their delusion . . .
See also ajñanavimohita; amūḍha; asaṃmūḍha; moha; vimuh; vimūḍhabhāva
mukta
See muc
muktasaṅga
3.9 free from attachment
18.26 freed from attachments
See muc
mumukṣu
4.15 while aspiring for release
See muc

naiṣkarmya
3.4 (na . . . naiṣkarmyaṃ puruṣo 'snute) man does not overcome activity . . .
naiṣkarmyasiddhi
18.49 (naiṣkarmyasiddhiṃ paramām) perfection beyond acts
nam
11.37 (kasmāt . . . na nameran) why should they not bow?
namas
11.31 (namo 'stu te) I bow before you
11.39 (namo namas te 'stu sahasrakṛtvaḥ punaś ca bhūyo 'pi namo namas te) You should receive honor a thousandfold—time and again, honor, honor to you!
11.40 (namaḥ . . . te namo 'stu te . . .) let honor be given to you
namaskṛ
9.34 revere
11.35 honor
nāmayajña
16.17 (yajante nāmayajñais te) they make a show of sacrificing
See also yajña
nānāvarṇakṛtin
11.5 (plural) in all their colors and semblances
See also ādityavarṇa; anekavarṇa; varṇa
naraka
1.42, 44; 16.16, 21 hell
naś
1.40 (dharme naṣṭe) with collapse of the tradition . . .
3.32; 4.2 (naṣṭa) lost
5.16 (jñānena tu tad ajñānaṃ yeṣāṃ nāśitam ātmanaḥ) but when knowledge of the self destroys that ignorance in men . . .
6.38 be lost
8.20 perish
10.11 (nāśayāmi) I put an end to . . .
18.73 (naṣṭa) cast out
See also nāśa; nāśana; naṣṭātman; praṇaś; vinaś
nāśa
11.29 (nāśāya) to meet their end
See also abhikramanāśa; anāśin; buddhināśa
nāśana
16.21 (nāśanam ātmanaḥ) . . . destroying the soul
See also jñānavijñānanāśana
naṣṭātman
16.9 having lost the reality of their lives
nibandh
4.22, 41; 5.12; 9.9; 18.7 imprison
14.5 tie
14.7, 8; 18.60 bind
See also bandh
nibandha
16.5 bondage
See also bandh
nibudh
1.7 (nibodha) observe!
18.13, 50 (nibodha) learn!
nidhāna
9.18 abiding essence
11.18 (paraṃ nidhānaṁ) ultimate foundation

11.38 (paraṃ nidhānam) absolute foundation
nidrālasyapramādottha
18.39 which arises from sleep, idleness, or negligence
nigrah
2.68 withdraw
9.19 stop
nigraha
3.33 coercion
6.34 (tasyā 'ham nigrahaṃ manye... suduṣkaram) it is quite difficult to restrain it, I think
niḥśreyasakara
5.2 . . . lead to supreme bliss
nirahaṃkāra
See nirmama
nirdoṣa
5.19 flawless
nirdvandva
2.45 free from opposites
5.3 free from the sway of opposites
nirguṇa
13.14 transcendent
nirguṇatva
13.31 not [being] subject to the states of matter
nirmama
2.71 (nirmamo nirahamkāraḥ) who says neither *mine* nor *I*
3.30 free from selfishness
12.13 (nirmamo nirahamkāraḥ) not selfish, not selfcentered
18.53 unselfish
nirmānamoha
15.5 humble, sincere man
nirvāṇa [227, 237]
nirvāṇaparama
6.15 (śāntiṃ nirvāṇaparamām matsaṃsthām adhigacchati) [he] attains the summit of freedom, the peace that is in Me
See also brahmanirvāṇa
nirvikāra
18.26 [he is] not changed
See also vikāra
niryogakṣema
2.45 detached from things
See also yogakṣema
niṣṭhā
3.3 basic rule
17.1 (teṣām niṣṭhā . . . kā) what determines their place?
18.50 (niṣṭhā jñānasya yā parā) [It is] the absolute culmination of wisdom
nistraigunya
2.45 (nistraiguṇyo bhava) transcend it (viz., the world's weave of integrity, passion, and sloth
nitya
2.18, 21 eternal
2.24 subsisting always
2.26 (nityam) continually
2.30 (nityam) for ever
3.15 ever
3.31 (ye me matam idam nityam anutiṣṭhanti) who hold to this my teaching
9.6; 11.52 (omitted)
10.9 (nityam) constantly
13.9 (nityam) always
18.52 (nityam) steadily
cf. śāśvata
nityābhiyukta
9.22 (plural) when their zeal is constant
nityasaṃnyāsin
5.3 (jñeyaḥ sa nityasaṃnyāsī yo . . .) clearly, constant renunciation is part of a man when he . . .
See also saṃnyāsa; saṃnyāsin
niyam
1.44 (niyatam) surely
3.7 restrain
3.8 (niyata) required
3.41 conquer
6.26 subdue
7.20 (prakṛtyā niyatāḥ svayā) to satisfy their nature's need
18.7, 9 (niyata) regular, required
18.23 (niyata) regular
18.51 control
See also niyata-; niyatā-; prayam; saṃniyam; saṃyam; udyam; viniyam; yata-; yatā-; yate-; yati
niyama
7.20 (taṃ taṃ niyamam āsthāya . . .) they resort to various regimens
See also niyam; saṃyam
niyatāhāra
4.30 (apare niyatāhārāḥ) others abstain from eating

See also niyam
niyatamānasa
6.15 controlling his mind
See also niyam
niyatātman
8.2 man of self-control
See also niyam
niyuj
3.1 (niyojayasi) you urge
3.36 (niyojita) driven
18.59 compel
nyāsa
18.2 abandoning [rites . . .]
See also saṃnyāsa

om
8.13; 17.23, 24 OM
[254]
oṃkāra
9.17 the sacred syllable OM

pada
2.51; 8.11 state
15.4, 5 place
paṇḍita
2.11; 4.19; 5.4, 18 educated
pāpa
1.36 atrocity
1.39; 5.10; 18.66 evil
1.45 crime
2.33, 38 demerit
3.13; 6.9 wicked
3.36 wrong
4.36 evildoer
5.15 fault
7.28 the impure
See also mahāpāpman; pāpman; pūtapāpa; sarvapāpa
[252]
pāpakṛttama
4.36 the worst of all evildoers
pāpayoni
9.32 (. . . ye 'pi syuḥ pāpayonayaḥ) no matter how vile their birth
pāpman
3.41 (omitted)
para
1.28 (kṛpayā parayā 'viṣṭaḥ) overwhelmed by emotion
2.59; 3.19 the highest
3.11; 5.16; 6.45; 8.28; 9.32; 11.1; 13.28; 14.1; 16.22, 23 highest
3.42a high
3.42b; 7.5 higher
3.42c (manasas tu parā buddhiḥ) the power of concentration transcends the mind
3.43 he [who is] beyond . . .
4.39; 7.24; 8.10; 13.12, 22; 14.1; 18.54, 62, 68, 75 supreme
4.40 the next [world]
7.13 (ebhyaḥ param) different
8.20 (paras tasmāt . . .) beyond that
8.22 (omitted)
10.12 (paraṃ brahman paraṃ dhāma) you are God, the highest abode
11.18 ultimate
11.37 (sad asat tatparaṃ yat) [you are] what exists and what does not exist, and [you are] beyond both
11.38; 18.50 absolute
12.2 greatest
13.34 the highest goal
17.17 utmost
17.19 someone else
paradharma
3.35; 18.47 someone else's duty
parama
6.32; 8.21b; 10.1, 12 supreme
8.3 (brahma paramam) the divine secret
8.8 (omitted)
8.15 perfect
8.21a; 18.68 highest
11.9 (paramaṃ rūpam aiśvaram) [his] highest, absolute form
11.18 (paramaṃ veditavyam) paramount necessary core of knowledge
18.49 (-siddhiṃ paramāṃ) perfection
See also kāmopabhogaparama
paramātman
6.7 (paramātmā samāhitaḥ) [he] has a self that is fully present
13.22 the supreme spirit
13.31 the supreme self
15.17 the supreme reality
parameśvara
11.3 highest Lord
13.27 the supreme Lord
paratara
7.7 higher
paraṃtapa
2.3; 4.33; 9.3; 18.41 Conqueror

prakṛtistha
13.21 (puruṣaḥ prakṛtisthaḥ) when the spirit exists in primal matter . . .
15.7 whose home is in matter
pralaya
7.6 the end [of the entire world]
9.18 [the world's . . .] dissolution
14.2 (pralaye) when the world is destroyed
14.14 (pralayaṃ yāti) he dies
14.15 (pralayaṃ gatvā) dying
See also pralī
pralayānta
16.11 (cintām aparimeyāṃ ca pralayāntām upāśritāḥ) they devote themselves to endless fantasies and anxieties, though they may die today or tomorrow
pralī
8.18, 19 dissolve
14.15 (pralīna) dying
See also pralaya
pramāda
See nidrālasyapramādottha
pramādamohau
14.17 carelessness and delusions, obsessions
pramāṇa
3.21 standard
16.24 criterion
See also aprameya
pramuc
5.3 (pramucyate) he is freed
10.3 (pramucyate) [he is] released at once
See also muc
prāṇa
1.33 life
4.29a the life-breath they inhale
4.29b breathing-in
4.30 (prāṇān prāṇeṣu juhvati) [they] offer nothing but their breathing
8.10 his breath, his life
8.12; 18.33 breath
See also apāna; madgataprāṇa; prāṇā-; prāṇendriyakriyā; prāṇin
prāṇakarman
4.27 activities of life
praṇam
11.14, 44 bow
11.35 bow down
prāṇāpāna
5.27 (dual) his breathing in and out
prāṇāpānagati
4.29 (dual) the course of their breath up and down
prāṇāpānasamāyukta
15.14 ignited by the breaths
praṇaś
1.40; 2.63 perish
6.30 (tasyāham na praṇaśyāmi sa ca me na praṇaśyati) I do not let him go; I never desert him
9.31 get lost
18.72 (praṇaṣṭa) . . . has come to an end
prāṇāyāmaparāyaṇa
4.29 who give themselves to breath control
prāṇendriyakriyā
18.33 activity of mind, breath, and senses
prāṇin
15.14 (plural) the living
prasad
11.25 (prasīda) give me your grace
11.31, 45 (prasīda) be gracious
11.44 (prasādaye tvām) I beg your grace
11.47 (prasanna) pleased
See also prasāda; prasanna-
prasāda
2.64, 65 clarity
See also ātmabuddhiprasādaja; manaḥprasāda; matprasāda; tatprasāda; tvatprasāda; vyāsaprasāda
prasakta
16.16 (prasaktāḥ kāmabhogeṣu) they are caught in the enjoyment of their lusts
See also bhogaiśvaryaprasakta; prasaṅga; saṅga
prasaṅga
18.34 attachment
See also bhogaiśvaryaprasakta; prasakta; saṅga
prasanna
See prasad
prasannātman
18.54 perfectly peaceful
prasannacetas
2.65 clear-minded [man]

praśānta
6.7 (omitted)
See also śānti
praśāntamanas
6.27 whose thought is at peace
praśāntātman
6.14 in total peace
prasidh
3.8 (śarīrayātra . . . na prasidhyet) the body would stop functioning
See also sidh
pratap
11.30 be scorching
pratijñā
9.31 understand
18.65 promise
pratiṣṭhā (verb)
2.57, 61 (pratiṣṭhitā) firm
2.58 (pratisthitā) . . . has become stable
2.68 (yasya . . . tasya prajñā pratiṣṭhitā) having . . . means attaining a steadfast judgment
3.15 (pratiṣṭhitam) established
6.11 prepare
pratiṣṭhā (noun)
14.27 ground
See also acalapratiṣṭha
pravyathitāntarātman
11.24 my heart in me is shaken
prayam
9.26 offer
See also niyam; prayatātman; saṃyam
prayatātman
9.26 the giver who gives himself
See also niyam; prayam; saṃyam
prayuj
3.36 (. . . kena prayukto 'yam pāpaṃ carati pūrusaḥ) . . . what or who makes man do wrong
17.26 (. . . sad ity etat prayujyate) SAT—good and real—relates to
prītamanas
11.49 your heart at ease
priyacikīrṣu
1.23 eager to please
priyakṛttama
18.69 (na . . . kaścin me priyakṛttamaḥ) no one renders Me service more precious

pūjā [250]
punarāvartin
8.16 (lokāḥ punarāvartinaḥ) worlds are cycles
punarjanman
4.9 (punarjanma naiti) he is not reborn
8.15 a new birth
8.16 (māṃ upetya . . . punarjanma na vidyate) for those who reach me there is no repetition
puṇya [252]
puṇyakarman
7.28 when one cultivates merit
18.71 meritorious
[252]
puṇyakṛt
6.41 meritorious
[252]
purāṇa
2.20 primeval
8.9 primordial
11.38 primal
15.4 (omitted)
purātana
4.3 of ancient days
puruṣa
2.15, 21, 60; 3.4; 9.3 man
8.4 man's spirit
8.8 (paramaṃ puruṣaṃ divyam) the Divine Being
8.10 (paraṃ puruṣaṃ divyam) the supreme Divine Being
8.22 (omitted)
10.12 (puruṣaṃ . . . divyam); 11.18, 38; 15.4 Divine Being
13.19, 20, 21, 22, 23; 15.16 spirit
15.17 (uttamaḥ puruṣaḥ) Highest Being
17.3 (ayaṃ puruṣo) everyone
[285]
puruṣavyāghra
18.4 (omitted)
puruṣottama
8.1 (omitted)
10.15; 15.18, 19 Highest Being
11.3 Supreme Divine Being
pūrvābhyāsa
6.44 former training
pūtapāpa
9.20 cleansed of evil

sama
2.38 (sukhaduḥkhe same kṛtvā) realizing that joy and grief . . . are the same
2.48; 9.29; 12.18; 18.54 equal-minded
4.22 even-minded
5.19 in balance
5.27 (. . . samau krtvā) who evens out . . .
6.13 straight
6.32 the same
13.27 [who sees in all creatures] alike [the supreme Lord]
13.28 alike
See also bhīmārjunasama; sāmya; tvatsama

śama
6.3 stillness
10.4 peace
11.24 all peace
18.42 serenity
See also śānti

samabuddhi
6.9 who is disposed equally toward . . .
12.4 (sarvatra samabuddhayaḥ) they have attained equanimity toward all

samacittatva
13.9 [to be wise, you should] practice equanimity

samadarśana
6.29 seeing the same [in all things]

samadarśin
5.18 (plural) [the educated] see no difference between . . .

samādhā
6.7 (. . . paramātmā samāhitaḥ) [he has] a self that is fully present
12.9; 17.11 concentrate

samādhi
2.44, 53 concentration
See also brahmakarmasamādhi; samādhā

samādhistha
2.54 established in concentration

samaduḥkhasukha
2.15 to whom unpleasantness and pleasure are alike
12.13 with equanimity toward pleasant and unpleasant things
14.24 dispassionate in pleasure and trouble

samaloṣṭāśmakāñcana
6.8 lumps of earth, rocks, gold are alike to him

sāman
See bṛhatsāman

samatā
10.5 equanimity

samatva
2.48 equanimity

sāmaveda
10.22 the Book of Songs
See also bṛhatsāman; veda

saṃgraha
3.25 totality [of the world; loka]
8.11 (saṃgrahena) concisely
See also lokasaṃgraha

saṃkalpa [242]

saṃkalpaprabhava
6.24 the outgrowth of conscious, stated purposes
See also asaṃnyastasaṃkalpa; sarvasaṃkalpasaṃnyāsin

sāṃkhya
2.39 the teachings of Reason
3.3; 5.5a man of reason
5.5b Reason
13.24 (sāṃkhyena yogena) through reason
18.13 (sāṃkhye kṛtānte) in the Philosophy of Reason
See also guṇasamkhyāna
[220, 237, 244, 255]

sāṃkhyayoga
5.4 (sāmkhyayogau) reason and discipline

saṃmoha
2.63a state of delusion
2.63b; 7.27 delusion

saṃmuh
3.29 (saṃmūḍha) obsessed
See also dharmasaṃmūḍhacetas

saṃniyam
12.4 restrain
See also niyam; saṃyam

saṃnyas
3.30 cast on . . .
5.13 (sarvakarmāṇi manasā saṃnyasya) mentally freed from all acts
12.6 dedicate to . . .
18.57 resign to . . .
See also asamnyastasaṃkalpa; saṃnyāsa; yogasamnyastakarman

See asakta; gatasaṅga; muktasaṅga; saṅgavarjita
sañj
3.25 (sakta) wedded to
3.28 (na sajjate) he is free [from them]
3.29 (sajjante) they are entranced by . . .
5.12 (sakta) attached
18.22 [one's knowledge] attaches itself to
See also saṅga
Śaṅkara [235, 239, 241, 243–245]
śānta
18.53 at peace
See also śānti
śāntarajas
6.27 [his] passion has quieted
See also rajas; śānti
śānti
2.66, 70, 71; 4.39; 5.12, 29; 6.15; 12.12; 16.2; 18.62 peace
See also aśama; aśānta; praśānta; śama; śānta; śāśvacchānti
śarīra
1.29 (śarīre me) within
2.22; 5.23; 15.8; 18.15 body
11.13 (devadevasya śarīre) embodied in the god of gods
13.1 (idaṃ śarīram) the human body
See also śarīrastha; śarīravānmanobhiḥ
śarīrastha
13.31 dwelling in the body
17.6 (śarīrasthaṃ bhūtagrāmam) the elements that stay together in the body
śarīravāṅmanobhiḥ
18.15 with body, speech, or mind
śarīravimokṣana
5.23 (prāk śarīravimokṣaṇāt) before he leaves the body
śarīrin
2.18 the embodied One
sarvabhāva
15.19 (sarvabhāvena) in all ways [of worship and love]
18.62 (sarvabhāvena) with your whole being
sarvabhūta
2.69; 7.9, 27; 9.7; 12.13; 14.3 (plural) all creatures
3.18 (na . . . asya sarvabhūteṣu kaścid arthavyapāśrayaḥ) he does not rely on anything in this world for any end
3.19 anything in this world
5.29; 9.4, 29; 18.61 (plural) all beings
7.10 (plural) all that lives
10.39 any being
11.55 any creatures
18.20 all realities
sarvabhūtātmabhūtātman
5.7 his own individual existence now being the existence of all
sarvadharma
18.66 (sarvadharmān parityajya) passing beyond appearances
sarvagata
2.24 [subsisting always,] everywhere
3.15 omnipresent
13.32 present everywhere
See also sarvatraga
sarvajñānavimūḍha
3.32 estranged from insight
sarvakarmaphalatyāga
12.11 (sarvakarmaphalatyāgaṃ . . . kuru) cease anticipating the effects of all your rituals
18.2 giving up the effects of all rituals
sarvakṣetra
13.2 (plural) all fields
sarvalokamaheśvara
5.29 the great Lord of the universe
sarvapāpa
10.3 (plural) [he is released at once from] all evil
18.66 (ahaṃ tvā sarvapāpebhyo mokṣayiṣyāmi) I shall set you free from evil
sarvārambha
18.48 (plural) all undertakings
sarvārambhaparityāgin
12.16 able to give up all he undertakes
14.25 able to give up all undertakings
sarvasaṃkalpasaṃnyāsin
6.4 he . . . has renounced all purpose
sarvatraga
9.6; 12.3 omnipresent
See also sarvagata
sarvavid
15.19 [he] knows all
See also vid

śūdra
9.32 laborer
18.41 (plural) the servant class
18.44 (singular) the servant class
[246]
suhṛnmitrāryudāsīna-
6.9 (suhṛnmitrāryudāsīnamadhyasthadveṣyabandhuṣu . . . samabuddhiḥ) disposed equally toward personal friends, allies, and opponents, those standing aside or caught between, foes, kinsmen
sukha
1.32; 6.27, 28b; 10.4 joy
1.33 (plural); 2.66; 4.40; 5.21a; 14.9; 16.23; 18.36, 37, 38, 39 happiness
2.56 pleasure
5.21b; 6.21; 14.27 bliss
6.28a (sukhena) easily
6.32 pleasant
13.6 pleasantness
See also antaḥsukha; asukha; āyuḥsattvabalārogyasukhaprītivivardhana; rājyasukhalobha; śītoṣṇasukhaduḥkhada; sukhin; susukha
sukhaduḥkha
2.38 joy and grief
13.20 unpleasantness and pleasure
See also śītoṣṇasukhaduhkha
sukhasaṅga
14.6 the love for happiness
sukhin
1.37; 2.32; 5.23; 16.14 happy
sukṛta
5.15 merit
14.16 rightly done
See also sukṛtaduṣkṛta
sukṛtaduṣkṛta
2.50 (dual) good and evil deeds
sukṛtin
7.16 (. . . bhajante māṃ janāḥ sukṛtinaḥ . . .) people act properly, and worship me when . . .
susukha
9.2 easy
See also sukha
svabhāva
5.14 material nature
8.3 highest nature
See also kārpaṇyadoṣopahatasvabhāva
svabhāvaja
17.2 (dehināṃ sā [śraddhā] svabhāvajā [trust is] part of their nature [of living souls]
18.42 (. . . brahmakarma svabhāvajam) the acts of spiritual leaders by nature express . . .
18.43 (. . . kṣātraṃ karma svabhāvajam) . . . are inherent in the acts of warriors
18.44a (. . . vaiśyakarma svabhāvajam) the work of those who produce wealth is by nature . . .
18.44b (. . . śūdrasyāpi svabhāvajam) the servant class by nature has . . .
svabhāvaniyata
18.47 proper to his own station
svabhāvaprabhava
18.41 (svabhāvaprabhavair guṇaiḥ) according to the state natural to [each class]
svadharma
2.31 duty of your own class
2.33 your duty
3.35; 18.47 one's own duty
svādhyāyābhyasana
17.15 to recite and study sacred texts
svādhyāyajñānayajña
4.28 whose sacrifice goes on through study or the pursuit of wisdom
See also jñāna; yajña
svarga
2.37 heaven
See also asvargya; svargati
svargadvāra
2.23 gate to heaven
svargaloka
9.21 (svargalokaṃ viśālam) the wide expanse of heaven
svargapara
2.43 zealous for heaven
svargati
9.20 (svargatiṃ prārthayante) [they] seek to attain heaven
Śetāśatara
[220]

tadātman
5.17 (tadātmānaḥ) [they direct . . .] their whole being toward it
tadbuddhi
5.17 (plural) they direct their meditations . . . toward it

tadvid
13.1 (plural) those who know him
See also vid
tamas
8.9; 13.17 darkness
10.11; 14.5, 8, 9, 10a, 10c, 13, 15, 16, 17; 17.1 sloth
14.10b (omitted)
18.32 (tamasāvrtta) slothful
tāmasa
7.12 (bhāvā . . . tāmasāḥ) states of mind arise from . . . sloth
14.18 [man] of sloth
17.2 determined by sloth
17.19, 22; 18.32 slothful
17.4 (tāmasā janāḥ) men of sloth
17.13 of the nature of sloth
18.7 [an act] of sloth
18.22, 25, 35, 39 of sloth
18.28 [a man] of sloth
tāmasapriya
17.10 (. . . bhojanaṃ tāmasapriyam) men of sloth by nature turn to victuals that are . . .
tap
9.19 scorch
11.19 burn up
17.5 (tapyante . . . tapaḥ) [they] practice . . . austerities
17.17 (taptaṃ tapaḥ) austerities . . . performed
17.28 (tapas taptam) deed . . . done in . . . austerity
tapas
5.29 (bhoktāraṃ yajñatapasām) [me] the enjoyer of sacrifice and spiritual exertion
7.9 ascetic fire
8.28 (plural) ascetic life
10.5; 11.48, 53 (plural); 16.1; 17.14, 15, 17, 18, 19, 27, 28; 18.42 austerity
17.5, 7 austerities
17.16 to be austere [. . . means . . .]
See also atapaska; pratap; tap; tapo-; yajñadānatapaḥkarma; yajñatapaḥkriyā
tapasvin
6.46 ascetic
7.9 holy man
tapasya
9.27 [whatever you] do in self-restraint
tapoyajña
4.28 who sacrifices with asceticism
See also yajña
tat
[254]
tatprasāda
18.62 his grace
tattva
6.21 [. . . its] truth
9.24 (na tu māṃ abhijānanti tattvena) but not all . . . recognize me as I am
11.54 (jñātuṃ draṣṭum ca tattvena) I can be known and seen . . . as I really am
18.1 (saṃnyāsasya . . . tattvam icchāmi veditum) I want to understand what renouncing means
tattvataḥ
4.9; 10.7 as they really are
7.3 as I really am
18.55a (omitted)
18.55b [knowing me] as I am
tattvavid
3.28 he who knows how . . .
5.8 knowing the nature of things
See also vid
tejas
7.9 burning strength
7.10; 10.36; 16.3; 18.43 majesty
11.30 (plural) effulgence
15.12a, 12b splendor
tejasvin
7.10, 10.36 majestic
tejomaya
11.47 ([rūpam] tejomayam) the form of my majesty
traiguṇyaviṣaya
2.45 (traiguṇyaviṣayā vedāḥ) the Scriptures speak to the world's weave of integrity, passion, and sloth
trailokyarājya
1.35 kingship over heaven, air, and earth
See also loka; lokatraya
traividya
9.20 (plural) knowers of the holy Scriptures
trayīdharma
9.21 the practice of the Scriptures
tṛṣṇāsaṅgasamudbhava
14.7 arising from cravings and attachments

jñānam . . .) that knowledge which perceives . . . that knowledge . . . is . . .
See also adhyātmavidyā; ahorātravid; akṛtsnavid; avidvat; brahmavid; kṛtsnavid; rājavidyā; sarvavid; tadvid; tattvavid; uttamavid; vedavid; veditavya; vedya; vettṛ; viditātman; vidvat; vidya-; yajñavid; yogavittama

vidhi
[240]

vidhidṛṣṭa
17.11 as . . . ordained

vidhihīna
17.13 outside the established liturgy

viditātman
5.26 (plural) who know themselves
See also vid

vidvat
3.25 wise man
3.26 the wise
See also vid

vidyā
See adhyātmavidyā
See also vid

vidyāvinayasaṃpanna
5.18 . . . of knowledge and good conduct
See also vid

vigatabhī
6.14 without any fear
See also bhaya

vigatajvara
3.30 without anxiety

vigatecchābhayakrodha
5.28 [who] is already freed from desire, fear, and anger
See also bhaya; icchā; krodha

viguṇa
3.35; 18.47 in [its] imperfection

vijitātman
5.7 [if he] learns to control himself

vijitendriya
6.8 controlled

vijñā
2.19 (ubhau tau na vijānītaḥ) both lack understanding
2.46 discern
4.4 make sense
11.31 know
13.18 understand

vijñāna
18.42 discernment
See also jñānavijñānanāśana; jñānavijñānatṛptātman; vijñānasahita

vijñānasahita
9.1 (jñānaṃ vijñānasahitaṃ) [I shall tell you] wisdom, and explain how it can be attained

vikāra
13.19 (vikārāṃś ca guṇāṃś ca) the underlying states and changes in all things
See also avikārya; nirvikāra; savikāra; vikārin

vikārin
See yadvikārin
See also vikāra

vikarman
4.17 wrong action

vimokṣa
16.5 release
See also muc; vimuc

vimuc
4.32 free
9.28; 16.22 (vimukta) released
14.20 (vimukta) [a person] gains release when . . .
15.5 (vimukta) set free
18.35 let go
18.53 (vimucya) freed from reliance on . . .
See muc; śarīravimokṣaṇa; vimokṣa;

vimūḍhabhāva
11.49 (mā te vyathā mā ca vimūḍhabhāvaḥ) have no fear, no anxieties
See also muh

vimuh
2.72 (nai 'nāṃ prāpya vimuhyati) who so reaches it is not again confused
3.40 (vimohayati) [the enemy] deludes
6.38 (vimūḍha) lost
15.10 (vimūḍha) deluded man
See also muh; sarvajñānavimūḍha

vimukta
See vimuc

vinaś
4.40; 18.58 perish
8.20 (yaḥ . . . na vinaśyati) which has no end
13.27 die

See also avināśin; avinaśyat; vināśa
vināśa
2.17 (vināśam . . . kartum) destroy
4.8 (vināśāya . . . duṣkṛtām) so that . . . the evildoers perish
6.40 (na . . . vināśas tasya vidyate) that man will not be ruined
viniyam
6.18 (viniyata) checked
6.24 restrain
See also niyam
viś (noun)
See brāhmaṇakṣatriyaviś
viṣaya
2.59 (plural) the realm of the senses
2.62 (plural) what the senses tell him
2.64 (plural) the sensual world
4.26 (plural) objects of their senses
15.9 (plural) what mind and senses enjoy
18.51 (plural) nourishment of the senses
See also traiguṇyaviṣaya
cf. indriyārtha
viṣayendriyasaṃyoga
18.38 the confusion of senses and sense-objects
vismi
11.22 (vismita) in wonder
viṣṇu
11.24 God
[219]
viśuddhātman
5.7 wholly purified
viśva (noun and adjective)
11.18, 19, 38b the world
11.38a all things
11.47 universal
viśva (proper name)
11.22 (viśve) the All-Gods
viśvatomukha
9.15 My face turned toward everyone
10.33 (dhātāham viśvatomukhaḥ) I turn everywhere, sustaining the world
11.11 facing in every direction
viśveśvara
11.16 universal Lord
vītarāga
8.11 (plural) who have vanquished passion
vītarāgabhayakrodha
2.56 when longing, fear, and anger have left
4.10 freed of passion, fear, and anger
See also bhaya; krodha; rāga
vyakta
2.28 (. . . bhutāni vyaktamadhyāni . . .) [no one sees the beginning] of things, but only the middle . . .
See also avyakta
vyakti
7.24 (avyaktaṃ vyaktim āpannam manyante . . .) [they] think I was unmanifest first and then came to exist
8.18 (avyaktād vyaktayaḥ sarvāḥ prabhavanti) all things are disclosed. They arise from the unmanifest.
10.14 (na te . . . vyaktiṃ vidur) they are not able to envision your form
See also vyakta
vyapetabhī
11.49 your fear is dispelled
See also under bhaya
vyāsaprasāda
18.75 Vyāsa's favor
vyavasāyātmika
2.41 [knowledge meditation attains] consists in commitment
2.44 consisting in commitment

yacchraddha
17.3 (yo yacchraddhaḥ sa eva saḥ) what he trusts in, that is what he is
See also śraddhā
yadvikārin
13.3 (tat kṣetram . . . yadvikāri . . . tad . . . me śṛṇu) learn from . . . about this field . . . , how it changes
See also vikāra
yaj
4.12 offer sacrifices to
9.15, 23 bring sacrifices
9.20 (yajñair iṣṭvā) [they] make sacrifice to me and . . .
16.15, 17; 18.70 sacrifice
17.1, 11 perform sacrifices
17.4 sacrifice to
17.12 offer [a sacrifice]
See also yajña
yajña
3.14a, 14b, 15; 4.25a, 25b, 32, 33; 8.28;

9.16; 10.25; 17.12, 13, 23, 27 sacrifice
4.23; 17.7, 11 sacrifices
9.20 (yajñair iṣṭvā) [they] make sacrifice to me and . . .
16.1 (. . . yajñaś ca . . . bhavanti . . . abhijātasya . . .) a man born to . . . he performs the required sacrifices
See also adhiyajña; ayajña; devayaj; dravyayajña; ijyā; japayajña; jñānayajña; madyājin; nāmayajña; svādhiyajña; sahayajña; sarvayajña; svādhyāyajñānayajña; tapoyajña; vedayajñādhyayana; yaj; yogayajña
[237, 240, 252]

yajñabhāvita
3.12 sustained by sacrifice

yajñadānatapaḥkarma
18.3 rites of sacrifice, gifts, and austerity
18.5 the work of sacrifice, gifts, and austerity
See also dāna; tapas; karma

yajñadānatapaḥkriyā
17.24 (yajñadānatapaḥkriyāḥ . . . brahmavādinām) those who speak with knowledge of the Eternal engage in acts of sacrifice, giftgiving, and austerity
See also dāna; tapas; kriyā

yajñakṣapitakalmaṣa
4.30 (plural) their impurities are taken away by sacrifice

yajñārtha
3.9 (yajñārthāt karmaṇaḥ) work for the sake of sacrifice

yajñaśiṣṭāmṛtabhuj
4.31 enjoying the food of immortality left over from sacrifice
See also bhuj; mṛ

yajñaśiṣṭāśin
3.13 (plural) [they] eat the remnants of sacrifice

yajñatapaḥkriyā
17.25 act of sacrifice, austerity . . .
See also tapas; kriyā

yajñatapas
5.29 sacrifice and spiritual exertion

yajñavid
4.30 (sarve 'py ete yajñavidaḥ) all these truly know sacrifice
See also vid

yajus
See ṛg

yakṣarakṣāṃsi
17.4 sprites and monsters
See also gandharva; rakṣas

yatacetas
5.26 (plural) who control their thought
See also niyam; saṃyam

yatacitta
6.19 of controlled mind
See also niyam; saṃyam

yatacittātman
4.21 with mind and body under control
6.10 restraining himself and his thoughts completely
See also niyam; saṃyam

yatacittendriyakriya
6.12 restraining the functions of his thought and senses
See also niyam; saṃyam

yatātman
5.25 (plural) they have dominion over themselves
12.14 controlling himself
See also niyam; saṃyam

yatātmavat
12.11 keep yourself in check, and . . .
See also niyam; saṃyam

yatavākkāyamānasa
18.52 [when he has learned] to control speech, body, and mind
See also niyam; saṃyam

yatendriyamanobuddhi
5.28 who masters his senses, thought, and meditation
See also niyam, saṃyam

yati
4.28 devotee
5.26 (plural) men of sustained efforts
8.11 ascetic
See also ayati; niyam

yoddhukāma
1.22 pugnacious

yoga
2.39 the tradition of Discipline
2.48, 50a, 50b, 53 Discipline
4.1, 2, 3, 42; 5.1, 5b; 6.12, 16, 17, 19, 23, 33, 36, 37, 44; 7.1; 18.33, 75 discipline
5.5a (plural) men of discipline
6.2 liturgical discipline

9.5 (me yogam aiśvaram) my sovereign technique; compare 11.8
10.7a use
10.7b (avikampena yogena) by applying himself without wavering
10.18 mystic power
11.8 (me yogam aiśvaram) my absolute power; cf. 9.5
12.6 (ananyenaiva yogena) disciplined toward none but me
13.24 (sāṃkhyena yogena) through reason
See also abhyāsayoga; ātmayoga; ātmasaṃyamayogāgni; ayogataḥ; bhaktiyoga; brahmayogayuktātman; buddhisaṃyoga; buddhiyoga; dhyānayogapara; duḥkhasaṃyogaviyoga; jñānayoga; karmaphalasaṃyoga; karmayoga; kṣetrakṣetrajñasaṃyoga; madyoga; mahāyogeśvara; niryogakṣema; sāṃkhyayoga; viṣayendriyasaṃyoga; yogeśvara; yogin; yuj
[219–220, 226, 244, 247, 255]

yogabala
8.10 the strength of discipline

yogabhraṣṭa
6.41 who strayed from discipline

yogadhāraṇā
8.12 (āsthito yogadhāraṇām . . .) [one should] concentrate on discipline

yogakṣema
9.22 a sure prize
See also niryogakṣema

yogamāyāsamāvṛta
7.25 [I am] concealed by the wizardry I apply

yogārūḍha
6.3 advanced to discipline
6.4 (yadā . . . yogarūḍhas tado 'cyate) he has advanced to discipline when . . .

yogasaṃjñita
6.23 (taṃ vidyād duḥkhasaṃyogaviyogaṃ yogasaṃjñitam) he will know that this loosening of sorrowful ties is discipline

yogasaṃnyastakarman
4.41 who through discipline has renounced action

yogasaṃsiddha
4.38 accomplished in discipline
See also sidh

yogasaṃsiddhi
6.37 enduring success [in discipline]
See also sidh

yogasevā
6.20 the practice of discipline

yogastha
2.48 (yogasthaḥ kuru karmāṇi) follow Discipline and perform your rites

yogavittama
12.1 (ke yogavittamāḥ) who knows discipline best?
See also vid

yogayajña
4.28 (plural) those who sacrifice through discipline
See also yajña

yogayukta
5.6 trained in some discipline
5.7 trained in a discipline
8.27 disciplined

yogayuktātman
6.29 wholly immersed in discipline

yogeśvara
11.4; 18.75, 78 Lord of mystic power

yogin
3.3; 6.8, 10, 15; 6.28, 31, 32, 42, 45, 46a, 46b, 47; 8.25; 12.14 man of discipline
4.25 (apare . . . yoginaḥ paryupāsate) the discipline of some is to revere . . .
5.11, 24; 6.19, 27; 8.23, 27, 28; 15.11 disciplined man
8.14 (nityayuktasya yoginaḥ) for him who is ever disciplined
10.17 you in your mystic power
See also yoga
[241]

yuj
1.14 yoke
2.38 gird
2.39 arm
2.50; 6.12, 19, 23 practice
2.61 restrain; compare 6.14
3.26; 4.18; 5.8, 12, 23; 6.14, 15, 18; 9.34; 10.7; 17.17 discipline
6.8 (yukta ity ucyate) [he] has true harmony
6.10; 8.10 train
7.1 persist in
7.22 fill

17.26 (yujyate) is fitting
18.51 direct properly
See also abhyāsayogayukta; ayukta; brahmayogayuktātman; buddhiyukta; dambhāhaṃkārasaṃyukta; kāmakrodhaviyukta; nityābhiyukta; niyuj; prāṇāpānasamāyukta; prayuj; rāgadveṣaviyukta; yuj; yukta-

yuktaceṣṭa
6.17 (yuktaceṣṭasya karmasu) disciplined in acts

yuktacetas
7.30 (plural) who concentrate their minds

yuktāhāravihāra
6.17 disciplined in eating, relaxation

yuktasvapnāvabodha
6.17 disciplined in sleep and wakefulness

yuktatama
6.47; 12.2 most disciplined

yuktātman
7.18 he has trained himself

ENGLISH GUIDE WITH REFERENCES TO THE SANSKRIT CONCORDANCE

Note: The terms listed with each English entry in most instances are not Sanskrit equivalents; they only indicate where in the Sanskrit Index relevant information can be found.

ENGLISH TERMS	SEE UNDER
A	
abandon	nyāsa
	saṃnyāsa
	tyāga
	tyaj
absolute	aiśvara
	para
act	karman
	kṛ
affect	lip
agitate	dviṣ
alike	sama
	sama-
All-Gods	viśva
Almighty	īśvara
alms-giving	dāna
Ancestors	uṣmapa
ancient	purātana
anger	krodha
anxiety	bhaya
	cintā
anyone	bhūta
anything	sarvabhūta
appearances	sarvadharma
arm	yuj
ascetic	yati
asceticism	tapas
atrocity	pāpa
attach, attachment	prasaṅga
	sañj
	saṅga
austerity	tapas
authority	īśvarabhāva
avoid	tyaj
awareness	cetanā
B	
balance	sama
	sama-
	sāmya
being	bhāva
	bhūta
	sarvabhūta
	sattva
best, better	śreyaḥ
bind	bandh
birth	janma-
	sadasadyonijanma
blameless	anagha
bliss, blissful	anāmaya
	sukha
body	śarīra
bondage	bandha
Book of Songs	sāmaveda
bothersome	duḥkha
breath, breathing	apāna
	prāṇa
	prāṇāpāna
C	
caste	jāti-
caught	prasakta
celestial race	deva

ENGLISH TERMS	SEE UNDER
changeless	avyaya
chaos	adharma
chariot fighter	mahāratha
check	viniyam
clarity	prasāda
class	varṇa
clear-minded	prasannacetas
cling	lip
	saṅga
command	prabhu
concentrate, concentration	buddhi
	manas
	samādhā
	samādhi
	samādhistha
confidence	śraddhā
confuse	moha
	muh
	vimuh
conquer	niyam
consciousness	buddhi-
	cetanā
constantly, continually	nitya
content	saṃtuṣ
	tuṣ
contrive	dambha
control	grah
	īśvara
	niyam
control	saṃyam
	yata-
courage	abhaya
craving	saṅga
	tṛṣṇā-
creator	brahman (m)
	īśa
creature	bhūta
	sarvabhūta
crime	pāpa
criterion	pramāṇa
cult, cultic act	karman
cycles, cycle of existence	punarāvartin
	saṃsāra

D

ENGLISH TERMS	SEE UNDER
danger	bhaya
darkness	tamas
darkness of mind	moha
deathless	amṛta
deceitful, deceptive	dambha
dedication	arpaṇa
delude, delusion	moha
	saṃmoha
	vimuh
demerit	kilbiṣa
	pāpa
demon, demonic	asura
	āsura
	bhūta
	rakṣas
desire	icchā
	iṣ
	kāma
	kāṅkṣ
	rāga
	saṅga
destroy	pralaya
detach, detachment	saṅga
	tyaj
devotee, devotion	bhaj
	bhakti
	bhakti-
	madyoga
	yati
die	pralaya
	pralayānta
	pralī
	vinaś
difference	samadarśin
difficult, difficulty	duḥkha
direct	yuj
discern	vijñā
discipline, disciplined	yoga
	yuj
	yukta-
discipline of work	karmayoga
disgust	dviṣ
disregard	tyaj

ENGLISH TERMS	SEE UNDER
dissolution, dissolve	pralaya
	pralī
divine	brāhma
	brahma-
	divya
Divine (the Divine)	brahma-
	brahman (n)
Divine Being	puruṣa
divine secret	brahman (n)
	parama
divine world	div
division (the four great divisions)	cāturvarṇya
	varṇa
duty	karman
	kārya
	paradharma
	svadharma
E	
earth	loka
earthly world	prakṛti
educated	paṇḍita
effects, effects of actions	karmaphala-
	sarvakarmaphala-tyāga
effort	yati
ego-centered	ahaṃkāra
embody, embodied	dehin
	śarīra
	śarīrin
end	pralaya
endless	śāśvata
enlightened	buddhimat
enrage	dviṣ
ensnare	bandh
envisage	cint
essence	nidhāna
established	pratiṣṭhā (verb)
estate	bhāva
eternal	avyaya
	nitya
Eternal (the Eternal)	brahman (n)
ever	nitya
everlasting	avyaya
everywhere	sarvagata
evil	aśubha
	mahāpāpman
	pāpa
	pāpman
	pūtapāpa
	sarvapāpa
evildoer	pāpa
	pāpa-
equally	sama-
equal-minded	sama
	sama-
equanimity	samacittatva
	samatā
	samatva
eternal	sanātana
	śāśvata
even-minded	sama
	sama-
even out	sama
	sama-
everlasting	sanātana
	śāśvata
exalted person	mahātman
exhalation	apāna
existence	bhūta
	prakṛtija
	sarvabhūtātma-bhūtātman
existent	sat
existent being	bhūta
externals of religion	śabdabrahma
F	
faculty of meditation	buddhi
fantasies	cintā
fault	pāpa
fear	bhaya
field	kṣetra
	kṣetra-
	dharmakṣetra

ENGLISH TERMS	SEE UNDER
	kṣetrin
	sarvakṣetra
fill	yuj
firm	pratiṣṭhā (verb)
fitting	yuj
flaw	doṣa
fleeting	aśāśvata
fool	muh
forbearance, forbearing	kṣamā
forever	nitya
foundation	nidhāna
free, freedom	asakta
	bhūtaprakṛtimokṣa
	brahmanirvāṇa
	mokṣa
	muc
	nirvāṇa-
	pramuc
	saṃnyas
	vimuc
fully present	samādhā
G	
generosity, generous, gift	dāna
gird	yuj
give	prayam
give up	parityāga
	tyāga
	tyaj
glory	mahātmya
goblin	rakṣas
god	deva
	mahātman
God	brahma-
	brahman
	deva
	devavara
	viṣṇu
godhead	brahman (n)
good	sat
	sad-
	śreyah

ENGLISH TERMS	SEE UNDER
GOOD and REAL	sat
grace, gracious	bhaj
	matprasāda
	prasad
	prasāda
	tatprasāda
	tatprasāda
greatest	para
great man	mahātman
Great Principle	mahat
	buddhi
greed, greedy	lobha
	lubdha
grief	duḥkha
gross elements	mahābhūta
ground	pratiṣṭhā (noun)
H	
happiness, happy	saṃtuṣ
	sukha
	sukhin
harmony	yuj
hate	dveṣa
	dviṣ
	pradviṣ
health	anāmaya
heart	pravya-thitāntarātman
	cetas
	manas
heaven	div
	svarga
hell	naraka
high, highest	para
	śreyaḥ
Highest Being	puruṣa
	puruṣottama
highest class of men	dvija
highest nature	svabhāva
historical circumstances	bhāva
hostilities	dviṣ

ENGLISH TERMS	SEE UNDER
I	
I	nirmama
immanent	guṇabhoktṛ
immortal	amṛta
imperfect, imperfection	doṣa
	sadoṣa
	yiguṇa
imprison imprisonment	bandh
	karmabandha
	karmabandhana
	muc
	nibandh
impure	kilbiṣa
	pāpa
infernal	āsura
infinite	abhāva
	akṣara
	amṛta
	sanātana
	śāśvata
inmost self	antarātman
integrity	sattva
	sāttvika
invisible	avyakta
J	
joy	antaḥsukha
	śukha
judge, judging, judgment	buddhi
	prajñā
just	dharmya
K	
know, knowledge	bodh
	buddhi
	jñā
	jñāna
	vid
	vijñā

ENGLISH TERMS	SEE UNDER
L	
laborer	śūdra
learn	jñā
	vid
leave	tyaj
life, life-breath	prāṇa
likes	rāga-
live, living, living being, living soul	bhūta
	dehin
	prāṇin
	sarvabhūta
loathe	dviṣ
Lord	bhūtamaheśvara
	bhuteśa
	deveśa
	īśa
	īśvara
	lokamaheśvara
	mahāyogeśvara
	maheśvara
	parameśvara
	prabhu
	sarvalokamaheśvara
	vibhu
	viśveśvara
	yogeśvara
lord	prabhu
lost	vimuh
love	bhaj
	bhakti
	kāma
	saṅga
lust	kāma
	kāma-
M	
magic power	māyā
make (set in motion)	prayuj
make sense	vijñā
man	dehin
	puruṣa

ENGLISH TERMS	SEE UNDER
manifest	vyakta
	vyakti
man of ritual work	karmin
master	ācārya
material	prakṛtisaṃbhava
material existence	prakṛti
material nature	svabhāva
matter	prakṛtija
	prakṛtistha
meditate	anucint
	dhyā
	paricint
meditation	buddhi
	dhyāna
meditative knowledge	buddhi
men	loka
mentally	manas
mentor	ācārya
merit, meritorious	puṇya-
mighty	mahātman
mind	buddhi
	cetas
	cint
	dhyā
	jñā
	manas
mine	nirmama
mislead	muh
monster	rakṣas
muddled	lip
mystic power	yoga
N	
nature	prakṛti
	svabhāva-
nature's forces	guṇa
nausea	duḥkha
necessary core of knowledge	parama
new birth	punarjanman
normal	prakṛti
O	
objects of sense	indriyārtha
	viṣaya
obsessed	anusañj
	saṃmuh
obsession	moha
	muh
offer	prayam
offering	arpaṇa
OM	akṣara
	ekākṣara
	om
omnipresent	sarvagata
	sarvatraga
opposites	dvandva
ordained work	karman
orient	jñā
other gods	anyadevatā
outcome of rituals	karmaphala-
own	ātma-
	ātman
	sva-
P	
pain	duḥkha
paramount	parama
passion	rāga
	rajas
	rājasa
	rajo-
path	dharma
patience	kṣamā
peace	prasannātman
	praśānta-
	śama
	śānta
	śānti
	tuṣ
people	loka
perennial	sanātana
	śāśvata
perfect	parama
perfect, perfection	siddhi
	sidh

ENGLISH TERMS	SEE UNDER
perish	vinaś
	vināśa
perplex	muh
persist	yuj
person	ātman
	dehin
place	pada
pleasant, pleasure	sukha
pleased	prasad
pollute	lip
	upalip
power	yoga
practice	yuj
praise	bhaj
prepare	pratiṣṭhā (verb)
primal	purāṇa
primal matter	prakṛti
	prakṛtisaṃbhaya
	prakṛtistha
primeval, primordial	purāṇa
principles of existence	adhibhūta
prison	bandha
prohibited	adharma
promise	pratijñā
purest birth	brāhmaṇa
purpose	sarvasaṃkalpa-saṃnyāsin
R	
Radiant Gods	vasu
realities	sarvabhūta
reality	anātman
	ātman
	bhāva
reason	sāṃkhya
rebirth	janma-punarāvartin
	punarjanman
	saṃsāra
reborn	punarjanman
regimen	niyama
region	loka
regular	niyam
relate	prayuj
release	pramuc
	vimokṣa
	vimuc
religion	dharma
relinquish	tyaj
renounce	saṃnyas
	saṃnyāsa
	tyaj
renouncer	saṃnyāsin
renunciation	saṃnyāsa
	tyāga
	tyaj
repetition	punarjanman
require	niyam
resign	saṃnyas
restrain	niyam
	saṃniyam
	saṃyam
	viniyam
	yuj
results of rituals	aphalākaṅkṣin
	aphalaprepsu
	asakta
	karmaphala
	karmaphalahetu
revere, reverence	paryupās
right	dharma
	dharmya
rite	karman
ritual, ritual work	karman
	kriyā
round of deaths	mṛtyusaṃsāra-
ruin	vināśa
ruler	prabhu
S	
Sacred Scriptures	veda
sacred study	brahmacārivrata
Sacred Texts	veda
sacrifice	brāhmaṇa
	ijyā
	nāmayajña

ENGLISH TERMS	SEE UNDER
	yaj
	yajña
same, sameness	sama
	sama-
	sāmya
Scriptures	veda
self	ātman
	dehin
	paramātman
self-centered, self-consciousness	ahaṃkāra
selfishness	nirmama
self-restraint	tapas
senses	indriya
	sarvendriya-vivarjita
	viṣaya
sensual world	indriyārtha
sentient	sarvendriya-guṇābhāsa
serenity	śama
servant, servant class	śūdra
sloth	tamas
	tāmasa
sorrow	duḥkha
soul	ātman
	dehin
sovereign	aiśvara
spirit	puruṣa
spiritual exertion	tapas
spiritual guide	ācārya
spiritual leaders	brahma-
spiritual man	brāhmaṇa
stable	pratiṣṭhā (verb)
stain	lip
standard	pramāṇa
state	bhāva
	pada
state of being	bhāva
state of mind	bhāva
states, states arising in primal matter, states of all existence, states of matter	guṇa
	nirguṇatva
	prakṛtija
steadfast	pratiṣṭhā (verb)
steadily	nitya
stillness	śama
straight	sama
study	svādhyāya-
subdue	niyam
subsisting always	nitya
success, successful	siddhi
	sidh
supreme	parama
Supreme Divine Being	puruṣa
	puruṣottama
supreme reality, supreme self, supreme spirit	paramātman
surely	niyam

T

ENGLISH TERMS	SEE UNDER
task	kārya
teacher	ācārya
technique	yoga
Terrifying Gods	rudras
thing	bhūta
think	cint
	vid
thought	cetas
	cint
	citta
	manas
tradition	dharma
	kuladharma
train	abhyāsa
	yoga
	yuj
	yuktātman
transcend, transcendent	nirguṇa
	nistraiguṇya
	para

ENGLISH TERMS	SEE UNDER
trust	śraddhā
truth	tattva
U	
unborn	aja
underlying states in all things	guṇa
understand, understanding	budh
	buddhi
	jñā
	jñāna
	prajñā
	pratijñā
	vid
	vijñā
undisciplined	ayukta
unmanifest	avyakta
unpleasant, unpleasantness, unpleasant things	duḥkha
unright	adharma
upright	ārjava
unselfish	nirmama
utmost	para
V	
vain, vainly	dambha
vile	pāpa-
W	
warrior	brāhmaṇakṣatriya-viś
	kṣatrakarma
	kṣatriya
	mahābāhu
	mahāratha
way of cultic work	karmayoga
wicked, wickedness	doṣa
	pāpa
will	manas
wisdom, wise	jñā
	jñāna
	jñānavat
	jñānin
	prajñā-
wizardry	māyā
work	karman
world	bhūta
	loka
	lokatraya
	trailokya
worship	bhaj
	bhakti
wrath, wrathful	krodha
wrong	adharma
	doṣavat
	pāpa
Y	
yoke	yuj

Acknowledgments

The very first of those I wish to mention with gratitude is V. S. Ranganathan of Tambaram, now professor of Tamil in the University of Allahabad. He opened my ears to the sound of Sanskrit poetry. Without such initiation, all understanding remains academic in the narrow sense of the word. Through his friendship, the two years of his instruction became something far more than a necessary scholastic exercise; the sessions with my friend, *paṇḍit* Ranganathan, became one of the great experiences in my life; quite unassuming, he witnessed to the actuality of human understanding on a worldwide scale.

I wish I could render truly adequate thanks to all who taught me Sanskrit in whatever stage and thus contributed directly to my interest in the Bhagavadgītā—for what a dull book it seemed to me when I first read it in translation! My thoughts go back to my first feeble, not very successful attempts, at the feet of Professor F. B. J. Kuiper in Leiden. They move on to the courses with Professor George V. Bobrinskoy in Chicago—at which time my progress was greatly facilitated by my friend and fellow student Edwin Gerow, now professor in Chicago, who even during those early days left me far behind as a Sanskritist. I feel especially thankful to the patience of my other professorial friend, J. A. B. van Buitenen, who spent many hours with me, explaining texts, including obscure religious materials such as would not have been his personal choice in literature. It is also Professor van Buitenen under whose guidance I read the Sanskrit text of the Gītā for the first time. When the present book appears in print, Professor van Buitenen's monumental translation of the Mahābhārata may well have reached the Gītā text. I wish I could have consulted it during my work! Last but not least, it will be in order to recall here the name of Professor V. Raghavan of Madras. To be sure, there is hardly anyone in Indic studies who is not in some measure indebted to him. However, Professor

Raghavan has not only been of great help to me in Sanskrit, but I owe it to his rare intuition that I met V. S. Ranganathan.

In most recent times, and to my immediate advantage in my Gītā translation, I have enjoyed in particular the criticism and encouragement by some colleagues and friends: Professors Norvin J. Hein (Yale), Willard Johnson (San Diego State University), and Guy R. Welbon (Pennsylvania). They and others have saved me from errors and pointed out the importance of this new translation when my spirits were flagging.

Invaluable help, unpremeditated, unexpected like grace, has come from students continually, since I guided my first Sanskrit class through the text at Brown University. I want to record my thanks to many former and present students, especially Richard Hecht (now assistant professor at the University of California, Santa Barbara), Karen Hurwitz, Ed Krafchow, Phyllis Herman (teaching at California State University, Northridge), Alexei Nicolai, Simone Wilson, Burt Thorp, and Jess Hollenback. I am grateful to Lisa A. Bonoff-Raskind not only for her share in readings of the text, but also for her active help in preparing the manuscript.

For the years I have been working on the translation off and on, Ellen T. Kaplan occupied herself with the English text, serving as my ultimate critical companion, sifting through words and phrases, rejecting redundancies of the pedestrian scholarly mind, and improving countless renderings. I bless my stars for her assistance. In this same paragraph I should also mention Sonja Bolle, my daughter, who listened to several of my readings attentively, with all her literary sensitivity, and who corrected me. A little bit of a comparable acknowledgment should go to my son Paul.

Some of my learned friends and helpers disagreed among themselves, thus stimulating me, in spite of their intentions, to hold on to some of my translations, especially when they were diametrically opposed to each other, with my translation exactly between them. One reproached me that I had made too much of the ritualistic and liturgical interests of the Bhagavadgītā's author; he wanted me to translate *karman* as "activity in general" in more instances than I did, and so on. On the opposite side was the advice from another critical helper, who insisted that I should demonstrate the ritual aspect of the teachings also in those texts where so far I had not done so. Could I do anything but conclude for the time being that I had steered a safe middle course? Needless to say, my gratefulness to the many teachers, colleagues, friends, and students does not diminish my responsibility in all cases where future work will prove me wrong.

I cannot omit a confession that I hope will not be misunderstood or misquoted. Frankly, I had not intended to venture a Gītā translation until much later. For years I had actually thought of it as an appealing project for an older, wiser, preferably emeritus professor, withdrawn in his study in the countryside of New England or the Achterhoek, resorting exclusively to his own books. Then, one day, Robert Y. Zachary of the University of California Press and cornerstone of the Hermeneutics series, asked me to evaluate a long poem he had received. It was Ann Stanford's rendering of the Bhagavadgītā. At Zachary's request, Ann and I spent one afternoon a week for several months going through the text line for line, changing, arguing, improving. Our work was interrupted by a severe illness that brought Ann close to death. When she recovered, she thought of only one thing: to get her translation in print. Herder & Herder had just established an American branch of their publishing house and were eager to bring out this work by a well-known poet. Ann Stanford and I had gone through the text of the first three or four chapters carefully, and hence we had dealt with some of the most crucial teachings of the Gītā. I only wish we could have gone through all the eighteen chapters, even though in that case I would have had to think up another project for my retirement. It would have been worth it, but fate decreed a different course altogether. Zachary was perhaps not part of fate when he kept urging me to complete on my own what had begun in such a promising fashion. I owe him a special debt of gratitude for his special role and his trust in me. Nevertheless, he too, just like all others mentioned, should not share in any blame, if blame is to be imputed at all.

Lastly, my work on the Bhagavadgītā has been supported by several Senate Grants of the University of California in the last few years; I am grateful to the research committees who assigned them.

April 15, 1978 Kees W. Bolle

Composition Trend Western, Inc.
Lithography Braun-Brumfield, Inc.
Binder Braun-Brumfield, Inc.

Text Linocomp Palatino
Display Linocomp Palatino & Palatino Bold
Paper 50 lb. P&S Offset vellum B 32
Binding Holliston Roxite B 53556